# Resisting Work

# Resisting Work

*The Corporatization of Life
and Its Discontents*

PETER FLEMING

Temple University Press
Philadelphia

TEMPLE UNIVERSITY PRESS
Philadelphia, Pennsylvania 19122
*www.temple.edu/tempress*

Copyright © 2014 by Temple University
All rights reserved
Published 2014

Library of Congress Cataloging-in-Publication Data

Fleming, P. (Peter), 1972–
    Resisting work : the corporatization of life and its discontents / Peter
Fleming.
        pages  cm
    Includes bibliographical references and index.
    ISBN 978-1-4399-1112-9 (cloth : alk. paper)
    ISBN 978-1-4399-1114-3 (e-book)
    1. Corporate power.  2. Corporate culture.  3. Work environment.  I. Title.
    HD2351.F55 2014
    306.3'6—dc23                                              2013042592

Printed and bound in Great Britain by
Marston Book Services Ltd, Oxfordshire

080414P

Once upon a time leftists and radicals talked
of liberation or the abolition of work. Now the talk
is about full employment.

—RUSSELL JACOBY, *The End of Utopia*

# Contents

# Acknowledgments

This book has benefited greatly from the many conversations and debates I have had with colleagues and friends over the past three years. My good friend Carl Cederström has been a wonderful sounding board for many of the ideas explored here—as has André Spicer, who continues to be a most supportive and critical source of inspiration for me. Gerry Hanlon kindly listened to me for many hours (usually at the Cat and Mutton Pub in Hackney, London) as I elaborated on the arguments made in the following pages, and—as always—the conversations that ensued helped clarify my ideas immeasurably. And my old friend Marc T. Jones, the most critical critic I know, still opens my eyes to the nature of capitalism, even after twenty years of intense dialogue.

Colleagues from my years at Queen Mary College, University of London, provided much intellectual support during the preparation of this book—including Arianna Bove, Matteo Mandarini, and Stefano Harney. During the early stages of the book-writing process, I presented papers at the Franklin Humanities Institute, Duke University, where I benefited from the generous support of Fred Moten and Ian Baucom. I presented portions of this book at Copenhagen Business School and the University of Innsbruck, Austria, where I was most fortunate to receive the great feedback and hospitality of Iain Munro,

Dan Kärreman, and Martin Kornberger. Many other events also helped hone my arguments, as did extremely useful exchanges with Kathi Weeks, Simon Critchley, Marysia Lewandowska, Martin Parker, Hugh Willmott, Andy Sturdy, Dirk Matten, Steffen Böhm, and Chris Land.

The conversations I shared with Mark Fisher, Tariq Goddard, and Alex Niven at a number of events related to this project remain deeply inspiring.

My new colleagues at Cass Business School, City University London—especially Cliff Oswick, Bobby Banergee, and Jean Pascal Gond—have been overwhelmingly supportive during the final stages of book production.

The team at Temple University Press, especially Micah Kleit and Joan Vidal, has been extremely helpful in the preparation of this manuscript and a pleasure to work with.

And finally, I offer a note of deep gratitude to Amelia Seddon for putting up with my being "lost in action" during the many days, weeks, and months spent writing this book.

# Introduction

*Why Work?*

A young university lecturer enters a London pub late Friday night with a backpack of undergraduate exams in urgent need of grading, within a matter of days, in fact—external auditors are already waiting to sign off on them. She wearily looks around, tired and irritated, moving toward the crowded bar to wait. What a mess this has become, and through no fault of her own. The impossible deadline for grading the 450 exams she received that day was apparent months ago, and she had dutifully alerted university management to the coming disaster should they fail to authorize the additional paid help.

The response was lukewarm, but affirmative. Then nothing happened. After two or three more worried e-mails to her supervisor as the deadline approached, they finally agreed. *"Of course. Don't be silly! Organize the support. The deadline needs to be met, and it's fast approaching!"* She went to work, frantically calling colleagues and former tutors who might be able to help. Three weeks ago, yes, but now they were taking a well-deserved holiday. Finally, after three anxious days, assistance was found. But given the short notice, they could not collect the exams on campus. She would have to deliver them herself. The backpack was handed over, strained small talk ensued, and finally she made her way home, relieved but depressed about how the whole process had been mismanaged by her superiors.

This real-life scenario conveyed to the author encapsulates the theme of this book. It suggests that many jobs in the West are now regulated by a new matrix of power—*biopower.* This is where *bios,* or "life itself," is put to work through our ability to self-organize around the formal rules, be resourceful outside the official workday, and use our social ingenuity to get things done. The presence of this power is especially obvious when the boundary between work and non-work dissolves. Both the formal and the informal spheres blend into the production process. The scenario also points to the way this type of regulation camouflages itself through moments of spontaneous self-planning, extra-employment networks and even generosity. The book suggests that there is something systematic and strategic occurring here, linked to the way in which capital accumulation is now organized, particularly in times of crisis and refusal.[1]

Our university employee interprets this biopolitical episode as mismanagement. It is this, but something else is happening here as well, since recent research indicates that most exploitative employment settings function similarly today. Neoliberalism in particular is experienced as incredibly disorganized and obstructive. Indeed, rather than being a one-off aberration, such disarray actually reflects its anti-democratic normalcy, especially today when it calls on us to be always poised to produce. Its ultimate aim is to secure its own untenable continuation rather than satisfy broader collective needs. Moreover, the lecturer's social virtuosity reveals another key topic investigated in this book, that of "the commons" and the modern corporation's parasitical reliance on it. Because neoliberal capitalism finds it almost impossible to reproduce itself on its own terms, it must draw on value outside of its official reach. Such value is embodied in the worker him- or herself, and the modern firm seeks to yoke this rich social excess to the lexicon of capitalist work relations. Today, this often takes the personified form of *self-exploitation,* as the above case demonstrates.

Let us depart the university and enter into an even stranger milieu: the modern business firm.[2] Something analogous is occurring here, too. A good deal of the real work does not seem to be occurring inside the corporation at all, but elsewhere. A large sports apparel conglomerate epitomizes this mentality perfectly. Here is a telling interview excerpt with the CEO (posted on YouTube as "Lessons in Leadership" [2008], emphasis added) that tells us why:

Interviewer: I'm sure you are a cool guy, but some of the young people who look at you, they just probably see some guy in a suit . . . and think, not so cool. . . . [H]ow do you keep parting me from my money and my kids? [*General laughter.*]
CEO: The main thing I do . . . every chance we have we keep rejuvenating our company with people who are the customer. . . . [I]n the areas of design, sales, and marketing, they all have to be *young people*. . . . [T]hey know the culture; they feel that it's part of their DNA; they can talk the talk and walk the walk. I'm not the guy who can do that. . . . I make sure those people read all the relevant magazines, they travel the world, they get into the marketplace, they look at customers, they watch our competitors, they go and hang out in high schools and just observe, they go to rock concerts, they go to the mall on the weekend. All that kind of thing they have to do to know how the market ticks. . . . [W]e're not that smart, to tell the truth. . . . [W]e sort of stumbled into it; we made shorts; we copied the guy in Australia. . . . [W]e kept on going.

The CEO summarizes the nature of the contemporary corporation very well. It needs to prospect and tap external social relations (e.g., tastes, cutting-edge innovations, and perhaps even "life itself") to generate profits, simply because it cannot do this itself. "We're not that smart." And might not this surplus intelligence that flourishes *despite* the capitalist enterprise also be the fulcrum of a new emancipatory movement? Perhaps, but that is taken up later.

While the corporation is now increasingly putting this life force to work, the sad irony is that for increasing numbers of employees amid it all, life has never felt so far away. Jobs utilize our public imagination and buzz of life, our vested abilities and genuine desire to self-organize, but the net payback is a moment of subtraction rather than freedom. Worry, fear, anxiety, and a nagging sense of purposelessness tend to result, or what Virno calls a lasting "not feeling at home" (Virno 2004: 34). The reason why is now becoming clear. When biopolitical institutions sap the best of the social common, they also leave us with the burnt-out remains. These negative externalities too are biopolitical: tired bodies, permanently anxious people, and numb personalities. This is why it is no surprise that recent research has discovered work-related stress is more dangerous to your health than heavy smoking ("Burnout Is Bigger Heart Attack Risk" 2013).

Yet so many of us strive to participate. In the current climate, the only thing that worries us more than our jobs is the idea of losing them. What makes working so painful today, especially in the wake of the 2008 global economic crisis, is the peculiar impasse it has now arrived at.

On the one hand, there has been a massive divestment in the long-standing assumption that work is intrinsically good for us. Compared to yesteryear, when it was one of the key icons of social and ethical virtue, even among a militant workforce, today the idea of working holds very little progressive purchase. A senior manager whom the author spoke with recently conveyed a view that resonates with those at the bottom of the hierarchy as well: "Work is shit." This is not an isolated opinion. According to one survey, almost 50 percent of the global workforce feels completely disengaged from their jobs, with U.S. and European workers particularly salient.[3] This might reflect the serious legitimacy crisis that the corporate system has suffered more generally. Even the *Harvard Business Review* recently admitted, "The legitimacy of business has fallen to levels not seen in recent history" (Porter and Kramer 2011: 4). In this context, where business firms are considered openly antithetical to the common good, it is no wonder that the joys of work feel like a distant memory.

On the other hand, however, the pressure of our jobs has never been more inclusive and totalizing. Almost everyone feels taken over by his or her work to the point where the suggestion that we could live without it seems preposterous. We are told to find a job no matter what, base our lives around it, measure our self-esteem against it, and feel guilty if we do not want it—even wreck ourselves in the name of it. This stalemate is particularly disheartening because it embodies a structural contradiction that goes to the heart of late capitalism more generally, although it may also harbor the image of an alternative to work. The ideology of work becomes all-pervasive precisely at the same moment its redundancy is apparent to all. This book aims to convince the reader that we can actually live comfortably and happily without work as we know it.

## Biocapitalism and the Myth of Economic Necessity

Why are we working now more than ever when its cultural legitimacy has reached an all-time low? The bills need to be paid, for sure. But something else is happening here. The rise of biopower in and around the workplace is inextricably linked to the shifting tactics of capitalist regulation. Following the 1970s structural crisis, the rise of neoliberal hegemony signaled to working people that the gains made after World War II were but a temporary indulgence. That this class offensive was justified with rhetoric about saving society from bankruptcy is no surprise. But history did not turn out as planned. This variant of capitalism was seriously unable to organize itself. As a result, a reconfiguration took place to save it. The management function was displaced onto workers themselves. It might have looked like freedom and empowerment, but it wasn't.

Neoliberalism now sees us constantly concerned with its problems, integrating them into our life problems in order to get things done. In the workplace, this did not do away with supervisors giving orders from above. But their power has been augmented by horizontal regulative forms like self-managing teams, the portfolio career, and emotional labor. All of a sudden life itself is drawn into the logic of production. With our bosses just as likely to be controlled in the same manner, this type of power is difficult to clearly target and oppose as we used to do under Fordism.

This undoubtedly represents a quantitative shift in capitalist regulation—more time spent in the office or worrying about it due to labor intensification and the lengthening of the working day.[4] But it is more importantly a *qualitative* change, too. Our jobs now become something very intimate to us, especially when they rely on interpersonal aptitudes and emotional intelligence to make things happen, as many occupations do today. And when the concerns of work are embedded in our very social being, it is difficult to check out or turn off. Its influence comes from above—a supervisor or deadline—but also from the side and below. We begin to live with the imposition of work and it with us. As a result, the objective necessity of a job—paying the bills—is conflated with our personal sense of individuality and social value.

But isn't this increased level of work simply a fact of life, freeing us from poverty and economic backwardness? Not at all. I suggest in this book that the ritual of working is now fairly detached from economic necessity and even contrary to it. The real reason we work so much today (or are obsessed with its absence, if we are now part of the growing reserve army of the unemployed) has very little to do with survival. The bills and rent need to be paid, but that has nothing to do with the biopolitical flows presently investing our bodies. This is explained nicely in Himanen's *Hacker Ethic* (2001: 49):

> "Survival" or "You have to do something to earn your living" is the answer a great number of people will give when asked why they work (often responding in a mildly puzzled fashion, as if this went without saying). But strictly speaking, they do not mean mere survival—that is, having food and so on. In their use, survival refers to a certain socially determined lifestyle: they are not working merely to survive but to be able to satisfy the form of social needs characteristic to a society.

In other words, the ritual of overwork today is a socially constructed fact rather than anything bound by physical necessity. Moreover, as a social meme, it has colonized almost every other sphere of life, which represents a particular neoliberal strategy of class domination. Rubbing salt into the wound is that despite all of this needless labor, many of us are still precarious, worried, and struggling. This has made the objective politics of work difficult to identify since it is literally everywhere. Indeed, appreciating the socially constructed nature of working life today has not yet translated into its utopian abolition (Rifkin 1995), reduction to more civilized levels (Gorz 2005), or some jobless dystopia (Aronowitz and DiFazio 2010). On the contrary, its scope and reach are growing.

While this description makes late capitalist regulation seem inescapable, the book is actually not about the inordinate power of corporations, a view that seems to characterize much critical thinking today. In fact, I suggest that the opposite is the case. The for-profit firm is an outmoded social institution that has outlived its utility for most of those involved. Society has left it behind, which is why it is clinging on to us so forcefully. Capitalism and its fetishization of private property are swimming against the tide. This is evident in the way the modern firm has noticeably become parasitical in nature, riding on the extra-commercial social qualities of what Marx calls "living labor." This is not to say that the large enterprise is not an imposing institution, as it certainly is. But it must increasingly gain sustenance from sources beyond itself: the living communities and rich sociality of the 99 percent (to borrow a term from the Occupy Movement) who have basically given up on capitalism as a workable ideal.

For example, take my current home in the city of London. Once we discard the tourist brochure on the street with all the other garbage, the bleak and abject reality following years of neoliberal brutality materializes.[5] The city should be impossible, and in some ways *it actually is.* The average income is close to the national average, but the cost of living is disproportionately above that figure. Rents, transport, subsistence, childcare, retirement expenditures, and so forth are massively mismatched by income. So how on earth do the majority of workers actually survive? How does the city continue? There is only one explanation (other than outlandish credit card debts). London can reproduce itself only if a hidden public takes up the slack. This is the extra-capitalist commons, the social dark matter of neoliberal society, which now might be stepping forward as a political force in its own right.

This social commons, however, is not always progressive. For example, think of the gender politics involved in the case of, say, a female secretary who has no choice but to double up with a higher-earning male counterpart. In 2012, the conservative U.K. government implicitly recognized this hidden sociality when it justified cutting youth housing welfare. The message? Let them stay at home with their parents rent-free. In this way, the commons functions as a shock absorber for an otherwise untenable London (and global) elite. But this social force that capitalism rides on is not only passive. It is also the central driver of productive value, without which the contemporary business enterprise would be unable to function. This is especially so under neoliberal conditions given its deeply anti-social precepts—hence the rise of biopower in the workplace.

## Entering the World of Work Today

I expand on these observations by way of four brief vignettes, based on real workers' experiences and recent reports of life on the job. They not only justify my rationale for approaching employment from the perspective of biopower and the commons but also capture significant permutations around work that this book is endeavoring to explain. While these employees are all from relatively well-paid positions, I suggest in the coming chapters that a wide variety of occupations are undergoing comparative transformations.

## "Off to the Toilet—Again?"

I recently gave a presentation on the rise of biopower in the workplace, explaining why so many employees find it difficult to "turn off." The reason, I proposed, is that for all intents and purposes, *we* (our bodies, social connectivity, and cognitive aptitudes) are now the firm's means of production. After the talk I was approached by a man who happened to be a former corporate lawyer. He told me that the talk resonated with his own experiences in this sector before he decided to escape and go back to the academic life. The event that hardened his resolve to quit was described to me as follows.

Long hours, stress, and deadlines meant that to get the job done well, employees often found themselves working outside of official hours, especially in the middle of the night. Hardly anyone took vacations, not because they were afraid of being sacked, as prevalent in the old days of Fordism, but because they simply would not know what to do. These employees were so saturated with their jobs that it was difficult to see anything of worth outside of them.

Eventually, a fellow team member that the former lawyer knew was forced to take a two-week vacation, as he had not done so since joining the company. So far, so good. The said team member arranged a beach holiday in Crete with his partner. Bidding farewells, no one expected to hear from him for another two weeks. However, the office soon noticed that every two or three days our would-be vacationer appeared to mysteriously clear his work e-mails in a frenetic, compact one-hour period. Upon his return to the office, they queried this unexpected work. His reply was telling of what happens to us under biopolitical capitalism. He could not face doing nothing all day on a beach. So he smuggled his Blackberry to the seashore, retiring to the toilet for an hour to clear his e-mails, presumably giving his partner some excuse about the quality of the previous evening's meal. Our former lawyer told me that this case of work addiction was enough for him to seriously consider leaving, which he eventually did.

The vignette touches on some salient themes that this book explores in relation to corporatized biopower (i.e., the extension of work into every facet of one's life), its parasitical nature (i.e., how non-work or free work is central to capitalist productivity today) and the disfigurement it wreaks on what we might call the bio-proletariat. First of all, we see evidence of what Gregg (2011) terms "presence bleed," whereby the template of productivity becomes evermore part of one's waking and sleeping life. In this case, the job is no longer a concrete task that can be delineated in time and space, and then forgotten once the workday is over. It is now somehow inscribed inside and between us as an inexorable pressure to produce. More specifically, work becomes ironically non-instrumental, as Weeks (2011) puts it, or *inessential*. Its biopolitical abstraction detaches the performance of working from specific tasks. This decoupling ironically rivets us even tighter to a job rather than freeing us from it because working paradoxically becomes *everything.*

The vignette also tells us what happens to our lives when work becomes a universal reference point. The notion of the social factory, first posited by writers in the Italian autonomist tradition, has sometimes been used to describe this socio-economic trend. The template of work escapes the factory, infecting life itself like some poisonous gas. As Hardt and Negri (1994: 9–10) put it:

> Laboring processes have moved outside the factory walls to invest the entire society. In other words, the apparent decline of the factory as site of production does not mean a decline of the regime and discipline of factory production, but means that it is no longer limited to a particular site in society. It has insinuated itself throughout all social forms of production, spreading like a virus.

In my mind, two important observations follow. First, because neoliberal capitalism cannot reproduce itself on its own terms, it actually needs non-capitalist spaces to take up the slack and absorb its shocks. Moreover, these social spaces are also active value creators for the firm, allowing it to remain organized while adhering to its own chaotic principles. This is what some have called the communist underbelly of late capitalist enterprise.[6] The social factory certainly appears to be a totalizing presence as work spreads into every aspect of life. But it can never be so, since neoliberal capitalism would implode without an external living commons—be it free time, artisanal enthusiasm, or life itself. Theorists of the social factory and corporate colonization often miss this crucial point when they describe it as an omniscient force. It isn't, and that makes matters far more serious.

Second, the way this autonomy *outside of capital and work* is positively lived now becomes a pertinent ethical question. For many workers like the one mentioned above, autonomous free time is experienced something like a black hole, an existential nothingness that evokes anxiety, sometimes anger and boredom, but mostly sadness (see Ehrenberg 2010 for the reasons why). Yes, I am on vacation, but every part of me is otherwise indexed to the job, and this is why my so-called free time feels so vacuous. This might also account for the growing number of advice columns and forums on the difficult art of "learning how to vacation" ("Learning How to Vacation" 2012). One employee interviewed in this telling *New York Times* piece confessed that after her holiday, "I hoped to return home at peace. Instead I was exhausted, defeated and irritable."

The neoliberal state, on the other hand, is more worried that its citizenry will start directing this free time toward socially progressive goals, which would also publicly reveal that we do not actually need to spend all of this time working. Perhaps this is why the U.K. government lately insisted that the unemployed work without remuneration in fast-food restaurants, and more recently, at the 2012 Olympic Games (see "It's Companies like G4S" 2012). The message is clear. You are not meant to enjoy your freedom from work! This is also why even being unemployed today weighs on us like a full-time job.[7] Indeed, even the playful spaces of childhood are deemed suspicious by the corporatized state. An array of entrepreneurial school programs designed to instill the virtues of continuous enterprise at an early age are commonplace in many schools (Beder 2009). In this sense, the ideology of work is dangerous because it has decoupled itself from income, task, and function and is now more about *who you are.*

### *"Try Measuring This!"*

The second vignette also demonstrates the need for renewed concepts regarding the nature of much employment today. It occurred after another presentation of mine, this time in the United States. After giving a talk on *biocracy* (discussed in Chapter 1), I was approached by a management consultant. She too found some of the ideas useful for explaining what she was experiencing at work. The aspect of biocracy that interested her was the way in which most performance measures (billable hours, in her case) were so obsolete that she and her colleagues would fill them out almost randomly. The nature of the job meant not only that she was *always* on call but also that so much discretion and unwritten knowhow were required that the firm's objective measurement system for tracking work was nearly useless. Moreover, it was not just concrete labor time that was difficult to quantify. Much of the informal work required to perform the job was completely omitted from the company's spreadsheet. And to make matters worse, it appeared that this immeasurability had become a kind of perverse open secret—management knew it, the client saw it, and the consultants lived it. But the company enforced the measurement system nevertheless, making it feel as if control were being exerted for its own sake.

Important here is the way the body or more accurately its spontaneous social resourcefulness is integrated into the firm's power relations to such an extent that metrics demarcating work and non-work time, for example, become meaningless. I demonstrate in this book that the utilization of living labor is crucial to the current phase of biocapitalism, not because of the corporation's strength, but because of its core weakness. Just as neoliberal institutions find it impossible to reproduce themselves, the corporate form too frequently discovers that its own directives are impossible to enact. For this reason, living labor finds itself working around the anti-social guidelines of capitalist enterprise, mostly at the cost of the workers' time and well-being.

If this social excess allows things to get done—while remaining inscrutable to the measures of capitalist rationality—it is only because the firm would otherwise be shambolic without it. Hence, the official edicts of managerialism often appear so needless for achieving any given task. This might seem strange until we realize that the business enterprise was never designed to functionally achieve collective goals.

assumption is, of course, the central weakness of functional sociology, especially in the U.S. tradition inaugurated by Talcott Parsons.
We must instead view corporations as primarily class-based systems,
both in terms of their low-paid periphery and the relationships within
the core. Management controls are essentially deployed to keep a lid
on the conflict of interests at the heart of the employment relationship.
Discussions by old-school business researchers are amusing in this regard because they assumed management was about coordinating activity to accomplish common objectives. Take these first impressions
of a worried researcher studying a well-known U.S. plant in the 1950s:

> Management is so preoccupied with its efforts to establish con-
> trol over the workers, that it loses sight of the presumed pur-
> pose of the organization. A casual visitor to the plant might
> indeed be surprised to learn that its purpose was to get out
> production. Certainly, if it had been possible to enforce some
> of the rules described . . . the result would have been a slowing
> down of production. (Whyte 1955: 65–66)

This might look like bad management, but it is actually a fairly accu-
rate definition of management in most situations characterized by class
conditions, for there is nothing common in the capitalistic endeavor.
This is why most of us find it so bewilderingly maladroit. Management
was invented not to help get things done, but to be obeyed.

Returning to our consultant: What exactly is being put to work
here that is above and beyond the numerical measures designed to
track her productivity? We must avoid the temptation to evoke bourgeois categories such as personal space, family time, goodwill, and
so on. No, what is being captured is something the firm structurally *cannot* and frequently *will not* (because of cost-saving imperatives)
provide itself: the unquantifiable richness of living labor that, as the
following chapters show, can never be entirely aligned with the capitalist agenda. It is frequently exploited yet intrinsically exceeds that
exploitation.

Two important qualifications must be made. First, "life" as defined here is not just the fleshy individual organism. It is also the
social aggregation that this body passes through, a stratum that conveys our *collective faculty* to act together. As Virno puts it, "The liv-

ing body becomes an object to be governed not for its intrinsic value, but because it is the substratum of what really matters: labor-power as the aggregate of the most diverse human faculties (the potential for speaking, for thinking, for remembering, for acting, etc.)" (Virno 2004: 83). In light of this, we must always think of the surplus or excess that the consultant's timesheet fails to measure in *social terms*. Otherwise we risk making the mistake that Marx warned us of long ago, fetishizing the individual worker and thereby missing his or her social character.

And second, this collective faculty of living labor can never enter into a functional relationship with its own exploitation. Even if there sometimes do appear to be moments of stability, there is no social equilibrium. The development of the excess/capture dynamic is always defined by struggle and non-coincidence, for if the living common was but a reflection of capital, it too would be immediately consigned to the category of dead labor.

## *"Bring Out the Guitar"*

If the logic of the factory has escaped the corporate precinct to infect ever more spheres of our lives, then the converse has occurred too. Perhaps the strangest aspect of life in the firm today is the managerial evocation of what used to be left alone as non-work under Fordism. This development is telling of why biopower becomes salient precisely when neoliberal capitalism enters into crisis. An example illustrates why.

In the city of London, a major trend in workplace motivation tools involves encouraging art, crafts, and music in the office. This may sound like a bad joke from the television series *The Office* (starring the frustratingly annoying David Brent, who secretly wants to be a pop star), but now life imitates art. A local commuter newspaper recently ran a story on one such company entitled "I Really Am a One-Man Band" (Chesworth 2012). The firm consults to clients with motivation, creativity, and engagement problems. As the CEO explains, "The company has successfully worked with a number of high-profile corporate clients in the City to integrate music into the working day." Learning and reciting a guitar riff or favorite song on the job is thought to breathe life back into the office, a social sphere that has long been drained of such leisurely and artistic activities. According to one enthusiastic client, "Within one hour I was playing 'Hey Jude' and after 10 lessons I have a modest repertoire."

We might put this appearance of non-work in the office down to yet another harebrained management incentive scheme. It probably is that, but is also symptomatic of more serious trends that are investigated in this book. If the corporation and its neoliberal institutional complex cannot reproduce itself, then management sometimes attempts to stage or replicate the buzz of life in the office so that productivity doesn't stall. Themes around non-work are crucial because they point to the social surplus lying *beyond* capitalist rationality, which, as we noted earlier, the business firm is conspicuously dependent on today. Hardt and Negri (2009: 152) emphasize the unframable nature of this social excess: "The affective and intellectual talents, the capacities to generate co-operation and organizational networks, the communication skills, and other competencies that characterize bio-political labor, are generally not site specific. You can think and form relationships not only on the job but also in the street, with your neighbours and friends. The capacities of biopolitical labor-power exceed work and spill over into life."

This non-site-specific social surplus is qualitatively beyond capitalism but is nevertheless its chief source of wealth and the catalyst for many post-capitalist emancipatory movements presently emerging. In terms of the corporation's interest in prospecting and capturing it, a whole host of examples from industry are evident. From replicating late night parties in call centers, to imitating slacker cool in IT firms (think of Mark Zuckerberg's Facebook trademark "hoodie") to workplace spirituality programs, the list goes on.

This trend is frequently interpreted by business commentators as a management-led concession, humanizing an otherwise dull and drab office setting. Perhaps. But more importantly, it is linked to the way capitalism needs to access *aggregate* living labor, which lies outside the algorithms of dead labor epitomized by the formal corporation. This aggregate excess is analogous to our agile ability to improvise around linguistic rules when speaking or choosing to remain silent. Rules on their own do not work here because of the infinite regress problem. They need a non-regressive backdrop of common knowhow, an excess that is difficult to measure or represent. This is why non-work is now such a prominent feature in many business organizations today.

## "A Banker in Disguise"

The final vignette puts the above cases and theoretical observations in the context of the serious legitimacy crisis that work is now undergoing. It is useful for understanding why biopower is assuming its present format and the rationale behind those attempting to refuse it.

The story relates to an encounter the author had in a London East End pub during a number of banking scandals, when the financial crisis seemed interminable and the legitimacy of business (and work itself) reached new lows. At the bar, another customer recognized my antipodean accent and struck up a conversation. He seemed to have a fairly working-class background, fitting for a pub in this area, and as the conversation developed he asked what I did. "A university lecturer," I said; "I teach and stuff." Because he looked a little bored by that answer, I reciprocated by asking him his occupation. "I'm an investment banker." I thought he was making fun of me, and then he explained. "I can't come into any of these pubs in a suit, it would be suicide." Bankers and anyone looking like they are from London's business community were so excoriated by the London population that this man felt it necessary to dress down to avoid attracting attention. His conversation became even more interesting after another round of drinks:

> It's not only because people think banking in the city is corrupt that makes them hate us, 'cause it's been like that for a long time; something else has changed. I think it's what we exemplify that really gets people angry. The whole system is rotten; *all* jobs are phony; no one is happy. The atmosphere has changed a lot. Everyone thinks work really stinks, that it's all been a bit of a con job, and we remind people of that—well, our suits do. Another beer?

The banking crisis certainly has made many of us 99 percenters very skeptical about the political, moral, and economic worth of the banking sector (and as I write, the LIBOR scandal involving Barclay's and HSBC is currently unfolding in the world's media). But as our disguised banker indicates, the sense of corruption seems to have cut deep into the public imagination, from suspicions about the mendacity of environmentally friendly products, to the sanctity of international markets or the social legitimacy of so-called democratic governments (especially following the bail-outs of the banking industry), to the *idea of work itself.*

One has only to read the hundreds of online blogs and forums to notice how many of us now feel duped by the very concept of work, about the societal worth of our overworked lifestyles and the merit of our so-called important jobs. What we might call the anti-work movement is no longer the reserve of marginalized militants (e.g., the Invisible Committee), or the material for fly-on-the-wall paperbacks (such as Sam's [2009] *Checkout*) or the inspiration for post-beat poets like Charles Bukowski. For a new generation of employees for whom precarity is the norm and the glaring statistics concerning income/wealth inequality are common knowledge, working has completely lost its cultural credibility.

Much of this is due to the economic reorganization of employment and its depressing class structure. Moreover, the young working poor are now a widespread facet of the middle class in many Western societies, which gives their dissatisfaction a strong generational dimension.[8] But a pervasive and trans-class malaise is evident here too. As Gorz (2005) argues regarding the results of a large-scale survey in Europe, this pervasive attitude is basically one of *pointlessness*. Indeed, it is interesting here to look at the tell-all question that downsizing consultants ask employees when deciding whether they should be fired: "If you did not come in tomorrow, would it make a difference?" If they answer yes, then they have to justify their job. If they answer no, they are dismissed because they are not adding value. But would not today's reigning attitude toward work be one that answers with a resounding *no*?

As Cederström and Fleming (2012) reveal, for the working multitude in a wide variety of occupations, most feel that what they do doesn't really matter to anyone, since their job seems so far removed from authentic social needs. And this brings us to a central problem, one that underlies the biopoliticization of employment as I see it. While the work ethic is now dead and buried, we nevertheless have to act *as if* work is a virtue of the highest order. In other words, its biopoliticization renders our jobs both pointless and also the most totalizing force in our lives. And this cultivates a political mindset among the workforce that is qualitatively different from previous manifestations of discontent.[9]

## The Commons versus Community at Work

To make matters more complex, capitalism itself has recently invented its own version of the commons in order to counteract the anxiety-ridden and fetid atmosphere found in jobs like the ones discussed above. In particular, the notion of community has been resuscitated as a possible antidote to the widespread discontent around work. We must distinguish this trend, which is congruent with the bio-exploitation evident in the vignettes, from the substantive social common that this book seeks to explore. The currently fashionable discourse celebrating organizational communities (i.e., having a shared sense of well-being and belonging at work) follows, I would argue, from the decline and failure of the corporate therapeutics movement in the 1990s. Its passing was fairly predictable because most employees—from the university lecturer to the health care provider—never really accepted the idea that one might be happy *and* overworked, satisfied *and* dominated, serene *and* exploited, free *and* micro-managed. Such contradictions might be temporarily surmountable in certain settings, such as the fascist state or totalitarian polity—but the suture can never really hold in the context of capitalist employment relations because of the a priori class antagonism.

The revitalization of workplace community, therefore, is indicative of a highly instrumental capitalist return to "the social" following the anti-social wave of neoliberal downsizing in the West and beyond. Consumer and brand communities are now viewed with a sanguine eye, as if the spontaneous collective identities that coagulate around specific brands might foster a feeling of homeliness in a world long stripped of solidarity. Likewise, the world of work has very recently been rethought in a manner that predicates community as a positive path out of the malaise that defines work for many today. Richard Sennett's contributions over the last few years, including *The Craftsman* (2009) and *Together* (2012), has called for the reevaluation of the social qualities of paid employment. He suggests that because most of us need to cooperate to do jobs well, we ought to officially acknowledge this fact rather than persist with outdated notions of isolated individualism, short-termism, and flexible contracts.

Erring more to the political Right, the conservative commentator David Brooks makes a surprisingly similar argument in *The Social Animal* (2011), whereby the collaborative capacities of people are celebrated as a panacea within an otherwise doomed civilization. For sure, the number of books on these themes continues to grow, with titles mentioning supercooperation, the gift, we-share, altruism and the unselfish gene. In my view, we ought to read most of these arguments as part of the arsenal with which a wounded neoliberalism is waging a new war—to both save itself and mollify an increasingly unhappy 99 percent. The type of community proposed by Brooks, among others, in fact undermines genuine emancipatory progress because it still believes that we might have the free joys of sociality *and* capitalism at the same time. And we know that isn't possible, as we shall soon see

Other popular tracts similarly promulgate the spurious belief that the commons might morally reform an otherwise self-destructive socio-economic paradigm. A prominent example is Barnes's (2006) *Capitalism 3.0: A Guide for Reclaiming the Commons.* On the surface, the book seems to make some useful points about what is occurring in the capitalist world today. Take its promotional descriptor:

> The Commons, our shared social, environmental and artistic inheritance, is under threat from market pressures to be sold off by profit-seekers. Our common heritage is being traded away to the highest bidder. By looking at current issues like Social Security and campaign finances, Barnes creates an economic model that both reinforces the strengths of our capitalist system, and abates its damaging effects upon the current culture and future generations.

Few would disagree. But the argument soon begins to unravel. It incorrectly posits the idea that we might have the structural features of capitalism (plus its alleged benefits of wealth creation, innovation, jobs, and so on) and an open, creative public commons. This oxymoron leads Barnes to make some confusing conclusions: "Capitalism 2.0 had its moments. It defeated communism, leveled national boundaries to trade, and brought material abundance never seen before. . . . But Capitalism 3.0 has a higher purpose. To help both capitalism and the human species achieve their full potential. To do that our economic machine must stop destroying the commons and start protecting it" (2006: 167–168). Claims like this do not make sense, for obvious reasons.

On the basis of the findings presented in this book, we can clearly see the ideological trap functioning in arguments like this. First, it ignores the axiomatic nature of the capitalist project and in some cases mystifies it. A system born around the private ownership of the means of production can never genuinely incorporate its own impossibility, that of an open and gift-oriented commonwealth (Nancy 2000). The massive enclosure movement in the early industrial period is an important indicator of the system's DNA. An open community might be fragmentally built around or against the anti-social nature of private property, but never in it.[10]

The second problem with the capitalism *and* the commons thesis is a little more complex and pertains to an argument I explore in this book. While capitalism is structurally bound to be adversarial to the commons it is also fundamentally reliant on it. This is especially salient under neoliberalism, since it is openly hostile to the collective labor that it is simultaneously dependent on to capture economic value. This is the central spirit of class antagonism in Western capitalism today and is gathering in force as we speak.

My criticisms of the commons and capitalism argument is just another way of stating what Marx said long ago about how a false society translates into a false social experience: "To say that man is alienated from himself is to say that the society of this alienated man is a caricature of his real community" ([1844] 2013). Society becomes an antinomy of its own reflection. This formula is complicated in the biopolitical era of work, however, because while community is impossible in the shadow of corporatized relations, it is also paradoxically what this institutional form now needs most. Human resource managers might invent tools to try and imitate the living commons in the office, usually by way of evoking non-work associatives, but its inherent *impossibility* is manifest to everyone.[11]

## Conclusion

Can this impossibility at the heart of contemporary capitalism be politically activated to oppose and escape work? There is no doubt that worker resistance is still alive and well today. However, under the shifting biopolitical conditions described above, the problem for anyone wanting to oppose work concerns identifying a suitable target. Is it the boss, our co-worker, ourselves? What kind of contestation can subvert a mode of power that invests life itself, flirts with our own self-styled interests, and promises us an authentic workplace community?

These questions are significantly different from those confronting the typical factory worker (that a good deal of employees around the world still remain) or the classic bureaucrat, both for whom life and work are clearly demarcated. The power of work over our lives today is so highly embodied and socialized, it behooves us to partially revise what we understand by resistance, its target, and its objectives concerning the future and non-future of work.

For example, the very word *resistance* is deeply problematic. We think of it as a secondary response to a primary power structure. We can no longer conceptualize counter-capitalist politics in these terms for two reasons. First, as I argue in this book, it is the capitalist enterprise that so often resists today, since it is increasingly assuming a reactive stance to the overwhelming emancipatory change sweeping through society, especially concerning the commons. Second, and building on the first point, much worker resistance is no longer *against* capitalism, fighting it to gain a better deal within its parameters. There is a growing perception that neoliberal capitalism is irrevocably bereft of any future promise. It is now the commons that is the vanguard first-mover, constituting new ways of life, making the corporation worthy only for abandonment.

This kind of refusal, moreover, has nothing to do with work-life balance programs, which have always been a ruse to reconcile us to our own exploitation. Nor is it related to idleness, laziness, or even illness (as with the Socialist Patients Collective's *Turn Illness into a Weapon* [1972]), all of which have been considered in the post-workerist literature. The problem with these practices is that they tend to reinforce the broader backdrop of a work-saturated society. This is where the radical autonomy of the commons comes into play. As I demonstrate in the following pages, biopolitical workers are not seeking to withdraw into solitude or bourgeois individualism, but to escape back into collective life, reclaiming the public labor *that we already are.*

We can already see the beginnings of a radical repossession movement among the growing disenfranchised working classes, which now includes almost everybody given the universalization of work. The common is being retained. From the cooperatives in southern Europe to the *fabricas recuperadas* (recovered factories) trend in Argentina in which deserted zones of production are reclaimed by the unemployed, self-valorization and detachment are central concepts for understanding what life looks like after work. New social movements around new approaches to labor are emerging in the United States and elsewhere as the manufactured nature of overwork and precarity are recognized.[12] Most importantly, these post-work worlds are not in some far-away, inscrutable future. Once we appreciate that it is, in fact, the living material that a semi-dead neoliberalism depends on to persist, another world appears before us—rich, enjoyable, and endless. How this joyous world might be grasped is swiftly becoming the central problem concerning the politics of work today.

# 1

# Come as You Are

*The New Corporate Enclosure Movement*

The best way to think about how biopower characterizes work today is to play a little thought experiment. Imagine if the sociologist Max Weber were to enter the offices and service outlets that make up a large majority of workplaces in the West today. There would be, of course, much that he would recognize. The filing systems might have been computerized and the old-fashion dark oak décor replaced by the glare of eco-friendly fluorescent lights, but the cubicles and background hum of rationality would be familiar.

Some features, however, would completely dumbfound our German time-traveler. Rather than the officeholder and office, the worker and their role being separated, rendering employees indistinguishable from one another, Weber would be shocked by the sheer personality expressed in the modern corporation. Far from being banished from the workplace, subjective resourcefulness is now a key source of value. Instead of eradicating play and fun, a whole consulting industry now aims to transform work into an enjoyable experience.

Whereas in Weber's time, bureaucracy was defined by expunging all non-official and non-work associatives from the job, today many employees are encouraged by "liberation management" to express their independence, unique personalities, and all that is different about them, including their sexual orientation and lifestyle. Indeed, one of the strangest aspects of contemporary management discourse is its explicit reliance on facets of life that Fordism would have deemed out of place in the office. In some large U.S. corporations, for example, workers are invited to express who they really are outside of their work roles. The management consultant Gurnek Bains and his coauthors describe this in terms of authenticity. On the basis of a number of empirical cases, they note how "enlightened" CEOs attempt to increase engagement among the workforce:

> A major reason why people don't feel a sense of genuine belonging to their organizations is that they have learned to be inauthentic and so have those around them. Take the example of Simon, a senior executive in a media company. He told us: "[F]or so long, I hadn't been bringing myself to work. I wasn't really prepared to let others see or know the true me. . . . [T]hen I woke up one morning and I realized, I'm living my life with these people, so what's the point in pretending." (2007: 248)

The language is curious in the way it frames the "true me" as something beyond the directives of the office, almost beyond manageability itself. The "true me" is signified by those parts of his character he would usually conceal from the corporate gaze, much of which can be expressed only outside of work. This shift in management practice has resulted in two important developments. First is the attempt to encourage and capture the informal organizational world, which in the past was viewed as a hazardous zone of autonomy by managers. Play, misbehavior, games, humor, and fooling around are not only permitted by liberation management; they are increasingly engineered through various exercises and events. One has only to think of the formidable number of studies documenting the rise of puerile role-playing drills in organizations, often devised by "funsultants" who bully employees into singing children's songs, wearing pajamas and even smiling while doing so (see Cederström and Fleming 2012 for a full summary of these distressing technologies of fun).

The second development is more proper to the sea change that this book investigates. Rather than badly imitate non-work memes in the office, the firm instead seeks to capture what workers *already are,* especially those self-sufficient and highly social qualities indicative of a life beyond calculative rationality. Kuhn (2006) calls this the lifestyle approach to labor management, where companies hope to engender more agile and creative performances by welcoming the whole person into the workplace. This may take banal forms such as informal dress codes or the obligatory tattoo displayed in the office. But some enterprises go much farther, dotting the call center with surfboards and electric guitars, permitting children to roam the hallways and intentionally leaving the office only half-furnished to evoke a warehouse atmosphere.

According to Florida (2004a), the aesthetic labor of the creative class (which includes almost everybody according to his overly expansive definition) demands increased self-expression and the freedom to be "complete people" (Florida 2004a: 222) in the workplace. As a result, organizations are increasingly relaxed about the presence of signs of life in the paper-littered cubicle, retail shop floor, health care center, and so forth.

If non-work signifiers are today found in the workspace, then the reverse has occurred too. The code of productivity has escaped the cubicle, infiltrating life and society more generally. Most employees, of course, still clock in and out as per usual. But an interesting trend appears to be gaining momentum. In their best-selling pop-business book *Why Work Sucks and How to Fix It* (2011), Ressler and Thompson note the prevalence of Results Only Work Environments (or ROWE) in U.S. industry. Many companies now focus on output indicators, rather than inputs as conventional management wisdom prescribes. As long as a project deadline is met, for example, firms do not care when, how, and where the work is done—be it in your underwear in the middle of the night or in a local café on Monday morning. As for the danger that workers might simply sleep all day? According to the authors, the exact opposite occurs: "It's not about giving people more time with the kids. ROWE is not about having more time off. . . . [Y]ou may even work more" (2011: 61).[1]

The spread of temporary work and zero hour contracts (where workers are on permanent call) is certainly linked to this development. But we can also note a broader change, especially in the way corporate managerialism understands itself in a wide range of employment settings. In his rather absurdly titled book *The Seven Day Weekend* (2007), the construction industry entrepreneur Ricardo Semler gives us a sense of this shift:

> Imagine a company where employees set their own hours; where there are no offices, no job titles, no business plans;

where employees get to endorse or veto any new venture; where kids are encouraged to run the halls; and where the CEO lets other people make nearly all the decisions . . . if you have the freedom to get your job done on your own terms and to blend your work life and personal life with enthusiasm and creative energy. Smart bosses will eventually realize that you might be most productive if you work on Sunday afternoon, play golf on Monday morning, go to a movie on Tuesday afternoon, and watch your child play soccer on Thursday. (Semler 2007: 13)

Of course, we should not give too much substantive weight to fanciful proclamations made by a multimillionaire CEO. However, there is now some empirical evidence indicating that these ideas are increasingly being adopted in a wide range of jobs. Many firms appear to be realizing that productive labor might just as easily occur outside office hours as during them. I argue that this is suggestive of a new form of power at work, one that aims to enlist social qualities that normally lie beyond the reach of corporate rationality. This is not to say that conventional management controls, such as bureaucracy or technocracy, have been supplanted. On the contrary. They have been augmented by what may be called *biocracy*, whereby bios or life itself becomes an essential human resource to be exploited.[2]

This chapter presents a brief overview of the main themes of this book. I develop the concept of "biocracy" by building on Michel Foucault's landmark studies of biopower. He argued that regulation in modern societies is not only exerted by traditional top-down hierarchies—overt bureaucracy, state judicial structures, or technological domination. It is also secured through infra-political means, by infiltrating and enrolling our wider life practices. Regulation is personified in activities usually reserved for aspects of life extraneous to formal governance structures. And when the key tension is not just between capital and labor but also between *capital and life,* we require revised concepts to understand how the workforce refuses its biopolitical capture.

## From Biopower to Living Labor

What exactly is biopower and how might the concept be used to understand the employment trends noted above? The idea was most famously explained in some of the last works of Michel Foucault, where he argued it was central for understanding sexuality (Foucault 1978) and the governmentality of populations under neoliberalism more generally (Foucault 2008). He considered biopower distinct from what he had earlier called "disciplinary regimes." Disciplinary power developed in the modern prison and is based on the strict training of bodies within tightly regulated spaces. Timetables, confinement, and the internalization of surveillance characteristic of prisons, he argued in *Discipline and Punish* (1977), subsequently proliferated throughout society to become a key model for the factory, hospital, school, and so forth.

Biopower is different. It concerns not only the physical organism but also broader ways of living as such, activities that have tended to be considered more of a secondary reproductive resource for powerful institutions. This kind of regulation does not seek to contain the subject of power. Instead it utilizes its inherent and self-productive qualities. This is how biopower assumes a virtual form because it transcends disciplinary demarcations, such as work and non-work. This is also, Foucault argued, how populations—their hygiene, bodily functions, familial conduct, and political alliances—are governed from afar in modern liberal societies.

The lectures entitled *The Birth of Biopolitics* (2008) are strikingly prescient in the way they highlight the then nascent neoliberal project as a sign of things to come. Foucault singles out economists like Gary Becker (1976) and R. E. Lucas (1972) as leading harbingers of a new type of domination. Their ideas around human capital particularly foretold the arrival of regulative measures that seek to index life more commonly to the needs of economic utility. Social adaptability, emotional intelligence, and our very ability to engage in useful human action are recruited in this respect. Value comes *before* the factory or marketplace, and this represents a significant break in capitalist reason, which has always sought to restrict life in name of productivity. This is why Foucault suggests that neoliberal thought implies a weird capitalism without capitalism version of society—that is to say, a version comprising the embodied reciprocity of non-corporate relations *and* the anodyne machinery of economic reason.

For sure, this fundamental contradiction runs throughout most corporate discourse today. It is the fantasy of the capitalist "other" that secures the capitalist faith in itself. Recall the claims of Semler (2007), the construction entrepreneur mentioned above, and his seven-day weekend that will never arrive. He appears to desire capitalism *and* its social transcendence, communal collectivism and private owner-ship. The pure impossibility of capitalism haunts its own reflexive self-awareness. Just think of the all-pervasive corporate social responsibility discourse that implicitly posits a non-capitalist supplement to make itself whole.[3]

I suggest that this trend is broadly symptomatic of how capitalism today is frenetically turning to the social common to protract its other-wise steady decline. Indeed, I argue that the arrival of biopower in the workplace signals a deepening crisis at the heart of the neoliberal proj-ect. As such, the disciplinary tropes of spatial confinement and docile bodies are less important in this biopolitical context. Life is accelerated rather than restricted, harnessed rather than coercively shaped anew. Timetables are too clumsy and wasteful in this respect. As Foucault explains in relation to U.S. neoliberalism, biopower instead aims to

> generalize the enterprise form within the social body or social fabric. . . . [T]he individual's life itself—with his relationships to his private property, with his family, household, insurance and retirement—must make him into a sort of permanent and multiple enterprise. . . . [I]t involves extending the economic model of supply and demand and investment-cost-profit so as to make it a model of social relations and existence itself, a form of relationship of the individual to himself, time, those around him, the group and the family. (Foucault 2008: 241–242)

Foucault's reading of this trend is notable for its foresight. How-ever, a central weakness is the way he needlessly downplays conflict and class struggle in the analysis. It is remarkable that Foucault theo-rizes the birth of neoliberalism without any indication of the hostility that accompanied it, as we saw with Thatcherism, for example. The neo-Kantian preference for an idea's internal consistency—as opposed to the messy political context in which it plays out—tends to mar Foucault's argument. This is where Italian autonomist thought, in-cluding Hardt and Negri (2009) and Virno (2004, 2008) among oth-ers, is useful since it places the birth of biopower within a capitalist framework.

The emphasis here is less on bare life (our naked and vulnerable biological organism) than on how forms of life become integral to the exploitation process. Whereas life used to be considered a reproductive force of secondary importance compared to the primary point of production, neoliberal doxa considerably blurs this border. The concept of biopower tells us why. As Hardt and Negri (1999) put it, "Life is no longer produced in the cycles of reproduction that are subordinated to the working day; on the contrary, life is what infuses and dominates all production. The excess of value is determined today in the affects, in the bodies crisscrossed with knowledge, in the intelligence of the mind, and in the sheer power to act" (Hardt and Negri 1999: 367).

Building on this insight, I suggest that three historical changes in corporate hegemony prefigure the rise of biopower at work.

First of all, the Fordist structural crisis of the 1970s was certainly born out of mounting inefficiencies bedeviling command and control systems of economic management. The oil embargo and economic drain of the Cold War no doubt exacerbated the situation. But while the falling rate of profit may have prompted the need for urgent change from the capitalist's perspective, what the rest of us got was more of the same, but only in a much nastier format. Neoliberal activists employed the mid-1970s crisis as a pretext to wage a dirty class war from above, both deepening the commercial ethic and confiscating the social gains made by labor following the post–World War II compact. If Fordism was bad for workers, it was nothing compared to the brutality that followed. There was, however, one flaw in the plan. On the ground, neoliberalism is so impractical and anti-social that it required the very thing it despised in order to keep going: autonomous living labor.

Second, a new appreciation of the working subject emerged that essentially aimed to enlist workers themselves to organize an otherwise inoperative employment infrastructure: hence the sudden focus in the 1990s on self-managing teams and empowerment, the self-styled learning abilities of staff, and the flexible portfolio career—the last of which had the added benefit of shifting many of the risks of capital investment onto workers themselves. The disease-like proliferation of the credit card soon followed, paving the way for even more original methods for externalizing the costs of exploitative employment practices.

And third, with the de-industrialization of Western economies, many jobs have come to include a highly socialized element, detached from external-specific tasks such as screwing on a bolt. The object

k is suddenly framed in terms of human capital, whereby the
ndent cooperative abilities of workers become central to profitability. Indeed, from the mid-1990s onward, there was a transformation in the corporate mindset. Enterprises no longer considered their
role to be compositional or educational (e.g., training and mentoring)
apropos of the workforce. This was not due to neglectfulness. On the
contrary, the corporate matrix simply appreciated that it required interpersonal qualities it couldn't muster on its own, social competencies
that developed from far richer social depositories. Without tapping
these intuitive aptitudes of labor it would not be able to survive this
specific configuration of capitalism. And so class struggle was born
anew but in a much more expansive form. The site of antagonism
spreads out from formal work time to encompass *life*, which in turn
gives rise to new understandings of future freedoms.[4]

## The Birth of Biocracy at Work

It is because biopower seeks to enlist these living attributes that typically lie beyond the time of formal exploitation that we see the sudden
corporate interest in non-work today. While not necessarily theorized
as a biopolitical tendency, many studies have noted this curious shift
in the organization of work. Andrew Ross's study of life at Razorfish,
for example, is striking in how it reveals the firm importing "lifestyle
components back into the workplace" (Ross 2004: 139). This might
not seem unusual at first. But we soon discover that the boundary between work and life was almost non-existent. And this was integral to
productivity, since "ideas and creativity were just as likely to surface
at home or in other locations, and so employees were encouraged to
work elsewhere. . . . [T]he goal was to extract every waking moment
of an employee's day" (Ross 2004: 52). So while it might be tempting to view this emphasis on lifestyle as a relaxation of management
power, the result is the systematic *extension* of capitalist regulation
rather than its repose.

The reason why is central to our investigation. Capitalism has
perhaps always required some non-coincidental externality to persist
given its internal contradictions. As Marx noted long ago, "The *real
barrier* to capitalist production is *capitalism itself*" ([1894] 1981: 206).
The nation state, civil society, and community sectors have all played
this role in the development of capitalist society. This constitutive

weakness, however, is immeasurably intensified under neoliberalism, for it would swiftly implode if it succeeded in transforming our world into a perfect reflection of its own principles (e.g., pure competition, pure individualism, no state, no public goods, and no mutualism). To maintain its hegemony, therefore, neoliberal capitalism requires currents of social life that lie beyond its otherwise unworkable precepts. This is why non-work or non-labor is so important today. Virno makes this point, which is useful to our argument:

> The productive cooperation in which labor-power participates is always larger and richer than the one put into play by the labor process. It includes also the world of non-labor, the experiences and knowledge matured outside of the factory and the office. Labor-power increases the value of capital only because it never loses its qualities of non-labor. (Virno 2004: 203)

One might object here. Why could such "experiences and knowledge" not be matured *inside* the factory or office? Do we not build social networks on the job as well? This is, of course, true. But I do not think this is what Virno means. Non-work is the fundamental supplement that makes capitalist rationality possible. We must really press ourselves to avoid approaching this issue in numerical terms, a larger or lesser quantum of space/time beyond work. As a qualitative or *immanent* social relation, the non-labor Virno is referring to is actually everywhere within the social body.[5]

We can see this more clearly if we examine the way capitalist reason operates, which is especially apparent under extreme neoliberal conditions. Unlike other modes of human action, capitalism cannot be articulated without a contextual reference point beyond itself. In other words, it gains traction through a fundamental *negation*—gathering itself only in the reflection of that which it is not: in this case, free and non-coerced social interaction inside and outside the workplace. Non-work (or non-labor) is the *counter-negation* of this negation not because it is somehow better than exploitative reason, but because it does not rely on an "other" to make itself whole. And just as the speaker doesn't undo the semantic rules he or she uses when speaking, social cooperation too engenders its own affirmative excess. This makes it inherently larger and richer than the reductive matrix that puts it to work.

Because living labor represents social knowhow accumulated within itself, it is paradoxically always more than what it is. And for this reason no one can own or subordinate it completely to the forces of economic exploitation. Embodied moments of collective expertise might occur *around* rationalization processes, but never within them. This is why, as we noted earlier, the exigency for some human externality is so noticeable within the neoliberal project. And this makes it a particularly transgressive economic ideology. For it is also patently *hostile* to the social common. To paraphrase that pugilist of New Right thought, Mrs. Thatcher, *there is no such thing as society.* For this reason, neoliberal governmentality takes on a *self-destructive* tone, since it conveys a built-in aggression to its own reliance on that which it must negate.

But don't we also observe a curious *schizophrenic* feature in the texture of regulation here? From the 1990s onward there is a veritable explosion of testimonials about the social in capitalistic discourse. Before that, the social was something that just sort of happened. Today its neo-corporate mediation is big business in its own right. We have corporate social responsibility, work-life balance, the big society in the United Kingdom, communities of practice and so on. At the very moment that free-market politics launches an open attack on the social commons, it also artificially celebrates it, simulates it in management jargon—indeed, captures it as a matter of urgency. This is neoliberalism's attempt to have capitalism without capitalism, and for that reason it ought to be considered all the more dangerous.

We are now closer to explaining why corporations are so desperately displacing the boundary between work and non-work at the moment. It provides easy access to the non-labor it cannot survive without. The spatial and temporal policing of this division has been a fixture of capitalist enterprise since early industrialism. And while its partial dissolution might be explained by the advent of mobile technology or a more family friendly management philosophy, I suggest that something else is occurring, reflecting the recent biopolitical importance placed on the independent life abilities of the workforce.

A very interesting illustration can be found in Michel's (2012) recent study of employees in a large U.S. bank. Senior management did something very unusual in order to enhance productivity. They transformed the work setting into a home away from home, removing all concrete demarcations that might have once separated work from home, leisure, and life more generally. This was presented in the parlance of freedom and increased benefits, since employees could now access the workflow process whenever they liked, include personal events and interests in the office schedule, and cultivate a workplace climate that was almost indistinguishable from living as such. Michel notes, "The bank erased distinctions between work and leisure by providing administrative support 24 hours a day, seven days a week, encouraging leisure at work, and providing free amenities, including childcare, valets, car service and meals" (Michel 2012: 336).

These so-called freedoms came at a cost. Michel closely documented the way in which existence in this lifestyle firm was completely overtaken by work. There were no boundaries to separate personal concerns from those of the job, prompting one employee to sadly note, "My work is my life" (Michel 2012: 344). But the first casualty of this biopolitical universalization of work was not family life, holidays, or hobbies. It was the *body.* Given the longitudinal nature of Michel's study, over a nine-year period, she was able to observe the physical impact associated with biopower at work. After years of dealing with a chaotic managerial paradigm, deploying broader life resources to get the job done, the physical organism ended up spent and broken.

Some companies go to even greater lengths to capture life on the job. Land and Taylor's (2010) investigation of an ethical textiles manufacturer in the United Kingdom tells us why. They report how managers painstakingly replicated themes indicative of life beyond work on the company's premises. To give the job and products a veneer of authentic chic, the firm openly promoted the leisurely pastimes of its workers, within both the organization's internal culture and its external identity: "In order to establish the authenticity of the brand, this immaterial labor of brand management drew upon the recreational activities of employees. This inscription of employees' lives into the brand created the economic value of the company's products, situating their 'lives' as a form of productive labor or 'work'" (Land and Taylor 2010: 408).

According to Land and Taylor, this systematic blurring of life and labor was much more than a marketing tool. It directly keyed into the value-creation process, especially when employees began to think of their jobs as something more than just work. Managers needed *more* from employees than anything the company could formally prescribe. Other studies have revealed an increase in similar corporate practices, including my own ethnographic investigation of a call-center firm, whereby sexuality, partying, and leisure were all prominent aspects of the office culture. The company philosophy was clear: treat your job as if it were a late-night party or an occasion for a romantic liaison—anything but work (Fleming 2009).

## The Coming Workers' Society?

It is perhaps now easier to see the downside for employees when their companies invite life itself into the workplace. The intention is not less work but the exact opposite. Not freedom from our jobs, but a multiplication of its pressures inside and around us. Not a more enlightened work-life balance, but an endless life of the stuff. Indeed, a definitive feature of biocracy is how the ideology of work moves in the opposite direction, from the office or traditional point of production into the broader private activities of employees. This is how biopower transforms a job into something we *are,* as opposed to something we merely *do* among other things. Foucault saw this coming when he observed neoliberalism's conspicuous emphasis on human capital and human resources. At the time he was writing in the late 1970s these concepts did not really make sense. But they do now, when jobs are highly embodied and personified. The tyranny of human capital lies in the way that it becomes very difficult to check out and leave it behind.

It is tempting to explain the extension of work time in Western capitalist societies by way of either psychological causes such as workaholism or structural ones like labor intensification. No doubt there is some truth in both explanations. But the introduction of biopower into the workplace does not simply represent a quantitative shift (more hours spent working or worrying about it) but also a qualitative one. Working becomes a way of life regardless of whether it is necessary or not.

Rob Lucas's (2010) autobiographical essay "Dreaming in Code" exemplifies this inessential but ritualistic element of biopower. The computer programmer describes a life so integrated with his job that sleep is even a place of labor, dreaming up solutions to problematic code conundrums in the middle of the night. He writes, "Dreaming about your work is one thing, but dreaming inside the logic of your work is another. . . . [I]n the kind of dream I have been having the very movement of my mind is transformed: it has become that of my job. This is unnerving" (Rob Lucas 2010: 125). Lucas's "sleep work" is symptomatic of organizational power relations that no longer rely on timetables and direct orders. This is a question of not only more hours—but *more of you.*

The nature of this biopolitical control is no more evident than when Lucas tries to resist his work. He explains with reference to some classic methods of opposing management:

> Given the individually allocated and project centered character of the job, absenteeism only amounts to self-punishment, as work that is not done will have to be done later under increased stress. Given the collaborative nature of the work, heel dragging necessarily involves a sense of guilt towards other workers. On the production line, sabotage might be a rational tactic, but when your work resembles that of an artisan, sabotage would only make life harder. . . . It is only when sickness comes and I am involuntarily incapable of work that I really gain extra time for myself. It is a strange thing to rejoice in the onset of a flu. (Rob Lucas 2010: 128)

The last part of the quotation reveals how visceral and interconnected biopower is with our bodies. And, of course, when we start to absorb certain management practices and pressures, it is inevitable that some may resist by hurting the body itself. I later call this a failed escape attempt for obvious reasons.

What about technology? Might not the oversaturation of life by work be explained by the adoption of mobile technology since that means we are always on call? This is partially correct, but we might do well to remember Marx's caution regarding the perils of technological determinism—that is, interpreting certain social relations as a reflection of specific technical advances. It is the social use that technology is put to that really counts, as Marx proposed regarding the factory, "since machinery in itself shortens the hours of labor, but when employed by capital lengthens them . . . any other utilization of machinery than the capitalist one is [considered] impossible" (Marx [1867] 1972: 568–569).

We should take this warning seriously, especially when so many political situations are explained away by technological inevitability. Technology is certainly an important facet of biopower in the employment sphere today, but more symptomatic of changing social relations designed to extract resources beyond the conventional site of production. A recent study by Melissa Gregg (2011) is helpful for illustrating this. Like those we discussed above, the media and IT employees she met were completely indexed to their jobs, to the point where one interviewee even continued to work when immobilized in a hospital's emergency ward following a serious accident.

Building on the argument above, let us ignore the technology as such and study the social organization that shaped its use. For example, the deployment of self-managing teams was crucial for *horizontalizing* the pressure to produce, resulting in employees feeling inexplicably guilty or disloyal if they failed to meet a deadline. This invariably encouraged work outside of official hours (usually at their own expense) in order to successfully complete certain tasks. Gregg refers to presence bleed (always being mentally on the job) and function creep (the widening array of informal work required to get a job done) as key features of this employment environment. Presence bleed is particularly insidious. It defines a situation where "firm boundaries between personal and professional identities no longer apply. Presence bleed explains the familiar experience whereby location and time of work become secondary considerations faced with the 'do to list' that seems forever out of control" (Gregg 2011: 2).

These social structures allowed workers' self-organizing skills to become a strategic resource for the firm, especially in relation to the sheer amount of *poise work* conducted after hours to meet onsite objectives. Mobile technology was certainly important in this regard. But it was the absolute social impossibility of *switching off the phone or laptop* that really mattered. That type of force is not inherent in the technology itself. Most importantly, none of these developments leads to freer or more democratic work processes, an assumption that frequently accompanies descriptions of high-tech jobs. Employees have very little say over what the overall task might be. And orthodox forms of upper management and direct supervision do not disappear, but strangely increase.

## Surplus Regulation

How do you measure a person, their social affability, skill, and know-how? How do you represent something that is intrinsically shared, embodied, and impossible to signify in units? If common living labor is now central to the capital accumulation process, then how it is translated into economic reason becomes a problem for the corporation. So the firm becomes obsessed with metrics. This is why traditional management methods like bureaucracy, surveillance, and direct supervision do not disappear under biopower. They actually proliferate. The advocates of liberation management and results-only work environments (ROWE) tend to downplay this. Even seasoned critics of capitalism like Andre Gorz (2010) fall into this trap. Because workers are exploited for their vested sociability, managers "do not attempt to dominate them by seeking to measure their individual performance" (Gorz 2010: 108). Gorz even refers to work under these conditions as analogous to a free-form jazz jam. But the mounting evidence suggests otherwise. It is no exaggeration to say that the biopolitical employee is probably the most micromanaged figure of all time.

Following Herbert Marcuse's concept of surplus repression (which allowed him to explain why there is more control under capitalism than is functionally required), I use the term *surplus regulation* to understand this facet of biocracy. As we have noted, in a society of control, one is never done with work and one therefore never knows when they are free from it. This might be a dismal predicament for workers, but a strategic problem for capital, since it never really knows when life has been exploited enough. The old metrics that once allowed the corporation to plan via the variance between fixed capital and variable capital, productive and non-productive labor, socially necessary time and surplus time have all been scrambled. When the inexhaustible facets of living labor come to the fore in the production matrix, it also inspires an almost limitless multiplication of surveillance and standardization.

This immeasurability of labor power is not entirely new. For example, in his seminal study of bureaucracy, Edwards (1979) argued that the immaterial nature of office work posed big problems for corporate performance metrics. He writes, "The distinct nature of each separate task meant that it was not possible to compare it *directly* with the performance of other workers or even the same worker at other times" (Edwards 1979: 88). But only with the rise of management systems like biocracy does the difficulty of measurement escalate exponentially. The person and the job are almost impossible to separate. Work time and non-work time intersect in complex ways. And no spreadsheet has yet been devised to draw any quantifiable equivalence between life and key performance indicators. For how do you give affect, sentiment, and resourcefulness a metric without inadvertently hypostasizing them? As Gregg (2011) observed in the study mentioned above, "No formal policies existed for them to manage online obligations; nor were there guidelines for appropriate response times. Employees operated on the basis of some vague and self-imposed ideas about what management would or wouldn't expect" (Gregg 2011: 52).

From capital's perspective, the predicament of immeasurability is met by activating time-tested forms of domination: not less but an overabundance of regulation—*just to make sure.* Indeed, it is not a coincidence that at the very moment that "trust," "empowerment," and "just be yourself" enter the lexicon of neo-corporatism, we also see a tremendous rise in management *distrust.* To appreciate why, it is important to remember the wider backdrop of class antagonism that inspires the introduction of biopower into the workplace. The redoubling of bureaucracy and technocracy aims to check what bio- power has unleashed and cannot fully represent. Often this involves the *needless* reduction of the body, its faculties and relations to the chronicle of work. And this is why so many management systems are perceived (even by managers themselves) to be rather pointless, ap- plied for their own sake rather than to achieve organizational goals.

## Mapping Biocracy Today

A potential difficulty with categories like the social factory or biocracy is that they lean toward overgeneralization, sometimes even assuming that everyone now works under the conditions described above—clear- ly an untenable proposition. If possible, we must be able to account for biopower's pattern of adoption and occupational distribution. For sure, similar problems have dogged well-used concepts like the knowledge economy, cognitive capitalism, and post-Fordism, whereby the major- ity of employees described begin to resemble the authors using such concepts: *academics.*

So, are some occupations more likely to display biopolitical ten- dencies than others? It would seem sensible to expect knowledge-in- tensive and service-oriented work to be especially relevant. However, it must be kept in mind that many jobs, even in menial and osten- sibly low-skilled occupations, now require vested proficiencies that biopower might enroll. Indeed, some of the most overly controlled and highly regulated occupations—say, the retail assistant or textile manufacturer—appear to require more than just direct subordination to achieve their objectives. Callaghan and Thompson (2002) found this in their study of coercive call centers' primary concern with recruiting attitude. Somehow this had become *the* crucial value-adding component of the job.

In his lectures on the subject, Foucault also notes the problem of overgeneralization in relation to biopower and its micro-power characteristics. The suggestion that society as a whole is regulated in this manner seems implausible. However, he states that "the analysis of micro-powers is not a question of scale, and it is not a question of sector, it is a question of point of view" (Foucault 2008: 186). What does he mean? Perhaps two things are happening here. First of all, he views this kind of power as diagrammatic or virtual, something akin to a virus or gas. Commenting on Foucault, Deleuze (2006) suggests that diagrams of power become operative precisely when they do not follow the typical trajectory of sectors, divisions, and classifications. Instead, it is a "function that must be *detached* from any specific use, as from any specified substance" (Deleuze 2006: 61, emphasis added). This does not make it any less concrete, indeed the opposite, because its directives work through our bodies.

And second, Foucault is investigating biopower as a *qualitative* tendency, perhaps limited in quantitative range presently, but potentially emblematic of things to come. In other words, just as the factory system was comparatively limited in scale and scope when Marx was writing (yet fundamental to his theory of what capitalist society meant for everyone else), so too might biopower represent an important trend underlying the capitalist system of employment more generally.[6] Of course, whether or not this is the case remains to be seen.

## Conclusion

At this juncture it is understandable if the analysis might seem somewhat pessimistic about the possibility of resisting biocracy. If the above propositions are correct, then it is easy to conclude that a new type of capitalist power has won the day. Indeed, this is close to what Jean Baudrillard (2010) surmised in the bleak lectures delivered shortly before his death. What we have described as biocracy he calls hegemony, something very different from simple domination. It is worth quoting him at length:

> We must distinguish between domination and hegemony. Until now, we were dealing with domination. A master/slave relation-

a symbolic one if you like, a dual relationship with the pos-
ᴜility of explosion, revolution, alienation and dis-alienation.
This domination has made way for hegemony, which is alto-
gether something else. There is no longer a dual relationship.
Everyone is an accomplice. Everyone is caught up in the network and submits to this hegemony. We are both victims and
accomplices; guilty and not responsible. Hegemony is within us.
If we want to resist hegemony and escape it using the means we
once used against domination (revolt, critical thought, negative
thought, etc.), there is no hope. (Baudrillard 2010: 116–117)

For Baudrillard, then, dialectical reasoning (the traditional way of
understanding industrial dissent) is problematic here since the target
of opposition is now somehow *us*. When the ideology of work becomes
integral to our gestures, desires, and worries, when we even dream
about work, how should we conceptualize resistance to capitalism?

There is little doubt traditional forms of resistance still have a
crucial role today, especially the strike and other forms of collective
protest. But what makes biocracy so effective is the way it convinces
people that refusing or even disrupting work is pointless. Our jobs are
synonymous with the living body itself, and how can you resist that?
This was noted by our sleep worker earlier. Rob Lucas found himself
so wedded to his job that sabotage or the go-slow seemed completely
irrational. It would merely create more stress for him and his teammates. And as Gregg also noted, biopower makes resistance seem un-
collegial, since "loyalty to the team has the effect of making extra
work seem courteous and common sense" (Gregg 2011: 85).

One might expect that the extra-close knowledge of their work acquired under biocracy might provide employees with an opportunity to
restrict or sabotage productivity. For example, in his excellent study of
deskilling or "de-lawyering" among temporary lawyers in the United
States, Brooks (2012) suggests that an unanticipated consequence of
enlisting the broad life abilities of employees was the deep expertise
they could subsequently use against management. No doubt this hidden knowledge might be used to slow down productivity and so forth,
but only up to a point. As Brooks points out, "Quitting or complaining
are perceived by the temporary worker to be futile (because the worker
is easily replaced) or even self-defeating (because workers may harm
their chances for future assignments). Other acts of resistance such as

absenteeism or tardiness are also not effective because the temporary worker is only paid for their actual time at work" (Brooks 2012: 15).[7] This leads to a strange predicament that would have looked impossible to the factory workers of Fordism. The more embodied expertise and independence that workers have, the less free they are.

When considering the rise (and perhaps fall) of biopower in the workplace, however, it is of utmost importance than we view it as symptomatic of a fundamental *crisis* in managerialism and neoliberal governance more generally—not a success. This theoretically places the employee (which includes managers and consumers as much as anyone else) in a very powerful position. And this is how we ought to approach the topic of resistance.

In the forthcoming chapters I propose that biopower can be and is refused through various kinds of collective *endpoints* or *exits*. We now know that biopower succeeds when it makes work appear universal and endless. This phantasmagoria of permanence or endlessness is one of neoliberalism's crowning achievements. Indeed, we have known for quite a while that capitalism exploits us primarily through *time*: time at work, time thinking about work, time preparing for work. What makes neoliberalism so much more radical than earlier modes of capitalist control lies in the way it *infinitizes* the otherwise finite register of work, erasing any sense of end or beginning. After that, there is no alternative to working life. Building on the arguments above, this occurs because our bodily capacities are enlisted by the job and we no longer perceive any boundaries between work and living as such. We are always checked in, but never quite know when or how.

While quitting might seem impossible to many of us today (in the manner described by Brooks [2012] above), it is this very perception that some are now refusing to accept. Effectively resisting work not only means countering the concrete time it steals from us. It also means disrupting the fantasy of its never-ending ubiquity. Some do this in self-destructive ways, which is perhaps understandable. The person thinks, "If I am the bearer of power, then I will hurt it by hurting myself. I will debilitate it by damaging myself." We must consider this a failed escape attempt because it mistakenly concedes life to capital, and thus resists by resisting life itself. No detachment from biopower is achieved; in fact, the opposite occurs.[8]

But there are less self-destructive ways to subvert biopower, which are discussed in the forthcoming pages. These types of opposition are inspired by the concepts of autonomy and self-valorization. The rationale goes like this. The biopolitical workplace is now conspicuously reliant on those rich qualities of social labor that forever lie beyond capitalism's reach. This is the commons. So why not collectively detach this commonwealth from the parasite of neoliberalism and repossess it for ourselves? The workers autonomy movement simply seeks to reclaim what it already is. This is why the praxis of political exit or departure has recently become important. But there is also the need to symbolically dispel two myths that neoliberalism uses to justify the current servitude of working people: (1) that without the corporation we would perish and be thrown back into the dark ages and (2) that constant work is a fact of life, necessitated by the expediency of human survival.

From this perspective it is capitalism that is the fetter or blockage to a progressive and democratic post-work future. And that future already exists in abundance before us because *it is us*. The corporation is the opposing party, not the workforce that invariably overwhelms its straitjacket of controls every day. We are currently witnessing a multitude of employees and would-be workers articulating the autonomy of the common. Some are struggling to be left alone by capital, developing producer cooperatives and exit routes through alternative economies. Deserted factories in Argentina and Greece are being reclaimed for democratic ends (see Greece Solidarity Campaign 2013). Others are "opting out" (Jones 2012) and "down-shifting" (Nelson, Paek, and Rademacher 2007) from the scene of biopower. The growing number of advice websites now dedicated to this end (e.g., leavingacademia.com) is telling. And we might also consider the invisible multitude of non-workers who chose not to enter the corporation in the first place, as Costas and Fleming (2009) discuss.[9]

This politics of exit differs significantly from earlier forms of worker militancy. The coming bio-proletariat no longer considers the employment situation something worth fighting over. Unlike its Fordist predecessors, these workers do not demand more work, less work, or better work.[10] They simply seek to exit the depressing site of late capitalist domination, a terrain that offers no collective benefits but would nevertheless like us to believe that we would be nothing without it.

# 2

# Common Matters

In a period of profound crisis, capitalism's desperate reliance on social qualities it cannot guarantee itself is easy to observe in most workplaces today. The double travesty of neoliberalism is straight-forward. It clearly diminishes our life chances in a drastic way, but it also enlists us to help with that goal. Because it cannot reproduce its own anti-social tenets alone, we are brought into the picture. And most of us really do not want to be involved—hence biopower's emphasis on things that look like *non-work*. Corporate capitalism wants everything about us that blooms before the moment of exploitation.

What exactly is this field of social action that precedes the arrival of biocracy? That is to say, if the biopolitical corporation is largely a parasitical figure that rides on pre-existing qualities or life itself, then how might we conceptualize this *prior* sociality? We have to reflect on this question to fully appreciate how biopower goes to work on us today—but, more importantly, the opposition that meets it.

When we survey how the corporation is often pictured, a dominant attitude is prevalent in scholarship and the popular imagination alike. Let us only in half-jest exaggerate the contours of this conventional wisdom to make the point. It goes something like this: Before we had international markets, the formal corporate entity, and so forth, life was decisively disorganized and brutish. This bleak world before the arrival of the modern firm might be described as a type of pre-industrial backwardness, a place of poverty, war, and abjection. Life before the corporation was a kind of living death, and it represented the ever-present possibility of being harmed, looted, and reduced to what philosophers, like G. Agamben (1998), have recently called *bare life*—an existence forsaken and bereft of rights. It is a world we ought to be grateful is in the past.

In this hyperbolic depiction, however, we can distill a basic underlying fantasy that still has much sway over the political imagination. It views the corporation as the ultimate protector from an ever-possible *social death*. Such an ideological conceit underscores many considerations of modern capitalism in mainstream economics, economic sociology, and history. For better or worse, the firm is considered a powerful and world-making governor of the modern social order. For example, in the much celebrated work of Alfred Chandler on the development of managerial capitalism in the United States, we can see this analytical subtext at work. In *The Visible Hand* (1977) the emergence of industry (inexorably linked with the rise of the railways and national markets) was guided by the acumen of a new managerial class. The taming of the natural environment, the end of obstructive indigenous practices of the pre-industrial period, and the rise of the complex multidivisional firm moved the United States into modernity. It is capital that defines the nature of business and society. It is the corporation (as a strategic self-authored entity) that lifts the nation into the light of prosperity, and it was the ingenuity of the nascent market mechanism to direct the best efforts of industry leaders that resulted in the betterment of all.

More recent examples come with a moral message—who can ever forget the trite claim by Thomas Friedman in his best seller *The Lexus and the Olive Tree* (1999) that international supply chains ought to deter countries from going to war? As the apologist for global capitalism continues, "No two countries who sell Big Macs ever went to war with each other." McDonalds to the rescue, it seems.[1]

Such a view is perhaps expected on the political Right. More worrying, however, is the way critical analysis has tended to see the firm (albeit in a negative light) as something of an institutional first-mover. A managerial or corporate elite is posited whose members employ and exploit alienated labor, invariably to the latter's impoverishment. Regardless of whether workers resist or not, they are still but a political reflection of capitalist agency. We can see this in the way many radical Weberian and Marxian studies view the predominance of corporations over our lives—creating worlds, disenchanting and impecunious worlds for sure, but worlds nevertheless.

Contra to this vision of the corporation as creator, the central proposition of this book is this: Capitalism and the corporation must be seen as entities that qualitatively *follow* from the social communities that are the true source of wealth we see in society today. That is to say, a detailed analysis of contemporary capitalism and its institutional antecedents reveals that the formal enterprise and market system involves a strong reactive element. They function as a kind of parasitical ossification defined more by rent and the capture of prior value in the living community. This is what social theorists have called "the commons."

Suddenly, of course, arises the voice of the concerned conservative: "Why be so critical of the free enterprise given the wealth and well-being it enables? Wouldn't society fall apart, go hungry, and suffer disease and servitude without it?" The answer is, of course, no. In fact, it is the very opposite. I reserve critical scrutinization of these ideological justifications of the modern corporation for Chapter 3, where the empirical examples speak for themselves. The present chapter undertakes the preliminary task of developing a philosophical foundation for thinking against the ingrained doxa *capitalism = life*. It does so by addressing the following questions: What are these social forces shaping the contours of the modern enterprise that is more than the firm itself? Is it merely another name for the working class? And does some kind of social naturalism or vitalism drive its *will-to-be-together,* to be in common? I argue that it is none of these things. But we do need a good understanding of its conceptual and empirical constituents if we are to develop a plausible critique of biopolitics at work.

## A Common World *despite* the Corporate "Leviathan"

The idea of the commons has received much attention in a new line of critical analysis that has attempted to avoid conceding so much power (over the imagination as much as anything else) to the corporate form and its corollaries. Rather than position the institutional flows of dead labor, for better or worse, as the primary architect of our lives as citizens and workers, this alternative line of inquiry posits the commons as something elementary that capital subsequently endeavors to capture. From this perspective, the corporation is an entity that generally subtracts, accumulating value by negating an a priori social positivity. The for-profit enterprise, then, does not so much create or even harness value, but taps it—encloses that which it cannot engender itself, since it always requires something that is other to its own crippling precepts. How can we understand this alterity that qualitatively precedes the capitalist institution of work?

## After the Leviathan

According to Virno (2008) among others, the dawn of political theory in liberal Western thought and then industrial statecraft *per se* was centered on the fear of the multitude—the affirmative, self-organizing, and communal relations that persisted despite the imperial interventions of the sovereign. It is in Thomas Hobbes's *Leviathan* ([1651] 2010) that we see this interconnection of community, power, and the state most fully inaugurated, developing a political vision that had, and still has, far-reaching consequences. As is well-known, Hobbes begins by returning to a figurative ground zero. What if there were no class, laws, or heritage, no conventions or codes that today keep the peace? The thought experiment revealed to Hobbes something frightful, a world of terror, disorganization, desolation, and murder. We are at heart thugs, and without external restraints or some kind of contract, most of us would not think twice about killing our neighbor for a loaf of bread. In other words, and as Hobbes puts it in his well-known phrase, life is "solitary, poor, nasty, brutish, and short" (Hobbes [1651] 2010: 78).

So enters the Leviathan—or the state, economic sovereign, and so forth—as protector and guarantor of order and *life itself.* Without it, the argument continues, we could never be together and would probably die alone. Our sociality needs to be pre-secured for us. The presupposition of a giant social contract allows a community to emerge, encouraging us to permanently suspend our negation of life so "that a man be willing, when others are so too, as far forth as for peace and defense of himself he shall think it necessary, to lay down this right to all things; and be contented with so much liberty against other men as he would allow other men against himself" (Hobbes [1651] 2010: 80).

So begins a long tradition of political thought that understands the people and their communities as a reflection of the vested sovereign who grants civil enjoinment, our very ability to live together. And to extrapolate, without the institutional support and policing gaze of the state, the corporate matrix or some other overarching authority, there would be general disorder. The watchword of the Leviathan is security, but also *fear,* which stems from some anticipated harm that might befall us.

There is, however, an alternative and less known tradition of thought that runs against this liberal legitimation of state and (now) corporate/market institutionalism. This alternative and somewhat subversive lineage begins with Spinoza, runs through to Marx, and resonates in the continental philosophy of Deleuze and Guattari (1987) and Nancy (1991).

So, why Spinoza? While it is often said he posited his own version of the Leviathan, I want to present an alternative reading of Spinoza, inspired in part by Negri's (1991) analysis of the subject. In his most celebrated philosophical meditation, *Ethics* ([1677] 1996), Spinoza outlines an image of the polity that is fundamentally at odds with Hobbes's version of it. Much of this conceptualization is embedded in theological reflection. Spinoza is often considered a pantheist (god is in everything, infinite) who seems to verge on radical atheism (god is in everything, making us god, and thus dethroning god as we traditionally think of "him"). This is not the place for an extended explanation of Spinozist theology. But a number of aspects are important for this discussion.

First is Spinoza's radical materialism. The abstraction of the people, the general will, or the state is replaced by a concrete and infinite "substance." Second, this substance, which might also be considered a variegated and singularized us, or, in today's philosophical parlance, multitude, is completely internal to its own unfolding. In other words, there is no external and abstract Leviathan pulling the strings, but only a self-productive *immanence.* Subsequently, every cause is now preconditioned by its own presupposed or absent effect. Third, in this world philosophy there is no such thing as mediation, such as the sovereign, the church, the state. Every point is but a resonance of every other point in the social universe. And fourth, this is a self-organizing and generative immanence, based on the love (Spinoza's highest form of knowledge) of the universal substance that extends through our bodies, but, more importantly, the relations between our bodies. *Autonomy* is therefore central to appreciating this substance. One can now see why Spinoza got into such trouble with the authorities.

According to one investigation of this alternative lineage of political thought conducted by Virno (2008), Hobbes was deeply suspicious of the governance principle that Spinoza envisaged in place of the Leviathan: *the multitude*. Unlike the civic people galvanized by their reflection in the sovereign and the sovereign in them, the multitude's inscrutability frustrated conventional codes of statecraft. It was a spontaneous sociality, without any fixed address and thus nomadic and non-episodic, outlandishly public in its secret methods of self-management, a kind of radical non-state public that ruthlessly defied the root etymology of "private": *deprivation*. Virno shows that this opaque political underground was dismissed by Hobbes as "leagues, or mere concourse of people, without union to any particular design" (Hobbes quoted in Virno 2004: 42). Virno is not romanticizing this radical counter-public lurking in the shadows of bourgeois society. For it can turn nasty: "Sometimes aggressive, sometimes united, prone to intelligent cooperation, but also to the war between factions, being both the poison and the antidote: such is the multitude" (Virno 2004: 40).

The Hobbesian mindset, however, does not find the multitude troubling simply because of its potential for counter-sovereign violence. It is the propensity for self-organization the Leviathan finds most disconcerting. The multitude is defined by its ability to make and enjoy a livable life without the sovereign—hence its importance in subsequent investigations regarding nonrepressive modes of communism and socialism. The radical insight of Spinozist thought is this: The universal substance allows us to logically deduce the possibility of a social existence that *does not fear itself.* The sovereign is now getting nervous. What's more, this is not simply a case of Hobbes seeing human nature as innately evil, while Spinoza sees it as intrinsically good. This has nothing to do with nature but its opposite, ethics: namely, the way we choose to practice the practices that resolutely practice us. This is why substance is best conceived as a universal moment of being-unto-sociality, and fear arrives when we mistakenly confer this togetherness to an external authority. This is also why Spinoza argued that knowledge of the substance is always *joyous,* since in its tremendous openness a series of multiplications occur. In other words, it adds to life, or more accurately, adds life to itself. And its concrete idiom is self-governance.

## *The Social as Loss*

What is so exciting is that the philosopher's third notion of love is precisely one of the earliest ideas of the social we have in European thought. The idea of unmediated trust is close to what he means, but this still does not quite pin it down. It is more a kind of gifted openness whereby we receive the other and the other receives us without recompense or proprietary rights. The "I" both engenders and retroactively presupposes an "ours." We are now very far away from private property, market individualism, and the state acting as absolutist guarantor. For us, the heirs of Hobbes and now in the grip of neoliberal authoritarianism, the message is inevitably radical. *We* are the state, and that state is fairly communist at that.

One way to think about this is to note how we move away from a *sociality of loss* to what instead might be called a *sociality of gain*. A sociality of loss involves a moment in which we give ourselves up, fear something might be taken from us, and are forever indebted to an authority or community for our well-being. Given the rather Augustinian milieu of the mid- to late seventeenth century, it might be worth revisiting the *Confessions* (1961) for an early Christian take on this subject. In an astounding passage, St. Augustine recalls how he was swept away by childhood friends while committing an awful burglary:

> I loved nothing in it except the act of thieving . . . and yet, as I recall my feelings at the time, I am quite sure I would not have done it on my own. . . . [B]y myself I would not have committed the robbery. It was not the takings that attracted me but the raid itself, and yet to do it myself would have been no fun and I should not have done it. This was a friendliness of a most unfriendly sort, bewitching my mind in an inexplicable way. For the sake of a laugh, a little sport, I was glad to do harm and anxious to damage another; and without a thought of profit for myself or retaliation for injuries received! And all because we are ashamed to hold back when others say, "Come on! Let's do it!" (Augustine 1961: 52)

St. Augustine is reflecting on the nature of a certain social relation. He understands it as a *sociality of loss* for the obvious reason that it is premised on the gratuitous harm to another. But something else more complex is being expressed here, for it is the subject himself (a young Augustine) who is crucially deprived. He opens himself to the group, yes, and bands together to steal something belonging to another. But St. Augustine is not only frightened by what the gang incited him to do. He is also terrified by the inexplicable power they had over him. He was no longer his own person. He was fundamentally negated, bereft of the power to produce himself through relations with others. This was the major setback he laments rather than anything to do with integrity or honesty.

Rather than being lost to the group, Spinoza's free and immanent knowledge of substance multiplies or enriches the subject precisely through shared openness. Sociality here is a mutual reciprocity that *adds* by imputing us with selfhood. Henceforth, we must abandon the obsolete dichotomy of the individual versus society. Society in this Hobbesian picture can yield only a false individual in this sense. The dualism is quite erroneous and foreign to radical politics proper. Instead, and after Spinoza, we have autonomous moments of singularity or qualities that are truly mine, but only through my relation to others. What we have come to call the individual is a wonderful thing for sure. But, as Spinoza discovered, this can be engendered only through what is for all intents and purposes an unmediated moment of being-in-common.[2]

Now we can understand why the Spinozist tradition of philosophy is so nervous about mediated institutions that force us together (or apart) in various shapes and sizes. The false formalization of sociality through the market mechanism, the state, or that worst kind of objectification—the competitive and deeply insecure neoliberal individual adrift in personal debt—all represent socialities of loss, a kind of anti-substance or non-life.

And as noted in the Introduction the common in this sense is not a community (*Gemeinschaft*) since that too is so often a manufactured substitute for productive human exchange, standing above, behind, and against "us" in an exploitative manner.[3] The contemporary communitarian movement in the United States, for example, basically throws a bucket of water on the autonomous free association that Marx beautifully dubbed the labor of fire. It is constructed around unification and closure rather than difference and openness. As such, a unifying identity will always be experienced as an authority that demands subordination ("We will accept you only if you forgo that which is not us"). It brings us together through a fundamental loss. Thus, there is no place for *Gemeinschaft* in the tradition of thought we are unpacking here, since it is yet another version of the Leviathan smuggled in through the back door.

## *The Social as Surplus*

We can now discern the strong Hobbesian tradition that underscores so many accounts of the modern corporation and its guiding emblem of work. It is posited as an agentic power first and foremost. It truly creates our world, perhaps impoverished and one-dimensional, but a world nevertheless.

When we putatively invert this *capital* = *life* formula, as the Spinozist tradition does with Hobbes, we begin to see that the laws of capital and the laboring multitude it exploits are not synonymous or equivalent. Labor is not a perfect reflection of capital or a minor composite of capitalism's life-granting powers. Like the state, the working multitude seems to express attributes *above and beyond* the codes designed to contain it. And this is why we might argue that the corporation is better seen as a subtraction or negation of the hidden public, which we are now calling "the commons." But what exactly is the nature of this living excess that the modern corporation both negates and yet is so conspicuously reliant on?

To answer this question we must return to Marx. When capitalism becomes a way of life (real subsumption) rather than an episodic imposition (formal subsumption), Marx argues that there must always be a *remainder* involved. In other words, real subsumption contains an integral lack, an internal variance that can never be closed. This excessive remainder Marx calls "living labor," a life essentially nonindexed to capital in its formal sense. The reasons why are complex. The anthropological tendencies in Marx have been much debated here. Is he not naturalizing living labor via some kind of primitive anarchism (man in his pure form) (see Absensour 2011)? I do not think this is necessarily the case. Marx seems to be suggesting something else. Capitalism is a historical configuration that clearly accumulates through a sociality of loss or exploitation. But it also paradoxically depends on a coversine sociality of gain, which is nothing other than the amplification of *capital's own absence*. In other words, the working class represents its own impossibility because it cannot be both itself *and* a wage-slave in the factory. Its affirmative power must also entail an inherent moment of self-negation, and this cannot help but spill over as excedents that capital both needs and is deeply hostile toward.

According to the labor theory of value, the commodity and capital more generally is but the congealed abstraction of this excess manifest as living labor. Marx's colorful description of capitalism as dead labor that sucks the living worker dry like a vampire is completely conditional on this non-capitalist supplement. This is why surplus value needs to include not only the value created above and beyond the costs of production by the worker but also a *social surplus*.[4] This stands for an unframable remainder to the capitalist accumulation process. Perhaps "remainder" is the wrong word to use here; what we are referring to instead are invariant qualities that are central to capitalism, but only because they correlatively *come before* the appearance of capital. For Antonio Negri (2008) this is a truly Marxian ontology. It is central to appreciating the post-capitalist world that latently lies before us, since "the productive act does not decree the death of labor; the productive act, rather, is the act that exalts and accumulates labor. . . . Live labor can never exhaust itself, can never be consumed" (Negri 2008: 160).

## *What Is Living Labor?*

We might debate the contradiction that appears to lie in an ostensibly anthropological category like living labor. Marx seems to be saying that labor is an immutable quality of us all, but at the same time he recognizes it as a historically specific ideology linked to capitalism. Some suggest that Marx is fruitlessly attempting to overcome a *bourgeois anthropology* through a pseudo-anthropological lens (see Shershow 2004). Weeks (2011) also points to this problem in much Marxist productivism when considering how best to understand work today. She writes, "The trouble with the category of living labor is that it is haunted by the very same essentialized conception of work" (Weeks 2011: 15; also see ibid.: 81). In other words, critiquing the myopia of work through the very category of work reproduces a core ideological trope endemic to capitalist society.

These criticisms are generally correct. They do, however, miss an important aspect of Marx's original analysis, a kind of generative *apo-*

*ria* situated between an ontology of labor and its historical transcendence. For is this not the very self-overcoming threshold (rather than paradox) that Marx is endeavoring to deduce in the moment of living labor? Man is man because he is not *all* man, the worker is a worker because he is not *all* worker, and so on. Elementary here once again is a prefigurative surplus that precedes what it formally follows, a living form non-identical to the calculative exchange relations that it otherwise observes.

Living labor thus always stands in advance of its own defining elements, always overcoming the limit of its own foundational moment.[5] This is how we should appreciate the social surplus that capitalism is increasingly reliant on today. And it allows us to return to the idea of the commons, a social force that exists as an unmediated or a priori extra to the work it is put to. Since it can never be captured or expropriated completely by capital, it embodies characteristics that are not only antagonistic (vis-à-vis capital) but also purely positive and non-dialectical. As Casarino notes in his excellent analysis of the topic:

> This surplus is the common-in-itself, the common as (its own self-producing, self-positing, self-referential) production, the common as potentially as such. This surplus is not measurable or quantifiable but also is not a thing. . . . [S]urplus is that which capital strives to subsume absolutely under surplus value and yet manages to do so only relatively because it is structurally unable to subsume without at the same time negating and foreclosing that which it subsumes—thereby enabling the emergence of a surplus common. (Casarino 2008: 22)

This self-positing moment of living labor is central for the autonomist reading of Marx and hence the importance of the "Fragment on Machines" from the *Grundrisse* ([1858] 1973) and its conceptualization of the general intellect in many of the discussions around this topic. This has very little to do with Marx's later analysis of cooperation in *Capital* ([1867] 1972), which is often misread as a homage to worker autonomy. He sees nothing laudable in that type of cooperation. It is a forced collectivity, or what we can call a sociality of loss, whose only redeeming feature is the counter-capital solidarity that might develop from it.

In the "Fragment on Machines," however, we see something different. Here, in the face of the intellectualization of labor, Marx pushes his own framework to its limits: what appears to be a process in which labor is rendered but a passive conscious organ in fact reveals a monumental insight on the other side of the coin. Labor is not only variable capital (i.e., working with machines and tools as a human factor of production); it is also coextensive with fixed capital itself because the worker's social intellect or interconnectedness becomes an inverted outcome of his or her apparent determination by the machine. When we become a living piece of fixed capital through such integration, something important occurs. The sum of our relations multiplies exponentially, developing not only alongside but also *outside* the capitalist accumulation process. The general intellect manifests an autonomy that exceeds the exploitative grid of production. This gives the social brain its general and open attributes, projecting its own self-causation ahead of the work process, which strives to catch up and contain it.

## The General Intellect at Work

Perhaps Paolo Virno (2004, 2008) has conducted some of the most groundbreaking research in this area. Two insights are useful for us. First is the homological framing of the communism of capital as a necessary prerequisite of the accumulation process, which is today seriously threatening to catapult capital beyond itself too. We might read this tendency as the coming supremacy of a *sociality of gain*. Virno follows the Wittgensteinian insight that a rule paradoxically cannot interpret itself without a preceding context of informal knowhow and collective sense making. Likewise, the formal structure of production cannot articulate itself without some a priori "common behavior of mankind" (Virno 2008: 35) or transindividuality that is always more than itself. As Virno writes, "The general intellect is the name that refers to the ordinary human faculty of thinking with words, and this in turn becomes the principle productive force of capitalism. . . . [T]he general intellect is that which precedes the determined rules and thus functions as the final criterion for their application" (Virno 2008: 41). Exploitative work cannot itself engender these qualities because it is composed of an exhaustible self-negation.

Earlier modes of capitalism required this animated connectivity of the general intellect too, but simultaneously viewed it as a dangerous substratum of self-determination that required disciplining. Today's era of biocapitalism, however, is different. And this is the second insight. The modern enterprise does not aim to eradicate this surplus common à la Taylor's Scientific Management of yesteryear, even though there is still much of that, of course. Instead, it seeks to put the commons to work. Indeed, as observed in the preceding chapter, neoliberal regulation and the corporate form could not survive without the commons, which is its central strategic and political weakness. Indeed, this is what the book's opening vignette of the young university lecturer hoped to convey. Her ability to activate spontaneous networks of cooperation got the job done despite the rules of domination.

As noted in Chapter 1, more cutting-edge advances in corporate managerialism now actively encourage the appearance of this non-capitalist general intellect, albeit in the highly mannerist form of liberation management and Results Only Work Environments. This enigmatic feature of post-industrial society is part and parcel of its crisis, since it needs to enlist counter-capitalist social principles to reproduce itself. The general intellect, like the virtuosity required to participate in the formal syntax of a language, is seen primarily as *potential*, an infinite and inexhaustible ensemble of variations that envelop any application of a rule. This potential yields a sort of *pure surplus* (think back to Spinoza's infinite substance). While we may see a good deal of liberation within this notion, it must really be approached as a new twist in how work now exploits us, as Virno also argues:

> The general intellect is the foundation of a social co-operation broader than that co-operation which is specifically related to labor. Broader, and at the same time, totally heterogeneous. . . . [T]he general intellect moves from common participation to "life of the mind," that is, from the preliminary sharing of communicative and cognitive abilities. However, cooperation *in excess* of the intellect, instead of annulling the co-actions of capitalist production, figures as its most eminent resource. (Virno 2004: 67)

Like Virno, we should be under no illusions. This forever-renewable social excess certainly lies outside of exploitation, but it is also now fundamental to what allows capitalism to survive, especially in relation to biocracy, discussed in Chapter 1. True, the communism of capital certainly shows us that the commons is always more than its imprisonment and thus a probable line of escape. But this doesn't make it any less exploitable in practical terms, rather, indeed, perhaps even more so.

Perhaps a more optimistic reading of this social excess might also be made. The materialization of the commons or general intellect undoubtedly ushers in new systems of regulation, without doing away with conventional modes of domination. But these aggregate social faculties are non-episodic in relation to exploitative work and therefore can never be completely assimilated by the corporate form. And this also opens up a new vista of politics, one that not only is organized around the capital versus labor divide but also pits the wealth of life more generally against capital. Indeed, "life lies at the centre of politics when the prize to be won is immaterial (and itself non-present) labor power" (Virno 2004: 83). It is in this surfeit of common life, in labor's infinite overabundance, that we might find hope for a redeemable sociality of gain.

## Capitalism as Resistance

Many of these ideas regarding the pre-operative autonomy of living labor can be traced back to the Italian *Operaismo* movement. In the writings of Tronti (1971), for example, we see an innovative redefinition of class politics associated with strategies of worker refusal. His study, as shown elsewhere in this book, is extremely important for understanding dissent in a biopolitical era. Again, the non-sequential reversal of the labor-capital nexus is developed, reminding us that capital is not the master in its own house. It exists within a class structure, of which the working class is the driving force, especially when it endeavors to escape.

### Capital Is Only the Fruit of Labor

It might still be true that the working class (which, I argue in later chapters, cuts through almost everybody today) reflects the demands of capital. But its power for self-abolition lies in that social excess we have already noted. It is more than itself and this is proper to living labor power as such. The same could never be said for the logic of capital. It cannot be more than itself, since it functions through pure subtraction. This is why Marx compares capital to a vampire. Through its circuits of exchange and manufactured necessity, capital grows only by appropriating that which is foreign to it. And thus capital is always pursuing living labor, desperately tracking its exit routes as it overflows the province of economic rationality. We must be very clear on this point. Capital might now be a new biopolitical Leviathan that enjoys total determination over society, but its control is a residue of past reactions to labor militancy. Dead labor is another name for past labor in this regard. And this is symptomatic of a profound weakness: "The labor theory of value means labor first, then capital; it means capital conditioned by labor-power, set in motion by labor-power. . . . [L]abor is the measure of value because the working class is the condition of capital" (Tronti 1966, quoted in Wright 2002: 84).

This way of conceptualizing the struggle between labor and capital, as I mentioned earlier, has been formulated elsewhere, especially in the Anglo-U.S. tradition of Marxist thought exemplified by Richard Edwards (1979) and E. P. Thompson (1963). We closely survey their arguments in Chapter 3. The gist of the *Operaismo* discovery, however, is that the engine of capitalist exploitation represents a major displacement. It is none other than the escape attempts of the workforce that shape the contours of capitalist geopolitics, especially in times of crisis.

The first wave of Italian workerism epitomized by Tronti (1966) and Panzieri ([1961] 2009) placed the autonomy of labor within a modified Marxian class analysis.[6] Because labor is the sole source of value, constituted by an indefinite living social surplus, the private firm must be viewed as a secondary blockage in relation to the common. It is hyper-reliant on a latent communist autonomy, holding it in abeyance to forestall the self-abolitionary tendency of the proletariat. Today, however, this independence of labor is both intensifying under present conditions—since workers are transformed into an embodied means of production—and increasingly rendering capital a tardy bystander to the production process. In this regard, Hardt and Negri point out:

> To reverse the conventional economic formulation, capital is increasingly external to the productive process and the generation of wealth. In other words, biopolitical labor is increasingly autonomous. Capital is predatory, as the analysts of neoliberalism

say, in so far as it seeks to capture and expropriate autonomously produced common wealth. (Hardt and Negri 2009: 141)

This excerpt is important because of its anti-Hobbesian appreciation of post-industrial class antagonism. As mentioned in the last part of Chapter 1, we might also now see *capital as a resistant force* and (from the point of view of living labor) a useless impediment to the full, lush expression of social commonality that it attempts to foreclose. Making matters more complex, however, labor's very struggle for self-abolition might also feature as a source of value. As the myriad of examples in Chapter 1 attest, perhaps capitalism is today cashing in on its own crisis, generating profits from that which attempts to surpass its own existence.

## Biopower against Forms of Life

There is no doubt that this story gets very interesting when labor struggle is set amid the biopolitical sea change in employment structures, whereby an incessant ideology of work is generalized throughout all of society—what we have termed "biocracy." But how does the concept of biopower relate to the surplus common as discussed above? To address this question, we best turn to G. Agamben's (2000) fascinating study concerning the ethico-political significance of biopower. According to him, biopower emerges with the historical conflation of *zoe* and *bios*. The former pertains to us as sentient beings not significantly organically different from other animals and living things (e.g., dogs and wolves). Bios is something else: it refers to contingent ways of living that project the social body beyond itself. This might be called a form-of-life, since it has an infinite number of possible enunciations (again, think Spinoza). A form-of-life functions by opening us to the stranger inside us and thus multiplies the tonalities of our social relations through unexpected adaptations.

Bios cannot be reduced to or contained by zoe because the latter is generally underscored by its opposite, death. That is to say, what all living beings have in common is their mutual finitude. Bios, on the other hand, is a prerequisite of life because of its intrinsic expansiveness. This has major implications. Since bios obtains to the very possibility of possibilities, it must logically link life to the potential for happiness. Why so? Because bios entails the power to make life worthy of itself as opposed to life that is not worth living (e.g., servitude and abjection). And this inevitably places bios in the realm of politics because it can be made, contested, reversed, and made anew. Stemming from the Hobbesian tradition investigated above, zoe and bios have unfortunately been conflated by the modern polis—and not for unstrategic reasons, since this is how capitalism uses life against itself. We all know what power tells us every day: "Your ability to live is seated purely in your body (i.e., health) and we will protect your body (i.e., regulation) from the dangers of the world you will inevitably feel (i.e., fear)." From the point of view of the law—be it sovereign, capital, or the corporate Leviathan—our bodies are always on the brink of loss. This often convinces us that nothing is to be gained from exiting power's structural map of itself.

We again arrive at a *sociality of loss* because it does not amplify or multiply our potential for creating a good life together. The vast beauty of necessity is used as a crude foil to propagate fear of the body and its social riches. Deleuze (2006) understood this ideological component of modern capitalism more clearly than anyone else. Its preserving command actually employs the language of life against bios, against a freely articulated way of being together. This is why any opposition to biopower means *fighting for life,* a bios free to enjoy its true limits, pains, and pleasures: "When power takes life as its aim or object, then resistance to power already puts itself on the side of life, and turns life against power" (Deleuze 2006: 76). Can these insights also help understand how the logic of work might be resisted as well? As I argue in the coming chapters, I believe they can.

## Conclusion

From Spinoza to Marx, to Deleuze and Hardt and Negri, the key to comprehending the commons or what others call the "multitude," appears to be this: It is a sociality of gain that is continuously escaping its own historical determinations. Such escape is what allows it to create its own specific trajectory, both inside and outside the bounds of capitalism. Its intrinsic *autonomy* is fundamentally linked to these perpetual currents of *exit.* What exactly is autonomy? Andre Gorz (1989) gives a useful definition for our purposes. He simply views it as tasks we freely choose to undertake together as ends in themselves. Importantly, this requires no shortage of time. There is indeed much labor involved, but only that which multiplies its own preconditions for being well together. Because this entails a kind of social timelessness, it chimes with a fresh register of political experience. As Negri's epiphany pertaining to Spinoza's thought correctly surmises, "Freedom is the infinite. . . . [H]ere then, begins life" (2008: 167–168).

If we can now consider neoliberal capitalism as a kind of stultifying impasse, obstructing the general intellect from becoming what it properly is, then the importance of exit becomes clearer. The refusal of work movement formulates its politics thus. We know that neo-managerialist capitalism is over-reliant on our living sociality of gain. We also know that the corporation is not what it claims to be, the guarantor of this living world, but the opposite, something that parasitically rides on it. Knowing all this, the real political question becomes obvious. If the corporation needs us, then do we really need it or its religion of work? Many are answering no. And when they withdraw their sociality of gain from the logos of loss, it is just another way of describing collective self-determination—that is, *democracy.*

But cannot this autonomy be cunningly cultivated within the enterprise, creating a friendlier, less hierarchical work environment while reproducing the codes of capitalist exploitation? In other words, and following Žižek's (2009) critique of Hardt and Negri, is the leftist celebration of autonomy not, in fact, a confused commemoration of new rhizomatic forms of corporate capitalism?[7] The answer must be a resounding *no.* For there can be no equilibrium or functionality between the multitude's autonomy and its exploitation. The class struggle here is not dialectical. Moreover, such criticisms of the commons generally confuse it with humanized management practices that permit pockets of limited freedom within the exploitation process. Within such employment situations, however, the ultimate goals of work are still not publicly discussed. Nor is the desirability of corporate capitalism itself.

This is why the ethical autonomy of commons must remain logically antagonistic to the precepts of capitalism. Its surplus sociality is radically exterior to the instrumental logic of modern work. Indeed, if the corporation ever fully valorized the multitude, it would collapse under its own weight. The autonomy of the commons represents an uncontainable class antagonism, which the capitalist enterprise could never incorporate without moving toward a future in which it was absent. The corporation recognizes this future like everyone else, since society has moved on. This is why, to reiterate Foucault's observation from Chapter 1, the neoliberal project is so perceptive of its own impossibility, a sort of capitalism without capitalism within its own rationale. But no matter how much liberation management expounds the virtues of cooperation, it simply cannot forgo its class nature, which remains archaic and outdated to the commons.

# 3

# Why the Corporation
# Does Not Work

*A Brief History*

In the best-selling book (and movie) *The Corporation* (Bakan 2005), we are presented with a very critical reading of the nature of the modern capitalist enterprise. According to Bakan, if the corporation—so defined as a limited-liability, publicly listed firm—were to be considered a person (as per company law) then it would display the traits of someone potentially insane, a psychopath. This person has a myopic understanding of the world, treats everyone around them as an instrumental means, displays little empathy or sense of personal responsibility, and is driven by selfish ends. And it is this institutional form that modern capitalism has set loose upon the world, sucking almost everything into its sphere of influence. Although a person, the modern enterprise is simultaneously the epitome of calculative *impersonality*. This makes it the ideal vehicle for monopolizing markets, exploiting labor, and dominating the natural environment. Workers, consumers, and the community are mere means for an instrumental and incredibly single-minded end—to make profit. Bakan draws a stark picture at the beginning of his book:

> Today, corporations govern our lives. They determine what we eat, what we watch, what we wear, where we work, and what we do. We are inescapably surrounded by their culture, ico-

nography, and ideology. . . . Increasingly, corporations dictate
the decisions of their supposed overseers in government and
control domains of society once firmly embedded within the
public sphere. (Bakan 2005: 5)

Following a long tradition of criticism of how corporations govern
our lives in detrimental ways given their singular focus on profit-maximization, *The Corporation* does a good job in revealing the dark side
of their omnipotence and power. As a mechanism for enriching the
ruling elite—especially in its most recent financialized and oligarchic
manifestation—its predominance is equaled only by the sheer emas-
culation it visits on everybody else.

Similar studies draw a depressing picture of the corporation's sway
over human existence. In Charles Perrow's *Organizing America* (2002),
an excellent analysis is posited regarding how the United States was
transformed into a society of organizations, much of which is highly
corporatized in nature. Why might this be problematic? It is a cause
for concern not just because almost every facet of the world becomes
a business transaction, rendering it dull and exceeding calculative,
as Korten (1995) points out in *When Corporations Rule the World*,
nor only because of the way corporations inherently erect pay walls
around basic resources like health, food, energy, and transport, which
simultaneously excludes large numbers of humanity (Patel 2011).[1] No,
the chief reason that the corporation is criticized and feared is the
undemocratic control it has over our lives, functioning for interests
that are seldom collective or shared by the "99 percent." For many, the
neoliberal state seems totally captured by the interests of big business,
making the whole idea of voting in general elections seem like a bad
joke.[2] Indeed, this story of the unaccountable and overly powerful
firm is now part of popular imagination, reaching a wide audience in
mainstream documentaries like M. Moore's (2009) *Capitalism: A Love
Story* and M.-M. Robin's (2008) *The World according to Monsanto*.

These investigations are important for correcting the conservative dogma that would like us to view the prototypical free enterprise
as somehow synonymous with democracy and political liberty. But
a secret subtext is present in these criticisms that this book seeks to
challenge. The implicit message reads like this: for better or worse,
we are *reflections* of the corporate Leviathan. It is the first mover, and
everybody else caught in its regulative authority is a product of that

predominance. In effect, it has created our worlds and we had better fight back before it is too late.

This depiction is partially true but misses a crucial aspect of how the corporation came to be what it is and what it means to work in one today. The problem, I believe, is that the style of criticism introduced above gives too much constitutive agency to the object of critique. Building on the discussion in Chapter 2, I demonstrate that the modern corporation is not a creator of worlds but an inherently parasitical entity, riding on the efforts of the workforce, especially their non-economic codes and desire to forge a well-being in common. In other words, the capitalist firm ought to be viewed as a machine of capture, an internal logic born not from its strength, but defining its weakness. This analytical change in emphasis also means the way we contest the corporation and its liturgy of work needs to be rethought, which is a key concern of this book.

At the beginning of Korten's (1995) lament about corporate hegemony, an interesting statement is made about how many view the modern enterprise today. A prominent U.S. newspaper found that "although corporations are providing profits and material goods in large quantities, most people believe that there should be *more to life,* and corporations seem to be unwilling or unable to provide it" (Korten 1995: 6, emphasis added).[3]

What I find interesting is that this "more to life" plays a double function in our current biopolitical era. First, while the private enterprise is officially deemed to be the purveyor of life as such, it is, in fact, intrinsically unable to deliver anything close to it. Chapter 2 discovered why: it primarily represents *dead labor* and a class blockage. Second, and this is the heart of the problem, corporate capitalism cannot survive without the social vitalism that forever lies beyond its unsustainable rules. This "more to life" is, in fact, the social surplus noted in Chapter 2, living labor that the modern enterprise must enclose and exploit. Without it, the firm becomes simply a reflection of its own dead principles.

Building on the theoretical reflections developed in Chapter 2, I argue that many critical evaluations of the formal enterprise miss too much of what really constitutes wealth creation in capitalist societies, especially in their current neoliberal phase, which will no doubt be remembered years from now as deliberately self-destructive. Indeed, we must stop portraying the firm as it would partially like us to see it: an all-powerful, preponderant force that creates the worlds in which we find ourselves. It does not create worlds because it cannot, *but we do,* and we do so often to avoid the suffocating logic of modern capitalism.

Something interesting happens when we survey the historical development of the corporate form from this perspective. Obviously, its professed correlation with rising living standards, innovative development, and democracy begins to look highly dubious. The corporate system actually impedes progressive patterns of modernity rather than hastening their advancement and diffusion. Indeed, a close genealogy of the corporation also reveals the strikingly accidental nature of its rise, making it something of an anomaly, as Schrader (1993) puts it— but a curiously inverted anomaly. Marx once noted, "It is not because he is a leader of industry that a man is a capitalist; on the contrary, he is a leader of industry because he is a capitalist" (Marx [1867] 1972: 450). We assume a leader of industry is naturally drawn to a capitalist calling because of his or her germane abilities, but the inverse is true. Similarly, we also tend to think that corporations are drawn to vital industries—transportation, communications, food and energy supply—because they are better at serving these needs of society. The approach thus undeservedly naturalizes the corporation as the guarantor of integral social value, just as Marx argued Comte did with the lords of capital in the footnote to the above excerpt. The anomaly becomes the rule.

None of this is to deny that the large for-profit enterprise is powerful. But its command is unmerited and in no way connected with meeting the social necessities that it so often takes credit for. To see all of this, we need to shift our standpoint to that of living labor. In doing so, the vast under-commons of networks, public knowledge, and open cooperation—*our world*—becomes evident. From this standpoint, the corporation appears decidedly oligarchic, unable to deliver on its own neoliberal objectives (e.g., market efficiency and innovation) let alone those of the 99 percent. Yes, it is certainly one of most powerful institutions in the modern world, but it simply cannot reproduce itself on its own accord, and never has done so, as I demonstrate here. I next present a brief historical study of how the business corporation, from the early industrial period to the present biopolitical period, has never really worked. It has always been an inherently parasitical political construct, and perhaps is nearing its end.

# The Birth of the Corporation

To even begin to speak of the corporation today, a number of difficulties must be addressed. To appreciate why, we must go back to some classic and conventional definitions. Legalistically, we tend to see the corporation as consisting of a joint-stock system of capital investment, usually publicly traded with limited liability, that slowly morphs into managerial capitalism as industry grows (see Bowman 1996). But we must expand this conceptualization when studying it under the present conditions of biopower. Just as work has strangely departed the point of production and become a gaseous template for multiple aspects of life, so too has the ideology of the corporation. Whereas it might have made sense to speak of the corporation or multidivisional firm as a discernible concrete entity in the past, with the rise of neo-liberalism in the West, we might do better to speak of *corporatization*. This approach can be further elaborated through the notion of managerialism, which is the modern firm's primary personification. It is no longer something practiced by an identifiable class of individuals we call managers but has become a diffuse part of everyday life (see Grey 1999). Similarly, given that biopower seeks to embed the principles of the corporation throughout all of society, we should be careful not to miss its more pervasive and capillary-like tendencies across different dimensions of life.

## Why Living Labor Precedes the Corporation

One way to understand this aspect of the modern corporation might be to approach it as something like a design, or what we called a diagram in Chapter 1. A diagram is powerful precisely because it inflects our behaviors and thought, our desires and imagination without needing to display a specific concrete enactment. This makes it dangerously contagious. The locatable corporate entity defined in traditional economic theory now jumps to the family, from the family to sexuality, and back again. Indeed, commenting on Foucault's conceptual discovery, Deleuze points out that the diagram plays a "function that must be detached from any specific use, as from any specified substance" (Deleuze 2006: 61).

Deleuze's argument entails something of further importance concerning how we analyze the corporation today. For him, any diagram of power contains an essential lack, a space that it is never able to completely dominate since it is not really calling the shots. This is why *"resistance comes first,* to the extent that power relations operate completely within a diagram, while resistances necessarily operate in a direct relation with an outside from which the diagram emerges" (Deleuze 2006: 77). And this externality, of course, is *life,* the very "more to life" that Korten (1995) alludes to in the newspaper survey above. In the following investigation, therefore, we ought to keep in mind that corporatization requires a non-numerically rich "other" for sustenance. And as noted in Chapter 2, this is the social excess that, though it is contrary to its own nature, the corporation is both highly dependent on and deeply aggressive toward: living labor.

Too many studies of why and how the corporation emerged in Western capitalism tend to omit this a priori extra-capital surplus called living labor. Workers ("the employee") are seen to be mirror reflections or, even worse, by-products of managerial force, even in times of conflict and upheaval. In the case of Fligstein's (1990) influential study, corporate control appears to have evolved under U.S. capitalism without labor. A similar omission can be found in Jacques's investigation concerning how the employee was manufactured, which surprisingly makes hardly any mention of radical labor history: "Capital and labor could be enemies, but they could not threaten each other's existence because each had come into existence through the opposition to the other" (1996: 63). This view was even momentarily supported by Marx in the pamphlet *Wage Labor and Capital* ([1847] 2008), when he posited an "inverse and reciprocal" relation between the exploited and exploiters—dialectics at its worst. For obvious reasons, he abandoned this method of analysis fairly swiftly.

A very useful corrective to these thoughts about the relationship between labor and the corporation can be found in Tronti's (1980) examination of capitalism in the Italian context. He argues that we must view the course of capitalist development in terms of a disproportionate rupture that is never a one-to-one relationship between opposing parties. This opens the door for a *non-dialectical* appreciation of class struggle. The moment of rupture is intimately linked to the autonomy of a socialized workforce, since capitalism requires living energies that cannot be reduced to capitalism itself. If the enterprise could, it would have removed labor from the process long ago. Capital cannot therefore be considered an innovator or founding force in society: "We too saw first capitalist development and then the workers' struggles. This is an error. The problem must be overturned, its terms must be changed and one must start again: at the beginning is the class struggle. At the level of socially developed capitalism, capitalist development is subordinated to workers' struggles; it comes after them and it must make the political mechanism of its production correspond to them" (Tronti 1966: 89, quoted in Negri 2009: xxiii).

An appreciation of class struggle must position aggregate labor as the driving determinant of the corporate form. Given the constitutive externality of living labor in the production process, employment regimes will tend to take on an important reactive character. Capitalism becomes a perpetual response, a resistant stance that gives birth not only to the corporation itself, but also the regulative measures it deploys to capture living labor, right up to the present travesty of personal debt among the working poor.

## The Early Corporate Form

This reactive characteristic of the corporation can be noted from its early inception. By the early to mid-nineteenth century in Europe and the United States, we see the materialization of large-scale enterprises and the subsequent rise of managerialism. Mainstream historians of the modern firm, including Drucker (1946), Chandler (1977), and Bowman (1996), usually suggest that the joint-stock company materialized when the needs of capital investment outstripped the partnership model of ownership. In England, the joint-stock corporation was, of course, banned by the Bubble Act between 1720 and 1825, after which was the substantial emergence of ever-larger incorporated companies. According to conventional history, selling stock was one way to accumulate larger amounts of funds for capital investment, driving the development of the railways (Chandler 1977) and the multinational enterprise (Robins 2006).

This narrative of the early corporate form, however, tells only part of the story. For example, if we consult the 1838 "Petitions and Remonstrances" pertaining to one of the earliest U.S. corporations—the Amherst Carriage Company—we see a founding *reactive* posture from the outset on the side of big business.[4] The petition to incorporate had little to do with raising capital for industrial enlargement. As concerned voices stated, "No such expenditures are required in this business, nor is a large capital needed" ("Petitions and Remonstrances" 1838: 7). Indeed, the local community argued that incorporation was more about deskilling journeymen, destroying the independence of blacksmiths, traders, and small industry owners, and thus gaining an impersonal monopoly over the local industry. It is fascinating to note that one remonstrance claimed that incorporation would ironically be an act of *anti-business,* stunting market efficiency and the quality of services.

The concerned citizens of Amherst understood the true rationale behind incorporation of the Amherst Carriage Company: to erode and exploit their founding self-determination and ultimately transform skilled artisans into waged workers while capturing their superior knowhow. "We believe that incorporation tends to crush all feeble enterprise, and compel us to wear out our days in the service of others. Incorporation puts means into the ends of inexperienced capitalists, to take away from us the profit of our arts, which has cost years of labor to obtain, and which we consider to be our exclusive privilege to enjoy" (10). The company was eventually incorporated under extremely acrimonious circumstances. It is clear from this documentation that something evidently predatory was underlying the nature of these early firms. Rentier capitalists saw the social independence displayed by the Amherst public as something to resist before it could be exploited. This strategy shaped the contours of the instrument that would best achieve that—the modern corporation. As Sellers (1991) states in his discussion of early industrialism in Jacksonian America, this unexpected arrival of corporativism eventually extinguished the ideals of self-determination and artisanal autonomy that inspired escape from the Old World in the first place. Worker and community democracy was the first victim of corporatization, something that was fiercely contested and in no way inevitable to the economic modernization process.[5]

We must, however, refine this argument in relation to the historical context of class conflict, since capital and its private ownership mean very little without considering the rupturing pressure of living labor. E. P. Thompson (1963) notes in relation to England, for example, that worker militancy in the first part of the nineteenth century was almost on the verge of becoming a revolutionary movement. Legal fervor around the enterprise in the United Kingdom (and the colonies) sought to contain this unrest through judicial and extra-judicial means. In the United States, railway construction was, in fact, largely controlled by workers, especially during the nationwide rebellion of 1877 (Montgomery 1988). Indeed, the use of the joint-stock mechanism not only created a major gulf between owners and managers but, more importantly, highlighted the conflicting interests between workers and capital. The hostility that followed (e.g., the great Railroad Strike of 1877) fundamentally shaped the strategies and structures of many firms as they endeavored to control the accumulation process. Whereas the paternalism of early nineteenth-century capitalism tended to soften the labor/capital divide, the sudden prevalence of corporate employment practices swiftly revealed the cold-cash nexus of exploitation. This proved decisive in inciting violent industrial unrest. Capital had to react, and those reactions radically styled the subsequent spirit of the firm, especially around its control strategies.

Conventional wisdom suggests that the joint-stock and limited liability format is a functional corollary to the growth of capital. This picture is complicated by a number of studies that demonstrate how this format was also driven by trepidation over advances made by labor (Jacoby 1985). In the U.K. context, Bakan (2005) makes an interesting argument. He suggests that limited liability protection was one way to bring workers on board, to integrate them ideologically into the perspective of owners and of capital itself. In 1851 the Select Committee on Partnerships made this intention clear, and in 1853 the *Edinburgh Journal* reported on the committee, especially its idea of creating a wider catchment of investors (that might "potentially" include workers) to curtail labor militancy: "The workman does not understand the position of the capitalist. The remedy is to put him in the way by practical experience. . . . Working men, once enabled to act together as the owners of a joint capital, will soon find their whole view of the relations between capital and labor undergo a radical alternation" (quoted in Bakan 2005: 12).

This kind of reaction to workers' struggles became a constitutive factor of the emergent corporate form, and continued to be so into the early twentieth century, especially with the use of welfare capitalism to appease the labor movement. For example, in the United States, Jacoby (1985) demonstrates this in relation to the increasing use of profit sharing and stock ownership in the mid-1920s. It can be read as a direct response to the workers' movement opposing rampant profiteering and intolerable factory conditions. In 1919 the shipyard workers' strike in Seattle and the massive strike at the U.S. Steel Corporation almost brought these industries to their knees. The softening of controls and the attempt to transform workers into minor capitalists changed the nature of the enterprise significantly.[6] Of course, this tactic failed miserably from the capitalist standpoint (Jacoby 1985). While the idea of capitalism without capitalism seemed like a good idea in besieged boardrooms, its insurmountable impossibility quickly became apparent among an increasingly educated workforce whose discontent was quelled only by the arrival of World War II.

A similar reactive pattern can be observed in subsequent developments around the firm. As ownership and the management function slowly separated in the twentieth century, something very mysterious happened inside the corporation, as noted by early commentators like Berle and Means (1932). The investment function (ostensibly the wealth-generator from the corporatist point of view) shrank in comparison to other activities related to the contemporary stock market, especially speculation. This is Kelly's (2001) main grievance with the modern corporation. The private property system codified through stock ownership doesn't actually create wealth, but extorts it, since a stock is merely the right to extract cash. This is especially evident in U.S. corporate capitalism from the 1980s to 2000, which shows that "you can't find any net stockholder money going in—it's all going out" (Kelly 2001: 34).[7] When we put this finding in the context of concentrated ownership—a strategy that the modern firm specializes in— then the parasitical logic of the modern firm becomes fairly obvious.

## A Labor History of Corporate Control

One of the most useful ways for demonstrating the labor-determined nature of the corporation is to examine the evolution of management control methods. A variety of detailed historical studies demonstrate how corporate regulation is especially shaped by the emancipatory escape-attempts of surplus labor. However, we must be careful how we approach the topic of organizational control. It is often said that some sort of hierarchical authority is necessary for coordinating large groups of people and tasks. But this is not entirely true, as the success of experiments in worker self-management attest. Instead, control should be viewed in relation to the class contradictions inherent in the capitalist work relationship. Its role is to keep a lid on an otherwise volatile situation. This is why so many employees complain that management control appears to *obstruct* getting the job done well, almost to be imposed for its own sake.[8]

## Class and Control

This class character of control can be observed in early capitalist enterprises, and has become a defining feature of work to the present day. Most notably, innovations in managerial control invariably emerge following periods of unrest and protest, which in turn inevitably fail and spark the search for new methods of containment. E. P. Thompson gives one of the most worker-centered studies of this trend in the development of English capitalism. In *The Making of the English Working Class* (1963), we see how labor struggles between 1780 and 1832 defined the tenor of industry in profound ways. Violence and regulation were central to the making of the English working class, but often this was as a reaction to the Jacobean calls for freedom and self-determination circulating at the time. Put another way, labor made their own history as they sought to escape regimentation and build a livable life. This social surplus profoundly shaped the structure of enterprise as it adjusted and readapted to deal with such unrest.

The factory system was one of the main results of the widespread conflict during the late eighteenth century. Adam Smith's iconic depiction of the pin factory and the superior output achieved by the division of labor makes it appear like a natural development in market-led economies. But its emergence was only tangentially linked to the evolution of mass markets. The key catalyst was the need to subdue the social turbulence that the age of revolution had inspired among the working multitude. Factories literally *followed* workers as they attempted to forge lives outside the confines of exploitation and serfdom. This is why Thompson sought to redress the historical record, especially studies that saw manufactories as constitutive and primarily drivers of society, dragging the workforce behind them. Contrary to this narrative, he writes, "It is an image which forces one to think first of the industry, and only secondly of the people connected to it or serving it" (Thompson 1963: 210). But the structure of the factory cannot be separated from the conflict it was designed to contain and consistently failed to do. Thompson painstakingly documents a counter-history, a history from below that seeks to reverse this image, revealing that the working class "was not a spontaneous generation of the factory system. . . . [It] made itself as much as it was made" (Thompson 1963: 213). And these self-producing qualities of labor could never be entirely determined by capitalist discipline.

In the United States, a similar account can be told. According to Richard Edwards, the nature of work organizations—from the early days of the incorporated railways following the American Civil War up until the large bureaucratic enterprises of the 1970s—was largely shaped by unsuccessful attempts to restrain opposing workers. The contested terrain of American capitalism centers on workplace control rather than legal, governmental, or corporate strategies. Workers' refusal of these controls set off the hunt for new methods of regulation, which in turn were subverted accordingly. This is how we should understand the development of the corporate labor process:

> The labor process becomes an arena of class conflict and the workplace becomes a contested terrain. Faced with chronic resistance to their efforts to compel production, employers over the years have attempted to resolve the matter by reorganizing, indeed revolutionizing, the labor process itself. Their goal remains profits; their strategies aim at establishing structures of control at work. (Edwards 1979: 16)

Using case studies of a number of large firms, including AT&T, IBM, Polaroid, U.S. Steel, and International Harvester, Edwards maps the emergence of three successive control systems shaped by the collective refusal of work. In the nascent factory system toward the end of the nineteenth and beginning of the twentieth centuries, simple control was key—this consisted of a foreman or supervisor physically monitoring the task and threatening force for non-compliance. The Pullman Factory Strike of 1894 and the 1919–1920 steelworks strikes revealed the fatal flaw with personal or simple control. Bosses were petty tyrants, supervisors prone to arbitrary authoritarianism, and the visible presence of line managers made them easy targets for retribution.

This set off a search for more effective forms of regulation that effectively revolutionized the firm. Technical control and the assembly line seemed to do the trick. Control became mechanized and impersonal. But the weakness with this system soon become evident too, as Edwards argues in relation to the wave of strikes in major automobile factories: "Technical control linked together the plants' workforce, and when the line stopped, every worker necessarily joined the strike. . . . [T]echnical control thus took relatively homogeneous labor and technologically linked them in production. The combination proved to be exceptionally favorable for building unions" (Edwards 1979: 128). Technical control was abandoned because it inadvertently radicalized the workforce.

Enter bureaucratic control, which transformed the large corporations of the 1960s and 1970s. This way of exploiting labor sought to convince workers to identify with the company rather than each other, and to see its success as inseparable from their own. This managerial regime is "embedded in the social and organizational structure of the firm and is built into job categories, work rules, promotion procedures, discipline, wage scales, definitions of responsibilities and the like" (Edwards 1979: 131).

Did this, for Edwards, represent the last frontier of control? He speculated that the key weakness of this regulative system is that it is unable to contain three emergent types of struggle. First, the bureaucratic career worker naturally demands more say over the job since his or her advancement is linked to it. Bureaucratic work thus requires more democracy to function well, which is anathema to the capitalist imperative. Second, the over-regulated, rule-laden workplace makes conditions ripe for work-to-rule tactics of resistance, as Edwards noted at a number of plants. This is because impersonal bureaucracy also requires a subculture of informal, personal knowhow, which can freeze the organization if it is withdrawn. And finally, bureaucracy unwittingly politicizes the corporation. As it becomes a realm of corporate law and due process, the firm is partially socialized and thus open to contestation at state level politics: "By constructing formal rights and responsibilities, capitalists have abolished the individual capitalist's responsibility for working conditions and replaced it with social responsibility. Thus does modern control resolve the problem of local conflict only at the cost of raising it to a more general level" (Edwards 1979: 162).

This extended analysis by Edwards demonstrates how the factory and the bureaucratic office might certainly be defined by an abundance of control, but they were always *failing*, outpaced by the social surplus of the workforce that escaped its determination. This significantly shaped the way the enterprise evolved over the course of a tumultuous, often violent, and militant era of capitalist development. The democratic corporation Edwards hoped to see emerge in the late 1970s, of course, never arrived. After the bureaucratic revolution came the neoliberal dream of total commercialization, and many of the jobs he studied were moved off-shore in search of a less recalcitrant workforce. And that strategy appears to have failed too (see Silver 2003).

## Management Ideology

Management control systems maintain asymmetrical relations of power, and these typically need to be justified to workers in some manner. This brings ideology into the picture. Would we not see a similar reactive pattern in the managerial discourses and ideas used to make organizational control seem natural and morally right? Industrial historians have debated the phases, timing, and determinants of management ideology for many years. In the 1950s, for example, Bendix's (1956) groundbreaking study traced the entrepreneurial and elite ideologies that emerged during the course of American and European capitalist development, including social Darwinism and natural selection. But he was still unclear on one crucial point, which shaped the debates that subsequently unfolded on the topic. What are the social forces that determine the content and shifts in any particular ideology in the business enterprise?

According to Barley and Kunda's (1992) highly influential study of U.S. capitalism, it certainly was not labor but broader surges or waves of economic activity. They used bibliographic data from business periodicals over a 100-year period to discern distinct cycles in the way management justifies the subordination of labor. These waves follow alternating logics between normative (or soft management styles like the human relations movement) and rational (or hard approaches such as scientific design). Distinct here are ideological surges and decline around industrial betterment (1870–1900), scientific management (1900–1923), welfare capitalism/human relations (1923–1955), systems rationalism (1955–1980), and organization culture (1980–1992). What caused these swings back and forth between people-focused and systems-focused justifications? Barley and Kunda suggested that it might have something to do with broader boom-bust waves in the economy often called Kondratieff Cycles. When a downturn begins, returns on capital dwindle and management concentrates more on labor, using normative ideologies to maintain productivity. When the economy beings to boom again, managers focus on rational procedures, since "profits hinge easily on capital investment and automation" (1992: 391).

What about labor struggle and strike activity? According to my argument, would not this be a central determinant of managerial ideology? For instance, would we not expect to see normative justifications surge during times of industrial unrest, since a more humanized management approach would seek to abate conflict? Barley and Kunda concluded that there is no data to support this assumption. However, in an excellent study, Abrahamson (1997) challenges this reading, agreeing with others such as Jacoby (1985) and Gross (1956) that labor activity might be a major force in shaping management ideology. He finds the long-wave explanation valid only up to a point since it does not explain the *postemergence prevalence* of normative and rational discourses. Using a much wider data set, Abrahamson discovers that *labor militancy* is indeed significant. For example, business leaders will switch to softer management approaches following periods of industrial unrest, since "the prevalence of human relations/personnel management rhetoric fluctuated with union activity until the mid-1950s" (Abrahamson 1997: 524). And concurring with Shenhav (2002), we see similar patterns between harder management approaches and moments of worker refusal.

Rather than labor being a dialectical reflection of capital, it seems that managerial capitalism *follows* labor, and is never able to catch up. For example, Taylorism was specifically designed to break down unofficial systems of autonomy, putting management in charge of the minutest job detail. It actually had very little to do with Taylor's much cited search for the one best way to organize work. His systems were more about what he perceived to be an excessively untamable workforce. Just look at the period in which Taylor's ideas were circulating. Between 1910 and 1914—from the bombing of the *Los Angeles Times* building through the infamous Ludlow Massacre in which seventy-four striking miners were murdered—the United States resembled a war zone. Business leaders seriously feared a workers' revolution. Taylorism emerged as an unpopular but decisive response.[9]

The human relations movement—which promoted communication, self-actualization, and a more caring management philosophy —can also be understood in these terms. Writers like Maslow and Mayo claimed that workplace harmony could be achieved through the diffusion of therapeutic technologies, reconciling an alienated workforce with their rationalized jobs. In his study of the classic experiments conducted at the Hawthorne Works of Western Electric between 1924 and 1933 (which is usually seen to be the beginning of the human relations management movement), Gillespie (1991) considers the anti-union motivations behind the experiments and subsequent applications. The use of counseling, for example, encouraged workers to voice their grievances in specific forums and was promoted as a more civilized method of managing the plant. But it was probably a little more sinister than that, especially given the way it effectively bypassed unions, shop floor stewards, and the like. Thus, "counseling provided a means of dealing with complaints before they escalated into union grievances" (Gillespie 1991: 223; also see Bramel and Friend 1981). Output restriction, pilfering, and absenteeism, for example, were stripped of their class character and transformed into personal pathologies. Indeed, if we place these management ideas in the context of the Great Depression, a period when capitalism's overthrow seemed briefly imminent, the writings of the human relations movement start to appear quite malign.[10]

The failure of attempts to democratize the corporation by the late 1970s, as noted by Edwards (1979) above, is reflected in some major shifts in the nature of managerialism itself. The coming era of neoliberal economic thought translated into management techniques that increasingly sought the vitalism of bios, in explicit ways. The corporation no longer expended time and money attempting to socialize, train, and motivate the employee, all of which were responses to the militancy of the post-war era. Indeed, a colossal reorganization in the nature of capitalist exploitation was taking place, which rendered these techniques largely obsolete. The firm was responding to living labor once again, but in an increasingly desperate manner, since capitalism needed bios in its fullest manifestation, something that frequently lay beyond its formal boundaries.

Two important aspects of 1980s capitalism prefigured the rise of neoliberalism and the type of biopolitical management tools that dominate large enterprises today. First, the massive wave of commercialization of society was a response to broader gains that labor had made in terms of relative income equality, class equity, and social mobility. By the 1970s, the corporation was indeed in danger of being socialized in significant ways (see Duménil and Lévy 2004). The reactive nature of the capitalist elite and neoliberal state was indeed brutal, but driven more by a core weakness than a position of strength. And second, two distinct logics begin to intersect and crosshatch in the late 1980s: (1) the demand for more "authenticity" and personal freedom among the workforce (e.g., working from home and flexible hours) and (2) the realization among the business elite that unadulterated neo-classical capitalism would tear itself apart without some sort of social buffer, especially amid the decline of the Welfare State.[11]

## Commercializing the Public Sphere

In order to bring our workers history of the corporation up-to-date, we need to examine the resurgence of capitalism via the prism of neoliberalism from the 1980s onward. The dismantling of the Welfare State and the rise of monetarism was an important driver behind the introduction of biopower into Western workplaces. Indeed, the first sign that something was terribly wrong when neoliberal thought fully unleashed the corporation on society—in the early 1980s—was the way it systematically and aggressively plundered the public purse. This makes sense today. Neoliberalism was clearly its own worst enemy, completely unsustainable even on its own terms, and therefore required the vast social wealth stored in the Keynesian state to prop it up. This confiscation of public wealth, once complete, then meant some other non-capitalist resource had to do its dirty work, pick up the slack, and absorb its extreme irrationalities. Enter biopower and its management techniques, termed biocracy in Chapter 1. But that is still to come.

The sale of railways in the United Kingdom, the fresh waterways in South America, the health care infrastructure in Australia, energy generation in New Zealand, and the bizarre mass confiscation of public assets in post-1989 Russia were not driven by only numerical gain. Brazen profiteering was certainly involved, resulting in what Freeland (2012) calls an *ultra*-ultra-rich plutocratic class. And let's face it; concerning the present Russian situation, Lenin would despair, Stalin would grimace, and Yeltsin/Putin would silently nod their approval.

Betrayal has a long history in this country. But an important qualitative transformation was also occurring here and elsewhere. The structural inability of capitalism to organize itself from the late 1970s onward meant that the capitalist imperative required access to public steerage. It could not supply such steerage through traditional economic means. Around this period, we see unprecedented cross-pollination between the public and private sectors, especially among senior personnel, resulting in a hybrid privatized Keynesian mentality (see Crouch 2011).

I suggest this privatization of the public operated in two ways, with uneven and differentiated effects that we are still yet to fully understand. First, the Fordist social agreement underpinning the Keynesian Welfare State certainly absorbed many of the social costs of exploitation. The post–Great Depression investment in public works, health care, and utilities saw the governmental apparatus functioning as an effective shock absorber to the externalities of corporate activity. But the state also found itself to be a vast reservoir of public wealth accumulated by past labor, something the global business sector subsequently sought to enclose. The corporate capture of the state is little more than the corporate capture of labor.

Second, and as noted above, the corporatized state could no longer act as the external reference point to the accumulation process, with the rise of biopower being an important corollary to this severe limitation.[12]

Privatization functions in an interesting manner. The sale, for example, of public transport represents an initial loss to the working public, following years of taxation and governmental reinvestment. But that is only the beginning of the losses; since many transportation systems, such as the railways, are natural monopolies, the public must continue to pay for these services, often at inflated prices and embarrassingly inferior quality.[13] This second and unending confiscation of public work feels much worse because it operates through a negative perpetuity, becoming something of an indentured way of life. Now we must work to pay for a service that our parents and grandparents worked hard to finance in the past via income tax.

The corporate privatization of the Welfare State can be equated, therefore, with not only the one-off appropriation of a vast history of collective labor but also a continuing parasitical exploitation of public goods that are rented back to us for a premium. Hanlon (2013) brings the point home regarding an important innovation, this time in health care:

> Sir John Charnley pioneered hip replacement treatment globally whilst working for the socialized medical organization the National Health Service in the UK. He experimented on himself by putting polyethylene into his own body and leaving it there for months to see how the body would react before he was prepared to implant it as a ball and socket into patients needing hip replacements—it was an outstanding achievement with a 95% success rate. . . . The NHS provided hip replacement treatment on this basis but not for profit. US firms took Charnley's work and provided hip replacements (less good ones as it happens) for profit—so who is credited with the innovation in this instance? (Hanlon 2013: 34)

What is interesting about this example is the way in which the division between public and private is no longer mutually exclusive. A false public sector emerges that is underwritten by the state but managed in the interests of for-profit enterprises. This dual system is sometimes complex. Value generated by past and present public reserves still persists underneath the corporate apparatus (e.g., governmental corporate tax credits), but within a system of permanent abeyance, with access often denied to those who labored to create it. In other words, the classic problem of "buying the same horse twice" becomes infinitely worse since many cannot even make the second purchase of social goods they already theoretically own.

Much the same can also be said for advances in medicine and the natural sciences, which overwhelmingly originate from public and volunteer funding bodies. According to Perelman (2002) the university is particularly prone to the new corporate parasite. He surveys a wide range of industries related to the military, medicine, technology, and alternative energy, arriving at a stark conclusion: "Recent spectacular scientific and technological advancements largely represent the fruits of earlier public investment in science and technology, even though private corporations later won the intellectual property rights. In short, as is the case so often in advanced market economies, costs are socialized, while benefits are privatized. . . . [I]ntellectual property rights have contributed to one of the most massive redistributions of wealth that has ever occurred" (Perelman 2002: 4–5).[14]

This concerted corporate enclosure of the public sphere is linked to a number of very important trends that move us into the biopolitical era. First of all, the social shock absorber that neoliberal society required following the decline of the Welfare State became *financialized*. This was certainly a way for the working and middle classes to maintain some kind of reasonable standard of living as real wages stagnated and social services were brutally dismantled—a weapon for resisting their coming precarity. But as Haiven notes, finance capital itself represents a moment of retaliation against the resultant autonomy of workers, "a direct capitalist response to the gains of labor in the Global North in the post-war period . . . a means by which capital responds to people's resistance by rendering capital more fluid and mobile, thus circumventing local forms of solidarity" (2013: 4).

Second, what Martin (2002) calls the financialization of everyday life essentially means that *debt* becomes a perennial presence for many. Given the massive inequalities that neoliberal corporatization creates, even the relatively well-off middle classes now must incur debt in order to live, to the point where some people even *acquire debt to work,* as the massive intern-industry reveals (Perlin 2011). This could be one reading of the post-2008 global financial crisis, since the external social surplus that capital requires to persist becomes partially internalized by capitalism itself. And as we now know, as soon as capitalism becomes a perfect reflection of itself, especially its suicidal neoliberal variant, catabolic crisis is never far away.

## Conclusion

Even a brief history of the corporation reveals how capitalism does not create our world. And we are certainly not laboring mirror images of its mechanisms since capitalism cannot function that way. Living labor and its qualitative surplus must forever lie beyond its otherwise exploited condition. And as it seeks to realize that surplus, the corporation shifts and turns as well. Indeed, the modern firm truly bears the imprint of that which is inherently antagonistic to it. And as we have seen, the opposite is not the case because living labor must always be more than a dialectical counterpart to the accumulation process.

The current era of biopoliticization ought to be seen as the most recent stage of this super-dependent character of corporate capitalism, however much it is credited with the wealth that others produce. Indeed, it is astounding how the failed firm and, increasingly, late capitalist society itself are still considered by many commentators to be the great provider. A recent review of Colin Mayer's *Firm Commitment* (2013) in a popular business newspaper gives us a good example of this fantasy world. The book itself is a fairly conservative criticism of the contemporary corporation, suggesting that is fundamentally a force for good, but has recently gone awry. Business managers need to rediscover the age-old axioms of commercial ethics, including trust and commitment, since "the corporation is capable of a richer array of commitments and controls than we as individuals are capable of realizing" (Mayer 2013: 9). The newspaper reviewer, however, finds these statements outlandishly shocking: "Few would go as far as Colin Mayer. . . . [W]hile accepting that it is a protean organizational form with the capacity for good, he worries that while it feeds, houses, educates and transports us, the corporation also exploits." ("Radical Tilt at Governance Failures" 2013).

Even when it is catastrophically malfunctioning before our very eyes, the corporation is still credited with everything that makes life possible. It does the work that allows us to eat; it provides shelter and transports us across the city, country, and globe. This fantasy world propagated by even the most rigorous economists and business commentators is strikingly bizarre for two reasons. First, the corporatization of society has proved to be an unmitigated disaster on almost every social measure: in terms of wealth distribution, class mobility, access to education, consumer price indexes, employee engagement measures, happiness indexes, and all the rest. Neoliberal society is a protracted nightmare rather than the utopian dreamworld Milton Friedman and Mrs. Thatcher promised. Life persists today *despite* the corporation, not because of it. However, its presence has become so ingrained in the moral imagination of some that envisaging a planet without it is analogous to that old nineteenth-century Russian parlor game where participants tried to imagine the world without people.

The second observation is more concerning, however. The wasteland of neoliberal society and its self-destructive institutions are not inactive, ignoring us as we make the best of a bad situation, but deeply *parasitical*. This is why so many workers today struggle to be *left alone* rather than included, a type of refusal that would have looked strange to their Fordist predecessors. Indeed, the corporatized elites of late capitalist society clearly recognize that the present system cannot provide us with a livable life. It cannot even maintain itself let alone existence for the remaining 99 percent. And this is where we enter the picture to make the system work. The arrival of biopower correlates precisely with a systemic failure in the current model of capital accumulation. As a result, the business firm now seeks life beyond itself, prospecting the multitude for ideas, resourcefulness, and more ideas. Moreover, this extraneous sociality simultaneously functions as a useful social buffer for extreme neoliberalism, albeit one that is now heavily in debt. And when that shock absorber itself goes into crisis, overburdened by personal debt for example, neoliberalism is more than happy to make money out of that too.[15]

# 4

# Corporate Culture and the Coming Bioproletariat

Two images of work thirty years apart reveal that the way capitalism exploits the workforce in the West has undergone some important changes.

The first image is of "Tech" conveyed in Gideon Kunda's ethnographic study *Engineering Culture* (1992), conducted in the 1980s. Everything about the firm exudes its brand and values, from the coffee cups and screensavers, to the prolonged teambuilding exercises and large Orwellian TV monitors in the foyer portraying a smiling image of the leader. When you arrive at Tech, you enter a culturally cleansed world, in which almost everything is designed to convince you that the 'clan' is where you belong. While this looks like a more family-friendly style of capitalism, managers at Tech were fairly clear about the objective. People work harder and longer when they are socialized into a strong, highly conformist environment: "Power plays don't work. You can't *make 'em* do anything. They have to *want* to. So you have to work through the culture. The idea is to educate people without them knowing it. Have the religion and not know how they ever got it!" (Kunda 1992: 5). Anything relating to life outside the firm is ignored. Like a cult or an overzealous lover, Tech is very jealous about any competing claims on the selfhood of its workers. Tech is *everything*:

Tom O'Brien has been around the company for a while; like many others, he has definite ideas about "Tech culture" and what it takes to get things done in Engineering. But, as he is constantly reminded, so does the company. When he arrives at work each morning, he encounters evidence of the company's point of view at every turn. First are the bumperstickers adorning many of the cars in the parking lot. "I LOVE TECH!" they declare, somewhat unoriginally. "This shit is everywhere," he says[;] "I got it in my own car." Inside the building, just beyond the security desk, a large television monitor is playing a videotape of a recent speech by Sam Miller (the company president). As he walks by, he hears the familiar voice discuss "our goals, our values, and the way we do things." "It's the 'We are One' speech," he notes. (Kunda 1992: 50)

Now jump ahead twenty or so years to 2011. The best-selling pop-management book *Why Work Sucks and How to Fix It* (Ressler and Thompson 2011) surveys a number of large U.S. companies in which the message could not be farther away from life at Tech. Good management should focus purely on results. Where and when the work is done, what you wear when you do it, what you think or feel when you do it, is of no consequence. If you are an anti-capitalist protestor, fine. If you have the most peculiar taste in hairstyles, so what? As long as the final result is of excellent quality, that is all that matters. In fact, the firm might actually make use of your nonconformity and extramural interests. This is how work time, for example, is treated by this new management approach:

Arriving at the workplace at 2:00 P.M. is not considered coming in late. Leaving at 2:00 P.M. is not considered leaving early. It's OK to grocery shop on a Wednesday morning, catch a movie on Tuesday afternoon, or nap on a Thursday afternoon. People have an unlimited amount of "paid time off" as long as the work gets done. There are no work schedules. (Ressler and Thompson 2011: 93)

The authors swiftly console the worried manager who thinks this may be a recipe for laziness, almost inviting the workforce to shirk their duties and relax on the job. It "doesn't mean that everyone is on a permanent paid vacation. As we have said before, you have more responsibility, not less. You are responsible to your team and customers to get your job done. You can't stick your coworkers with your job while you hit the beach" (Ressler and Thompson 2011: 105). This chapter demonstrates two points about this shift in management ideology. First, the Ressler-and-Thompson scenario is indicative of the rise of biopower at work. Second, employees in this type of firm work a lot more—*much more*—than those described by Kunda over twenty years ago.

Indeed, one of the most significant shifts in how the workforce is regulated has occurred in Europe, the United States, and the United Kingdom since the 1990s. And its effects on the labor/capital divide are now just becoming apparent. I suggest that the use of biopower in the workplace (and the concomitant importance of the commons) is perfectly exemplified by the decline of the once popular culture management trend in the West. Corporations no longer endeavor to craft "designer selves" through cultural control and other socialization technologies. Instead they simply channel life itself into the production mechanism. The once near obsession with corporate clans, families, values, and culture reached its zenith in the late 1980s, and its decline points to the preference for a more holistic type of power: biocracy.

For many human resource managers, the central dysfunction with culture management systems described by Kunda was fairly obvious. Employees tended to feign enthusiasm and cynically distance their authentic feelings from the firm.[1] In today's biopolitical enterprise, however, workers no longer screen or defer the personal side of themselves as they may have done in a strong cultural setting. Companies in the service sector, education, IT, and many other industries now demand natural social performances in order to get the job done well. They want to see the buzz of life in the office, often indicative of a world beyond the workplace, and utilize social indicators that workers carry with them *all of the time.* Sexuality, lifestyle, and personal idiosyncrasies are no longer deemed the enemy of production but rather encouraged and employed.[2]

What exactly occurred to bring about this change in management practice? Why did large firms change their mind about the multiplicity of life being displayed and performed on the job? Answering this question may provide us with a more in-depth appreciation of the use of biopower at work. The peculiar abandonment of culture management marks the arrival of a new form of regulation—what we have labeled in earlier chapters as biocracy. It has no interest in building the ideal employee from scratch. Instead, it exploits what the workforce already is, using the idiom of self-determination and personal authenticity. It asks us to just be ourselves in the hope of evoking our life abilities and sociality. This chapter continues the overall theme of the book by demonstrating that the so-called freedom to express life itself at work should not be understood in terms of liberty, as many business commentators would have us believe. Rather, it represents an important facet of biopolitical control that aims to enlist the whole employee, including social qualities that we now know capitalism itself finds difficult to stimulate.

The shift away from internally sealed cultures to more porous systems of control reveals how workplaces are now exceptionally *dependent* on the self-management abilities of labor. A close analysis of the transition shows its striking correlation with the crisis of neoliberal corporatism in particular. Moreover, we can also note the new styles of dissent that emerge among the workforce. These oppositional strategies by living labor both predate and undermine these biopolitical tendencies as per our discussion of surplus sociality in earlier chapters. In this sense, it would be a mistake to assume that biocracy goes uncontested—in fact, it is the *result of contestation*. The excedents of social labor constantly overwhelm the rules of exploitation, which is one reason why the modern corporation is constantly seeking new methods for containing its latent post-capitalist future.

## The Rise and Fall of Corporate Cultures

The rise of corporate culturalism is frequently said to represent an important break from earlier modes of regulation in Western capitalism. From the early days of industrialism in the West, the key labor management problem could be articulated thus: how do we enjoy the benefits of control without simultaneously killing the so-called human factor increasingly required in many jobs? Popular management commentators celebrating the wonders of culture management in the early 1980s believed they had found a simple solution: *indoctrination*. Socialize workers with values, beliefs, and commitments so that they emotionally identify with their own subordination. As

Kunda put it in his ethnographic study of Tech, under this form of control "members act in the best interests of the company not because they are physically coerced, nor purely from an instrumental concern with economic rewards and incentives. Rather they are driven by internal commitment, strong identification with company goals" (Kunda 1992: 11).[3]

Popularized by Peters and Waterman's (1982) *In Search of Excellence* and Deal and Kennedy's (1982) *Corporate Cultures,* many firms in the United States began to rethink the normative and emotional qualities of the workforce. A good deal of inspiration was derived from Japanese models of management, which effectively blended capitalistic rationality with pre-modern patrimony. Because the Japanese miracle in the 1970s and early 1980s resulted in economic growth far outstripping the lumbering economies of the West, North American and European firms endeavored to follow the strong culture approach too. Indeed, a whole raft of corporate techniques that were developed in post-war Japan, including Total Quality Management and self-managing teams, were introduced into Western organizations. One of the major obstacles to embedding these new management systems was not culture clash, as some suggested, but unionized opposition (Grenier 1987), and hence the concomitant popularity of change management technologies and hired consultants. This effectively psychologized the resistant individual, labeling them irrational or even pathological.

## Contextualizing the Rise of Corporate Culturalism

It is important to see this managerial preoccupation with corporate culture in both a scholarly and historical context. That twenty-five years ago both academic and practitioner literature was obsessed with culture is no exaggeration. While popular management writers were praising the benefits of transforming the company into a family or clan, academics were also exploring the nature of business cultures. Some were prescriptive in their studies (such as Schein's [1985] influential schema) while others aimed to be more analytical and even anthropological in their investigations of how values affect work.

As Parker (2000) rightly observes, it is difficult to say whether there was anything overwhelmingly new in corporate culturalism as opposed to earlier attempts to normatively align the workforce with the principles of economic exploitation. We can see similar efforts to emotionalize the work ethic long before Peters and Waterman arrived on the scene, including the human and neo-human relations movement. According to Barley and Kunda (1992), as discussed in Chapter 3, the rise of corporate culturalism in the United States was the latest surge in normative controls that follow broader macro-economic cycles of expansion and contraction. Ramsay (1977) noted similar cycles of control and commitment in the United Kingdom, showing that corporations become interested in soft models of management on a periodical basis.[4]

But for the critics of corporate culturalism, there is something significantly different happening here. As opposed to the human and neo–human relations movement that aimed to have employees discover intrinsic fulfillment through task completion, corporate culturalism is more emotionally focused. It seeks to foster an all-encompassing environment in which our very personhood becomes a loyal reflection of the company. There is something monolithic, totalizing, and singular about this method of management, transforming the firm into something other commentators might term a greedy institution (Coser 1974) or total institution (Goffman 1961). As Hugh Willmott similarly argues in his classic critique of this trend, "What is new about corporate culturalism is the *systematizing and legitimizing* of a mode of control that purposefully seeks to shape and regulate the practical consciousness . . . of employees" (1993: 523, emphasis original).

This criticism was fairly typical of the way corporate culturalism was received in academic circles by the early 1990s. But culture management had caught the eye of sociologists earlier, especially in relation to a new capitalist tactic for reforming the strike-ridden economies of the West. In Edward's (1979) detailed historical study of regimes of control in corporate America, the management of culture was seen as yet another attempt to obfuscate the clash of interests between labor and capital. But what made it different was the anti-union flavor of this form of socialization. What Edwards terms the "IBM-Family" approach to business management sought to wrest loyalty away from unions and reconstitute labor in the image of managerialism itself. When this type of control is functioning, workers see little difference between their own well-being and that of the enterprise, making overt industrial action less attractive to workers, at least in theory.

These observations are important for positioning the rise of culture in the context of broader economic conflict, especially between labor and capital. Indeed, it is no coincidence that corporate culturalism came to prominence at the same time that a vast recomposition of class relations was taking place under the neoliberal agenda. This class element of the trend deserves more attention than it has received if we are to grasp the political significance of this management tool in the early days. As unions were dismantled and Fordist governance structures rolled back, corporate culturalism precipitated both an ultra-rationalized economization of the employee (we no longer talk about groups, teams, or departments, but responsible individuals) and the simultaneous reconstitution of workers as a reflection of shared norms ("we are all in this together")—a rather paradoxical premise from the beginning.

### "Strength Is Ignorance; Slavery Is Freedom"

One of the most cited and insightful criticisms of corporate culture management is an article by Hugh Willmott (1993) entitled "Strength Is Ignorance; Slavery Is Freedom." It draws parallels with George Orwell's *1984* to reveal the totalitarian aspirations of this method of regulating workers. It is worth paying close attention to this investigation for a number of reasons. It reveals the dimensions of this once popular form of control, but also allows us to draw some keen distinctions between it and the biopolitical objectives of much neo-managerialism today.

At first glance, it is surprising that Willmott chose Orwell's classic tale of totalitarianism to shed light on the more controversial aspects of corporate culturalism. For all intents and purposes, and like *Animal Farm, 1984* is usually read as a warning about the evils of dictatorial communism. More than anything else, *1984* is about the maintenance of power through pure naked force and violence (or its paranoid anticipation). Can we really draw analogies from this story to garner insights about management fads in liberal democratic societies?

Although the comparison is strained for this reason, Willmott does successfully demonstrate that if we distil this management ideology down to its basic principles, we find some frightening authoritarian tendencies. Willmott declares from the beginning that he uses little empirical data in his argument. Instead, he explores the theoretical (and consequently) moral foundations of corporate culturalism. Two lines of critique are developed. First, and using Orwell's now commonplace terminology, corporate culturalism relies on an untenable Doublethink, since it paradoxically promises practical autonomy (to think or do as we wish) while demanding this be achieved within a monolithic value-framework. This is an impossible incongruity. As Willmott puts it, "The benefits of participating in a strong corporate culture (and thereby further strengthening its totalizing effects) are sold by stressing the benefits for the individual employee who, it is claimed, not only enjoys greater practical autonomy but is transformed into a winner" (1993: 526). The real message underlying these strong cultures might read, "You can do what you like, just as long as you do what we tell you."

The second criticism concerns the conviction that strict adherence to *one* set of values might be healthy or acceptable, especially in societies defined by pluralism and free thought. Is there not something tyrannical and rather creepy in this method of management? Willmott does not use a Marxian or even Foucauldian framework to develop this line of critique. Instead, the grand theoretician of cold bureaucratic rationality is favored for the job: Max Weber. The feature of corporate culturalism Willmott finds most disconcerting is its overreliance on instrumental rationality to preclude all other value-standpoints. Indeed, the proponents of corporate culturalism are disingenuous on this point. They ask us to believe that this warmer method of management mitigates the negative side effects of instrumental rationality. This is why Peters and Waterman (1982) assert that all of those irrational, uncontrollable, and unmanageable aspects of the workforce can now be fostered.

It is in this manner that strong corporate cultures create flexible synergies between the emotional needs of employees and the economic aspirations of the firm, effectively rendering obsolete the old divide between labor and capital—or at least this is what the corporation would like us to believe. Willmott's counter-argument is unforgiving. Corporate culturalism forcibly binds the sentimental domain of the workforce to a singular set of values in order to *deepen* instrumental rationality. It renders behavior even more predictable, calculable, and certain from a one-dimensional economic (or instrumental) viewpoint.[5]

This brings us to the real problem. What truly justifies the evocation of *1984* for Willmott is the way corporate culturalism openly prohibits alternative value-standpoints. For Weber (adhering to a neo-Kantian understanding of moral maturity in an enlightened age), the true engine of democracy is *substantive rationality* or the open evaluation of diverse qualitative ends. That is to say, are the broad goals our so-called rational societies strive toward rational in themselves? Substantive rationality requires both an environment that encourages dialogue about diverse value perspectives and the agentic capacity of individuals to reflect and decide. Of course, corporate culturalism is not keen on any of this. Only one set of values is permitted, and if you do not like them, to quote Peters and Waterman (1982: 72), "you get out." For Willmott, this must place corporate culturalism in the worst tradition of anti-democratic thought, reminiscent of fascism and Stalinism, since it aspires to "extend the terrain of instrumental rational action by developing monocultures in which conditions for the development of value-rational action, where individuals struggle to assess the meaning and worth of a range of competing value standpoints, are systematically eroded" (1993: 518).

Corporate culturalism is sold in the garb of freedom, as a method of management that does away with more repressive Fordist controls. But Willmott demonstrates the opposite. It actually increases the level of workplace monitoring. At least in the bureaucratic office of yesteryear, we could think what we liked. Now even our thoughts are policed, but perversely in the name of self-expression. For Willmott, the autocratic consequences are clear. If you want to subscribe to values dissimilar to the dominant discourse then you are in big trouble, and this prospect encourages a secret life of guilt and fear. As our dependence on these monolithic norms intensifies, we become afraid of real freedom, true choice, and ultimately our own existential responsibilities. And in the unlikely event that anyone does openly challenge the company, then, to paraphrase Willmott, they soon discover the iron fist beneath the velvet glove.

## The End of Corporate Culture: Putting "Life Itself" to Work

The critical studies of corporate culture conducted by Willmott and others are very important for revealing not only the controlling aspirations of this method of management but managerialism *per se*. It is not my intention here to claim that cultural controls are no longer relevant or important in the world of work. They obviously are. But I would suggest that the symbolic systems of large enterprises have undergone significant changes of late. Most workers are no longer bombarded with the cult-like socialization tactics identified by Willmott and Kunda. Nor are they emphatically implored to think of the firm as their family. Perhaps this is indicative of the massive evacuation of legitimacy concerning work more generally. Not even lucratively paid investment bankers see much moral worth in it, according to Michel (2012). We are living through a profound crisis in corporate capitalism, one that sees otherwise pro-business publications like the *Harvard Business Review* openly concede that the legitimacy of business corporations and their attendant institutions have slumped to an all-time low. Demanding or even inviting employees to love their firm, emotionally bond with it, and consider management their family would certainly be a tall order, even for the most charismatic of leaders.

Other historical shifts are also important to note, especially concerning what capitalism needs from the workforce today and the profound limitations it has to generate them on its own accord. This new imperative is especially evident in emergent types of corporate discourse that eschew cultural conformity and emotional identification. As opposed to the clan-like preclusion of non-work influences described so well by the critics above, diverse extra-employment identities are now actively encouraged on the job. Even dissent and slacker-cool attitudes appear to be welcome.

As the jargon of liberation management and Results Only Work Environments alludes to, the independent social competencies of workers are now deemed a crucial economic resource. Andrew Sturdy and I observed this in our study of a call center that encouraged workers to just be themselves (see Fleming and Sturdy 2011). The discourse of personal authenticity was a vehicle to mine, capture, and utilize the social intelligence of employees. This was especially the case in relation to emotional labor and the need for off-script gregariousness. One call-center trainer explained to workers how this works: "The key to persuasiveness (with customers) is openness: the more open the conversations the greater potential for success and customer satisfaction." Management viewed the central productive capacity of its workforce as already present, preformed, and developed. They simply had to persuade employees that it was OK to use it on the job.

Thus motifs of individual freedom and self-expression must be viewed as proxies for the real prize that biopolitical capitalism seeks today: *the commons.* But what is common or social about personal authenticity and emotional intelligence? Are not these individual attributes? No. We must avoid falling into the trap of perpetuating individualist readings of embodied skill and other forms of human capital. These are thoroughly social qualities. Andre Gorz explains this point very well:

> What companies regard as their human capital is a free resource, an externality that produced itself and continues to produce itself, while companies merely tap into and channel this capacity. This human capital is clearly not purely personal. The production of self does not happen out of nothing. It takes place on the basis of shared culture transmitted by primary socialization and common forms of experiential knowledge. (Gorz 2010: 12)

That is to say, human capital consists of a certain social surplus, which the present investigation has demonstrated will always exceed the algorithms of economic exploitation.

Having said this, and building on the discussion in previous chapters, the social factory of neo-corporate hegemony should never be granted constitutive powers it does not deserve. We must see its predominance as something secondary to the value creation process. This is why we see the corporate form today riding on the extra-corporate sociality of workers, relations that are difficult to reinvent within the parameters of managerial authority and instrumental rationality. Ironically enough, this freer social life might have even been developed to escape the regimentation of capitalism. More specifically, we can note three moments of post-corporate culture capitalism here, all of which indicate the new importance placed on life itself and its bioexploitation in the workplace today.

## From Conformity to Diversity

It is the suffocating uniformity of corporate cultures that keenly concerns Willmott and other critics. As Willmott correctly states, "The space within organizations for expressing and developing awareness of, and allegiance to, alternative norms or values is reduced and, ideally, eliminated" (1993: 532). But not long after the first appearance of critical studies of the trend, popular management commentators also started to have serious reservations about the utility of cultural conformity. Even the original proponents of strong cultures—including Tom Peters (1994)—were changing their minds, arguing that slavish adherence to a monolithic set of values might actually smother the creative, innovative, and entrepreneurial capabilities of employees. According to Foster and Kaplan (2001) human resource managers quickly realized that the staid conformity indicative of corporate culture made workers increasingly complacent and drone-like when imaginative solutions were required. By the late 1990s management ideology was suddenly preoccupied with eliciting the whole person in the organization, permitting individual differences and unique professional/personal backgrounds to be integrated with the job.

Indeed, the closed communities of highly managed cultures effectively resort to *depersonalizing* the worker, since any facet of the individual that did not reflect the firm's values was symbolically castigated as hazardous. In this highly conformist climate, "cultural diversity is dissolved in the acid bath of the core corporate values" (Willmott 1993: 534). Now the opposite seems to be the case. In keeping with the view that the market, rather than the clan, is becoming the guiding metaphor of workplace relations, Peters claims that "chaos is with us . . . but the way to deal with it is to pursue variation, not to manage or stifle it" (1994: 51). If employees are to be motivated and compliant, they must be free to display their diverse identities in the office. It is simply astounding to see how management rhetoric abandoned authority in favor of freedom during the late 1990s and early 2000s. Almost overnight the corporate sector discovered the benefits of life at work, whereby lifestyle differences, sexual orientation, and consumer tastes were openly celebrated.[6]

This has a number of important implications when considering the key distinctions between culture management and biopolitical regulation in the contemporary workplace. For Willmott, diverse standpoints are a vital democratic antidote to the totalitarian conformity of culture management. The terrain is different today, however. Workplace democracy is increasingly shut down precisely by using the language of diversity. Indeed, all manner of assorted views are welcome in the office, since what David Courpasson (2006) calls "soft constraint" employs the idiom of political liberalism rather than totalitarianism. The message now is "Be yourself, say what you like, but submit to the demands of economic necessity." As opposed to the rule of law demanded by bureaucracy and culture, the putative freedom to be yourself even extends to dissent. Accordingly, if management is to retain a role, they ought to hire and nurture employees who are troublemakers: insolent, uncomfortable with the norm, and willing to thumb their noses at authority.[7] This is why the ethos of the unruly youngster is often drawn on—"go for youth" (Peters 1994: 204)—even if this conflicts with liberal concerns around age discrimination.

The language of liberty in this capitalist discourse harbors a dark side, which points to the human costs of biopower at work. The emphasis on identity and difference belies a more disconcerting injunction underlying this management technique. When it comes to the work environment, the so-called freedom to be yourself really means freedom *to do it yourself.* In other words, the social overheads of production will no longer be borne by the firm. Training, motivation, and emotional aptitudes are now entirely the worker's responsibility. Even basic everyday management has largely become the responsibility of workers as they endeavor to get the job done under impossible neoliberal conditions. And as such, more of 'life itself' must be drawn on, otherwise one risks retrenchment.

The strong cultures trend of the 1980s might therefore be viewed as the last management ideology that viewed the corporation as some kind of *guarantor,* perhaps a vestige of the New Deal social compromise. The old system told workers: "If we employ you, then we will exploit you, but also train you, manage you, and find ways to motivate you, using techniques such as culture management." The cost to the worker was forgoing individual freedom. The capital/labor interface no longer functions quite like this. Employees are accountable for almost every aspect of what happens to them on the job and beyond. As a CEO interviewed by Pink (2011: 32) noted, "If you need me to motivate you, I probably don't want to hire you." The quip seems insignificant, but represents a tremendous shift in the nature of corporate hegemony compared to yesteryear. Employees now function more as always-potentially-terminated agents, free to be themselves, but also wedded to their work through *fear.* This is the perverse underside of liberation management and workplace authenticity.

## From Labor to "Life Itself"

A further move away from culture management is evidenced in the way it increasingly focuses on moments of *non-work* as a source of value and ideas. Previous chapters have explained why this is the case. This permutation is nowhere more apparent than in the business advice of Bains (2007). For him, productivity (or what we will call exploitation) is simply a question of "whether employees are able to bring their full selves into work and whether their job utilizes all of their capabilities . . . characteristics in their private lives that they could bring into play at work" (2007: 219). This is when the contemporary corporate infrastructure displays signs of what we have termed biocracy, whereby the independent life abilities of the workforce are enrolled as a productive force.

Critics of corporate culturalism correctly draw parallels with the mind-control tactics usually found in offbeat cults and sects. These institutions are total and monolithic, distrusting to the point of paranoia any foreign agents that might contaminate the scene. As Kunda (1992) observed among the culture architects, the diluting influence of non-corporate life (e.g., family, hobbies, and leisure) must be minimized since it can upset the tightly policed story. For example, one worker interviewed by Kunda (1992: 38) made reference to a colleague's family troubles: "In the office you keep that kind of shit to yourself." Pluralistic life projects pursued beyond work might reduce the desirability of complete allegiance to the firm. It is for this reason that Willmott (1993) laments, "Far from enabling the active process of comprehending the possibility and necessity of choosing between competing values and their associated life-projects, identification with a single set of values is demanded" (529).

The post-industrial workplace complicates this picture. It has significantly displaced the old boundaries that once delineated work from non-work. If employees in the 1980s and 1990s believed their life projects were unwelcome in the organizational sphere, then today they are enthusiastically encouraged and turned toward productive ends. As previous chapters have noted, this is because many useful qualities desired by the contemporary firm lie beyond its official remit, and modern management methods are increasingly designed to tap them. The rise of the lifestyle organization seeks to capture essential creative and cooperative energies and index them to economic rationality. For example, employees of large music stores are encouraged to wear their own attire rather than a corporate uniform. Why? Because they have a much better fashion sense than anything prescribed by a dull middle manager. And this creates a consumer-conducive atmosphere. Similarly, training in the knowledge industries is almost non-existent, since companies know full well that the members of their workforce train themselves, on their own time and expense. The closed social system defined by corporate culturalism that Willmott outlined has been partially replaced by the Google-Model of production (Hanlon 2013) whereby the extra- (and sometimes *anti-*) economic qualities of living labor are harvested for exploitative ends.

Grassman's (2012) intensive semi-ethnographic study of a well-known knowledge-based enterprise in London is illuminating here. When asked about the climate of the firm, an employee observed, "You are encouraged to be how you want. . . . [T]here is no common denominator other than there is no norm[;] it is almost not like going to work because you do not know when it begins or ends" (Grassman 2012: 159). Three important facets of biocratic management systems are important for us in relation to this study. First, the enterprise has moved away from explicitly constructing an organizational norm that all of its workforce must subsequently adhere to no matter what. Instead, deviation and difference, ironically, become the new unstated norm. One reason, I would suggest, is that a wider ideological catchment area is generated by companies that depend on abilities they can neither foster nor predict, nor numerically evaluate. This is an important point. It is precisely management's incapacity to completely regulate its workers that gives rise to biocratic systems.

Second, Grassman's study reveals the typical blending of work and non-work utilized by biopolitical management methods, which now appear to be so vital for tapping the general intellect of the workforce. We also observe this in the lifestyle firm Ross (2004) investigated too, since porous boundaries help perpetuate the illusion of freedom while extending the logic of production deep into society. In this sense, the cultural management trend discussed above was still wedded to a Fordist image of the factory. It believed that the most industrious employee performances were generated through containment. But when society itself begins to resemble a factory, demarcations typical of the

Keynesian order become an impediment to prolonged productivity. From capitalism's perspective, we need to be at work all the time in order to make an otherwise unworkable paradigm function.

Third, and pointing to the most injurious facet of this type of capitalist regulation, firms are able to dissolve the boundaries between work and non-work without fearing that employees might shirk their duties or relax. This is a fascinating facet of organizational control that previous generations of workers would have found unfathomable. Symbolically blending work and leisure, home and office, and relaxing the spatial/temporal regimentation of our jobs—none of this results in less work; it does just the opposite. Abolishing the strict requirement to clock in and out actually overloads (rather than frees) our social imagination with the manufactured necessity of work.

This last point is important for a number of reasons. The language of freedom and liberation is equated with some kind of life *beyond work,* something that the culture management techniques of the 1980s would have considered a dangerous distraction. Of course, this life after work so vivid in the biopolitical imagination *never arrives.* Also, stress, mental fatigue, and breakdown, all of which were typical under culture management as well, become generalized social norms. The architects of strong cultures in the 1980s and 1990s were embarrassed by burnouts. They preferred to consign these "causalities" to the unspoken realm of office life. This might be put down to the prudent fear of legal culpability among the large corporations. Now, however, mental and physical atrophy are individualized lifestyle pathologies that seemingly arise by choice, as implicitly expected by the firm, but whose costs are carried by the employee. For in the end, it is their life and no one has forced them to overwork.

A further issue arises here. Although biopower and its virus-like ideology of work appear particularly virtual or immaterial, in fact, the opposite is the case. We are dealing with a very concrete and embodied form of influence. Michel's (2012) research of biopower in a city bank is poignant because the externalities of biocracy were especially physical. Many of these high-paid employees left their jobs prematurely aged and decrepit. Broken and wrecked bodies, obesity, and dangerously high blood pressure are some of the costs for doing neoliberalism's work. Biopower sucks up the fruits of life and leaves us, or at least our caregivers, to deal with its negative externalities.[8]

## From Political Inclusion to Discursive Escape

The corporatization of life as noted so far raises important questions around how we might resist biopower at work. There are important changes around this topic too. To see this, let us return to Willmott's central criticism of corporate cultures. He was deeply concerned with the totalitarian manner in which it precluded alternative value-standpoints. Consequently, value diversity might be considered emancipatory given the "affinity between the practical realization of autonomy and the development of democratic organizations of social institutions, in which the virtues of competing values are freely debated" (Willmott 1993: 534). A rather Habermasian solution pertaining to deliberative dialogue is offered as a radical remedy to the totalitarian spirit of corporate culturalism. A truly democratic reconstitution of corporate life would place it in the context of a plural social universe, as one sphere among many others, and thus open up its meaning/organization to multiple points of view. And following Habermas (1987), such democratic consensus requires open debate and discussion, as well as the positive recognition of those who are speaking, no matter their rank (Scherer and Palazzo 2007). Whether this enabling critical dialogue entails minor modifications in power relations (via micro-emancipation [Alvesson and Willmott 1992]) or more significant interventions, open and free communicative exchange is a crucial prerequisite.

In the context of a closed social institution that aims to remain pure and untainted by outside life projects, this speaking the truth to power (Foucault 2001) certainly holds much democratic promise. But today there seems to be a major world-weariness concerning the idea of asking to be recognized by power and voicing our demands. Why so? I believe it reflects a pervasive disillusionment with the cultural status of work life itself. Compared to yesteryear, in which the worker was held as an iconic social ideal, recent times have seen a major decline in legitimacy of this view. The employee today rarely desires more, less, fairer, or better work, but simply a silent and unceremonial escape or *exit* from the scene of paid toil.

Following a major theme in this book, such disaffection may be partially responsible for the turn away from *recognition politics* in today's workplaces. But it is also indicative of a new kind of resistance among the emergent bioproletariat. We might term this *post-recognition politics* because it does not implore to be seen, heard, or counted in corporate-sponsored debates. The concept is prompted by the observation that many of us are worried that dialogue with power not only fails to curb corporate control but may also justify its continuance. As the Invisible Committee (2009) points out, an emergent workers' militancy is increasingly aware of this pitfall. It refuses to enter into dialogue with corporate officialdom since any sort of exchange may inadvertently reinforce the terms of an unwinnable game. Suddenly we are using its language, its expectations, and its political baggage.[9]

The rationale underlying post-recognition politics is fairly clear. If the biopolitical corporation is conspicuously over-reliant on human qualities lying beyond its structures, then why not valorize this social autonomy toward more democratic objectives? In this sense, the self-determination that Willmott champions in his critique of culture is still tremendously relevant. But he assumes it can happen within the logic of the modern firm, through heated dialogue and pluralist debate. Workers are very pessimistic about this possibility today (Gillick 2009). Resistance inspired by post-recognition politics seeks self-determination *outside* the corporate project by repossessing the social independence that many jobs enclose for capitalistic ends. Gorz calls this a democratic reclamation of work, whereby "social relations, co-operative bonds and the meaning of each life will be mainly produced by activities that do not valorize capital. Working time will cease to be the dominant social time" (Gorz 2005: 73). The political efficacy of this post-work imaginary and its new sense of social time are investigated in more depth later.

## Conclusion

The transition from culture to life occurred quietly as commercial conditions required more of the worker in the field of exploitation, and that field of exploitation became scattered and diffuse. The endogenous cognitive attributes of workers are not fixed by the space and time of employment, and this independence is what neoliberalism in crisis needs the most today. I would suggest that this imperative is now one of the most defining features of capitalistic management presently.

It is interesting to note that culture management often backfired in practice because of the high expectations it fostered among workers. The humane and caring side of its discourse often clashed with everyday realities of capitalist power relations. Indeed, there is something unmistakably innocent (and even nostalgic) in the aforementioned critical studies of culture when we reread them in today's context. They seem to point to a time when corporations still worried about their internal and external legitimacy, and spent significant resources on ideological programs designed to convince how wonderfully beneficent they were. But since the 1990s (a period that coincides with the rise of biopower in the workplace), we have witnessed the travesty of post-Enron capitalism, criminal oil wars in the Middle East, Wikileaks revelations of predatory profiteering, bank bailouts confirming how democratic governments are but instruments of the elite (at the expense of the 99 percent, to quote the Occupy Movement slogan), and so much more. After all that, the idea that employees might seriously believe in the corporation—let alone emotionally bond with it—seems inconceivable.

In these so-called end times (Žižek 2010) governed by a self-destructive capitalist realism, it is difficult to imagine that corporate culture might have once mattered. Today, there is an uneasy feeling that no one really cares whether we identify with our work or not—least of all the firm itself. Legitimacy is out of fashion. Power no longer feels the need to disguise itself. And as a result, perhaps more pressing questions are coming to the fore, along with even more urgent democratic solutions to the problem of work.

# 5

# "Free Work" Capitalism

In an advertisement aired on a digital music website popular in the United Kingdom, listeners were told that they too might contribute to the stylistic direction of the service. Only a few moments of their time would be required. This was an opportunity to influence the product that they and thousands of others had come to love, shaping and collectively managing its future on-line delivery. The advertisement concluded with the alluring phrase "Some might call it work . . . but we don't." The idea was clear. Listeners would lend their time to a for-profit enterprise without payment, but one should not think of it as work. Such activity is more akin to any other labor of love, such as uploading an artistic homemade film on YouTube or creating freeware code solutions on the weekend. This was nothing to do with a dreary and unfulfilling job, but closer to pleasure, self-determination, and perhaps living itself.

I suggest that we use this opening example as a guiding image for investigating an emergent mode of capitalism that has been widely adopted in contemporary workplaces. According to classic Marxism, productive work can be exploited only if it passes through the circuits of wage-exploitation. Wages and productivity are closely calibrated to ensure that surplus value can be clearly expropriated and the illusion of equity maintained—a fair day's wage for a fair day's work. All broader life concerns of the workforce that cannot be tallied against the objective measure of paid time tend to be considered by industrial capitalists as irrelevant at best.[1]

As Chapter 4 revealed, the move from corporate culture to life itself aims to place the workers' life abilities, social attributes, and self-management skills at the forefront of the exploitation process. And just to remind the reader, none of this means fewer supervisors above us giving orders—on the contrary, since biocracy represents an augmentation of traditional management structures rather than their replacement. However, as the ideology of work escapes the office and more living space is indexed to our jobs, often prompted by the unworkable realities of neoliberal reason itself, we invariably find ourselves doing productive work outside the formal employment situation.

The rise of *free labor* capitalism is a concrete outcome of the trend introduced in Chapter 4. For example, think of the university worker with which I introduced this book. Not only was productive work conducted outside of official paid hours (on a Friday evening, in this case) but the stress and attentiveness that it required overflowed the paid/non-paid divide. And the cost, of course, was borne by her and the social networks that came to assistance. Think also of how training in the knowledge industries is almost nonexistent since companies know full well that most workers train themselves on their own time (Cederström and Fleming 2012). A leading business model in the United Kingdom intends to transform the workforce into self-employed individuals so they must bear job-related expenses, including retail uniforms and social security payments.[2] And as mentioned in Chapter 4, a number of commentators have also pointed to the way Internet websites such as Facebook utilize the same strategy among their users (Terranova 2003; Land and Böhm 2012).[3] When life itself is put to work, a good deal of the productivity expected or even demanded by the firm falls beyond its remuneration systems, and we end up working for nothing.

The normalcy of working for free, I argue, is playing a major economic role in business today, especially when the social intelligence of employees becomes intrinsic to the job. As we have noted, because capitalism will not (and frequently cannot) generate these life qualities itself, new methods of power have emerged to capture them. This changes the nature of the employment relationship considerably. Whereas Fordism's classic dichotomy between official and unofficial work time treated them as distinct spheres, today the two are increasingly interchangeable. This is emblematic of the coming biopolitical enterprise in Western economies. Socially acquired skills among the growing immaterial workforce are rendered profitable by exploiting pre- and post-corporatized spaces, which in turn often escape the hard metrics of enterprise (Lazzarato 1996).

Of course, these self-fashioned facets of the workforce (e.g., capabilities born from cooperative relations) have perhaps always been valuable to the firm. The classic sociological studies of Blau (1955) and Gouldner (1954), for example, observed the striking importance of this implicit self-organizing. Only in the present context of biocracy, however, does social labor power become a widespread capitalist concern—and not for progressive reasons. As Callaghan and Thompson (2002) put it in their study of a customer service enterprise, management aims to recruit and exploit readymade human qualities ("we recruit attitude") instead of raw material that might be costly to subsequently instruct.

We might expect that this development is due to the post-industrial displacement of traditional boundaries between work and home, paid and unpaid labor time, fixed and variable capital (see Felstead, Jewson, and Walters 2005). It might also be indicative of the way neoliberalism significantly diminishes our chances of having permanent and secure employment while simultaneously glorifying its unconditional centrality. As Gorz notes, this perversely encourages us to frame our job "as an asset one should be prepared to make sacrifices to possess" (Gorz 2005: 56). Unpaid labor time and effort might be one such sacrifice, which enterprises will exploit to their advantage. The massive reliance on unpaid interns in U.S. and U.K. corporations is sustained by this dynamic of precarity, which increasingly defines wider employment patterns, too (Perlin 2010).[4]

This chapter also suggests that the rise of free-work capitalism is indicative of qualitative changes in the nature of the labor/capital relationship. Labor is no longer simply variable capital but also fixed—not external to the valorization process but intrinsically part of it. We *are* capital, and that social embodiment defies the calculative systems once used to direct the exploitation process. This points to the private enterprise's growing dependence on the worker's otherwise independent abilities, especially within an impractical neoliberal economic world.

Because the value that drives post-industrial capitalism lies far beyond its own formal structures, a symbolic distance emerges that becomes a problem for corporate managerialism. For example, it would be exceedingly difficult to train a customer service worker to be naturally conversational and genuinely personable on the phone with a customer (Fleming 2009). Thus, when these human qualities become central to revenue creation, the management function follows a different logic, one that seeks to enclose rather than compose behavior onsite. This also encourages many of us to assume the responsibilities of paid work regardless of whether we are formally checked in or not, and hence, note the importance of worker-led attempts to defy the normalization of unpaid labor (like the Work Your Proper Hours Day in the United Kingdom, designed to curb unpaid overtime in the service sector).

As Chapter 6 addresses more fully, the refusal of work movement emerging in the West and elsewhere appropriates this vast gap between productivity and wages for its own cause. Its first demand is a living wage, irrespective of one's individual productivity, since it is capitalism that no longer respects any equivalence between the two. But that is not enough. Radical independence from capitalism might be good, too. This repossession of social labor time does not require the construction of some blueprint for a future society. It merely focuses on the autonomous wealth that labor already is. In this sense, perhaps it is neoliberal thought that begins to look decidedly utopian (i.e., a nowhere place), not the 99 percent calling for its demise.

## The Scattered Points of Production

The heightened importance of free work for today's economic system is not really registered by the corporation or capitalist state. This is partly due to the way biopower compels us to work, transferring the responsibilities of the job onto the individual and social networks, thus rendering it synonymous with the joys and worries of life as such. Researchers frequently miss this element of working life, too. Exploitation is considered a practice of spatial and temporal confinement since control is the central motif of exploitation. It still is, of course, but the act of production has been dramatically generalized. The embodiment of the accumulation process confounds earlier logics of confinement, rendering time-tested borders porous to a certain extent. Our employers are no longer totally reliant on the factory walls, time-sheets, and direct surveillance as they used to be.

It is also important to note that this free work variant of capitalism is not entirely new. According to Graeber (2011), early industrialism relied on unpaid work before coinage could properly supply the wages owed to the nascent working class. In early 1800s England, for example, the shortage of payable cash meant that factory workers often toiled without pay, taking what they needed from the shop floor. Moreover, the extended family found other ways to support the working proletariat until wages finally arrived. What came to be called "pilfering" was largely condoned by bosses and owners until the factories could completely integrate the workforce into the wage-exploitation matrix.[5] Are we witnessing a return to this pre-Fordist condition given the proliferation of free work and credit card debt today?

## *From Sociologies of Containment to Biocapitalism*

In order to understand the capitalist utility of free work we need to partially revise the conceptual tools bequeathed to us by traditional theories of work. As critical labor process theory has rightly shown (Braverman 1974), most management regimes are concerned with the transformation of labor power at the *point of production,* in the main confined to tightly controlled locations. Surplus value is formally generated inside the perimeter of this locale. Even the much-studied strong culture fad discussed earlier treated the organization as something like a closed cult in this regard, aiming to shape employees into a faithful reflection of the enterprise.

This way of conceptualizing the capitalist work process—and in particular productive and unproductive labor—follows a long tradition of critical thought. After Marx and Weber, we are able to identify how capitalist profit is created by regulating people's behavior in a specific time and space. Unproductive activities that do not directly support economic efficiency are openly and punitively excluded from the workplace.

In the administrative office, for example, this entails the methodical rationalization of work, ascribing human activity algorithmic rules to ensure predictable outcomes. This is why the defining feature of bureaucracies is their impersonal mood. The official position and the distinctive individual holding the office are strictly separated.

As Weber puts it, "The more bureaucracy is dehumanized, the more completely it succeeds in eliminating from official business love, hatred, and all purely personal, irrational and emotional elements which escape calculation. This is the specific nature of bureaucracy and it is appraised as its special virtue" (Weber 1946: 220; also see Crozier 1964). Productive work is strictly delimited, formalized, and clearly measureable.

A similar process of dehumanization can be noted in classic studies of factory employment. Beynon found at Ford, for instance, that even talking was banned. As the company motto sought to remind workers, "When we are at work, we ought to be at work. When we are at play, we ought to be at play. There is no use trying to mix the two" (1973: 25). Of course, many studies have also revealed that individuality, play, and humor still flourish in these austere environments. But they are forced underground and frequently considered a dangerous zone of autonomy by managers (see Ackroyd and Thompson 1999).

Where is the point of production, however, when some work in their sleep, as Rob Lucas's (2010) study revealed in Chapter 1? For sure, the integration of ever more aspects of social personality into the production process partly dismantles the usefulness of the boundary between work and life. And as a result, the act of labor diffuses widely into the world. Now we enter the realm of biopower and its economization on free work. How did this occur in corporate practice given the above antecedents? And why is it such an important mechanism for exploiting the workforce today?

## *The Managerial Turn to the "Tacit" Workplace*

An important precursor to the corporation's attempt to valorize what Marx would have dismissed as unproductive labor and Weber as purely personal occurred in the 1990s. The unwritten rules of organizational processes were suddenly deemed crucial to the management function. Some popular business commentators even claimed that the implicit knowhow, informal expertise, and social competence of employees should be considered key success factors in modern firms. There was only one catch: these qualities often flourished *outside* the formal dictates of economic rationality, and even more worryingly, *against* the authority of supervisors. And how might that be managed?

That the unofficial sphere plays a major role in organizational effectiveness was observed long ago. In *Patterns of Industrial Bureaucracy* (1954), for example, Gouldner noted the significance of "indulgency patterns." Here, managers would indulge the workforce's unsanctioned and even moderately illegal activities. Such tolerance helped maintain overall factory discipline. Blau (1955) noted similar patterns in his study of bureaucratic culture, especially the hidden social world that resided among staff. Its productive importance was no more evident than when employees contested senior management's informal policies and yet followed the official rules to the letter. An invisible economy of goodwill and discretion was withdrawn and the organization came to an abrupt halt. Instrumental rationality, it seemed, required something *beyond itself* to function well. But what?

Management sought to address the question in the 1990s by instrumentalizing this hidden abode of work. There are a number of reasons for this move that are theorized more thoroughly herein. Suffice it to say that the human factor gained sudden importance when local knowledge and self-management became a key facet of profitability, especially in an emergent post-Fordist environment that required real people rather than living automatons. However, managers quickly realized that this informal world of productiveness could be only incompletely accessed through routines. Its true vibrancy flowed from unmanaged worker initiatives, which until now had been either ignored or feared by capitalism.

This is when the idea of the tacit workplace (usually drawing on Michael Polanyi's [1966] classic investigations) assumed a prominent place in corporate jargon. According to Peter Senge (1990), for example, the learning organization required elaborately orchestrated cultures to encourage workers to give up their implicit knowledge. Once this occurred, a crucial body of expertise might be integrated back into the organization's operating procedures. Otherwise it was likely to be lost if an employee left the firm or used against the firm during periods of unrest. Senge gained inspiration from the Japanese Toyotist method of manufacturing, where high levels of productivity were achieved by tapping rather than suppressing the informal workforce, using techniques like *Kaizen*. And at the same time, academic circles also pointed to the exciting possibilities of learning and enabling bureaucracies (Adler and Borys 1996), especially ones that might nurture worker-centered communities of social competence (Lave and Wenger 1991).

The drawback, of course, was soon obvious (see Collins 2001; Nonaka and von Krogh 2009). The management of social-intuition through formalized systems represented something of a paradox. It is like trying to read a fairy tale written in mathematical formula. Formal structures like self-managing teams or enabling bureaucracies could not help but ossify the very qualities they sought to engender (Barker 1993). Just as managed fun exercises in the office are generally experienced as humiliating or silly (Fleming 2009), so too does creativity and learning tend to resist formal planning. So if management authority could not engender the informal riches of the tacit workforce, then it certainly could try to enclose them.

## Capturing "Life" on the Job

The paradox noted above has today inspired an alternative corporate approach. A good deal of recent management thinking has concluded that it is very difficult to force workers to yield their goodwill and non-commercialized knowhow within a formal setting. While this unseen world of value is of increasing importance to capitalist reason, it is frequently born *despite* or even *against* the corporation. Fostering it would be analogous to forcing a child to play, which frequently results in the opposite outcome since the command context ruins the experience. Moreover, the hands-on development of learning cultures that might yield such tacit knowledge is costly to the enterprise (Foster and Kaplan 2001). It requires consultants, training, and massive amounts of ideological conditioning to convince members of an otherwise distrustful workforce to give up their expertise.

Thus emerges a new and distinct method for exploiting living labor. These processes seek to access the independent competencies of employees through moments of *capture* rather than composition. We might term this a new corporate enclosure movement. Now the personal is truly political, or more accurately, the *social* is now politically personal. And much of this human effort is *free*, since it is often developed on people's own time in self-managed environments, outside or against the formalities of economic rationality and private property.

This sea change in management thinking is increasingly evident in the business literature, which marks a significant departure from themes more typical in such publications. The *Harvard Business Review*, for example, now celebrates all manner of insights about harnessing the voluntary efforts of workers. An article entitled "Harnessing Your Staff's Informal Networks" (McDermott and Archibald 2010) is telling in this regard. In order to tap subterranean innovations, a hands-off, non-interventionist approach to supervision is recommended. Success requires a radically altered managerial gaze, one comfortable with measuring performance mainly through results rather than inputs. Indeed, as the article continues, "If your smartest employees are getting together to solve problems and develop new ideas on their own, the best thing to do is to stay out of their way" (McDermott and Archibald 2010).

A similar theme is evident in human resource management thinking concerning a holistic approach to the employment relationship. HR managers no longer see the corporation as responsible for the workforce's skill or enthusiasm about the job. These are expected to be part and parcel of what is already hired. Corporations are merely mechanisms of access for its otherwise precarious personnel. Whereas the old corporate cultures of the 1980s attempted to significantly re-educate people into the desired profile, the new wisdom tells them to arrive at work already knowing what to do. And if they do not, they should swiftly acquire the knowledge from their cohort, which is an important skill in itself. This is why so many non–work-related attributes are now observed at work—because they breathe life into customer service roles, staid office environments, and occupations that require self-direction. As two management consultants recently put it, "People are inherently creative and want to engage with organizations; they don't want to have processes imposed on them. . . . [A]t most companies, however, managers are behind the times: They cling to their hierarchies and their control over the definition and creation of stakeholders' experiences" (Ramaswamy and Gouillart 2010).

Much of this chimes with Tom Peters's (2003) idea of liberation management. It assumes that agile and vibrant organizational performances are achieved not when workers are forced to become yet another cardboard cutout of the "organization man" (Whyte 1956), but when preformed competencies are unleashed. In customer service environments, for example, the aesthetic sensibilities of a bookstore employee cannot be mechanistically induced by clinical management programs. Companies must enclose them instead. And the same managerial logic applies to a growing number of occupations in the West and perhaps beyond.

This kind of corporate strategy also views the external environment in a very different manner. Rather than frame the state, civil society, protest groups, customers, and the volunteer sector as external stakeholders that ought to be kept at a safe distance, a more entrepreneurial ethos is evident. Money can be made from the innovative social networks lying beyond the formal enterprise. An exemplar of this trend can be found in the book *Wikinomics,* by Tapscott and Williams (2008). They argue that collaboration, open-source innovation, and peer sharing are now leading forces in corporate revenue generation. Some of the most profitable business ideas can be sourced from the everyday activities of consumers, amateurs, and enthusiasts as they invent creative solutions on their own or together. Analogous to the music company mentioned at the beginning of this chapter, modern society is said to increasingly resemble Wikipedia, in which no one owns anything and social value is derived from decidedly *communist* principles. As Tapscott and Williams (2008: 123) argue in relation to "harvesting external ideas" from society, or what they call the "ideagora":

> The corporate R&D process must look two ways. Towards its international projects and competencies, and towards the external marketplace to leverage new IP and capabilities. Innovation must extend beyond the boundaries of the firm to the very fringes of the Web, where companies will engage with customers and a dynamic network of external collaborators. Ideagoras are places where companies can tap a wealth of new ideas, innovations and uniquely qualified minds.

Despite my reference to communism, these commercial models don't herald the end of capitalism or private property. The principles of capitalism are actually extended with the aid of communal interactions both inside and outside the enterprise. As the authors of *Wikinomics* continue, "By tapping open platforms you can leverage world-class infrastructures for a fraction of the cost of developing them yourself" (Tapscott and Williams 2008: 147).[6]

It is on this basis that we see intellectual and creative property being prospected and commercialized through predatory patenting systems (Perelman 2002). From the Human Genome Project to all manner of medicines, the natural commons is currently being plundered on an unprecedented level. Similarly, fashions and styles developed by underground subcultures are swiftly patented and commodified by large multinationals (Lash and Lury 2007). This is partly linked to the way consumption is now framed in *co-productive* terms, whereby users are enrolled to conduct unpaid R&D work (Arvidsson 2006). So-called budget airlines also understand this principle well, shifting much of the customer service labor onto the customers themselves without compensation. As the recent *Harvard Business Review* article "Building the Co-creative Enterprise" (Ramaswamy and Gouillart 2010) implies, these costless inputs are vital for business today because savings identifiably correlate with an increase in the productive moments that many enterprises cannot secure on their own.

## Toward a Critical Theory of "Free Work" Capitalism

Mapping these management techniques over the last few decades reveals how the point of production in Western organizations may still be predominantly centered at the office, retail showroom, restaurant, or university lecture hall, but there has also been a considerable de-centering. Important types of value-adding activities can be found outside of the formal zone of paid employment. And concerted efforts have been made by corporations to capitalize on tacit elements of the working self that previous systems would have impugned.

This invariably makes exploitation increasingly difficult to resist today. With many of us now embodying the 24/7 work template and with new methods of corporate regulation that seek to tap independent reservoirs of wealth outside its formal boundaries, exploitation has become a fact of life. This has rather sad psychological consequences. How else could we explain why so many workers are more afraid of *not being exploited* than exploitation itself? The alternative, according to this pervasive mindset, would feel like abnegating something integral to living more generally.

I believe the increasing prominence of free work capitalism requires a new set of concepts in order to be explained within the current climate of crisis and decline—concepts that point to its intimate relationship to biopower and biocracy at work. This is why the critical scholarship on internship exploitation is important, although tangential to my argument here. Interns are unpaid employee replicas. As far as the corporate sector is concerned, they help cut costs in a quantitative sense. What we see in the biopolitical management of free labor is something slightly different, more of a qualitative permutation around the laws of exploitation. Work is installed in the texture of the social commons and is largely incalculable from a numerical stance. This is symptomatic of a central weakness of the corporate form. It now requires a vast amount of cooperative social work but is simultaneously built on precepts anathema to it.

This raises an important issue. The reason biopolitical conditions render work into a virus-like template is not because our jobs are more immaterial (as the cognitive capitalism thesis would imply). Biopower has nothing to do with post-industrial jobs or the rise of the symbolic analyst as famously described by Reich (1992). Something else is occurring linked with class struggle. First of all, work has become largely ritualistic in nature and generally disconnected from concrete questions of necessity or survival; indeed, the very opposite is the case if we survey the life chances of the working poor. Second, the basic axioms of neoliberal thought—including private property, economic rationality, instrumentalism, and competition—are so antagonistic to social life that corporations need to secure them through other means. Biopower fulfills this need in an exemplary way. As a consequence, our shared interest in a livable life becomes riveted to the pressures of work.

Any critical theory of free work must therefore explain the prominent reliance that capitalism has on the independent and non-exchangeable qualities of working people today, which it can neither acknowledge nor secure on its own terms. This is why it is amusing to reread American neoliberal economists like Becker (1972) and R. E. Lucas (1988) in this light. Theories of human capital and human resources sought to extend *homo economicus* to the very heart of society and individual personality. Despite all of this quantification, however, they still could not define this crucial social supplement that remains impervious to capitalist metrics. In his classic analysis, a baffled R. E. Lucas (1988) finally gave up and simply called it "factor X."[7] We now know what this is—the social cushion of living labor that perpetually exceeds its own exploitation; in other words, *class antagonism*. We now turn to the various dimensions of free work capitalism for a better understanding of this claim.

## Free Time

If capitalism exploits us mainly through the time it steals from us, then unpaid time preparing for, worrying about, and performing our jobs is perhaps the classic signature of biopower in the workplace. R. E. Lucas's (1988) factor X is here the unquantifiable amount of social time required to support paid employment. As I noted earlier, time does strange things when biopower meets capitalism. The presence of work is perceived to be universal and without end, to the point where some see jumping off a high building as the only exit if things go wrong. The illusion of permanence is an impressive political achievement of neoliberal capitalism. We may hate our jobs, disconnect or even hurt ourselves to avoid them, but there is no future without them. Quitting or being fired only intensifies this inescapable presence of work as we struggle to find another job. Such an impressive ideological suture of time is designed to close down alternatives.

The perverse truth, of course, is that biocracy thrives on expansive networks of non-capitalist time to maintain the workday. In other words, today's typical business firm actually *requires* the workforce to have a life away from work in order to have material beyond itself to exploit. This kind of social reality largely remains in a state of permanent abeyance. Once again, neoliberal capitalism has its cake (i.e., the costs of work borne by the public intellect) and eats it too (i.e., private profits). As Virno correctly observes, unpaid labor is now definitive of capitalism as such, since "the old distinction between 'labor' and 'non-labor' ends up in the distinction between remunerated and non-remunerated life. . . . [T]he crucial point here is to recognize that in the realm of labor, experiences which mature outside of labor hold predominant weight" (2004: 102).

If your employer ordered you to work for nothing, you would justifiably tell them where to shove their job. This is where biocracy comes to capitalism's assistance. How does it actually harness all of this necessary free time? Melissa Gregg's (2011) excellent study briefly mentioned in Chapter 1 is illuminating here. So much of the work she observed in her investigation of post-industrial work is conducted outside of official hours. These employees are highly mobile given the nature of their jobs and the use of technology. But none of this makes the job more orderly. Gregg uncovered a world of constant stress, anxiety, and almost painful levels of corporate disorganization. That these working people are saturated by their jobs cannot, however, only be put down to labor intensification or the use of mobile technology, both of which present quantitative explanations. I am interested in the *qualitative* shift that also transpires here. This is where work-induced stress becomes a way of life, almost expected and sometimes even *desired*. The telltale sign is work done without any immediate justification, just as it was needless for our "sleep worker" Rob Lucas (2010) to toil for the firm in his dreams.[8]

Reading Gregg's study from the viewpoint of biopower reveals the presence of two interconnected labor processes. The first is conducted at the formal point of production during office hours, which is measured and remunerated accordingly. The second type is unrecognized and non-remunerated because it *must* occur outside of official hours, along with the inevitable negative fallout among loved ones. This might entail preparing for a Monday morning meeting on Sunday evening. It might also include problem-solving on one's own time, especially when the impediments of neoliberal management begin to erode one's ability to do the job well. For example, Gregg (2011: 62) reported on Sam, a casual reporter who confronts the idiocy of capitalism on a daily basis, as this incident reveals: "Technical problems meant [Sam] had to think of other ways to file the story. One solution was to try to burn a disk and Express Post it to Sydney by the due date. But given that she worked outside of business hours she couldn't use the office stationary to make this happen overnight, and paid for the package herself out of her $100 pay check."

## Free Self-Organization

The above quote reveals another dimension of free work capitalism that helps biopolitical variants of employment sustain its otherwise unworkable structures. If a good deal of work occurs coincidentally to the formalities of the job, then it also involves a high degree of autonomy and self-organization. Commentators often depict this devolution of control as a gesture of corporate humanism. Workers are now empowered to make their own decisions, develop creative solutions, and experience work in a more fulfilling manner. This fundamentally distorts the truth for two reasons. First, management was never about coordinating the work process or making things easier. As a number of seminal studies reveal, most notably Marglin (1974) and Gordon (1996), management primarily represents a *class function,* shoring up that specific relationship even if it means making jobs more difficult to accomplish. This is why clandestine self-management and autonomy is often a basic defense mechanism among the workforce, especially when job security is low. And second, because of neoliberalism's grave internal contradictions, for reasons we have noted throughout this book, it invariably turns to worker self-management to get things done. Most of us therefore experience work as highly controlled from above, co-present with life as such, and impossible to get done well.

Chapter 2 called this self-governing capacity to organize *social surplus.* It can be observed literally everywhere in the workplace today, outrunning and confounding the instruments that seek to objectify it. To understand what this excess means we ought to take a closer look at *economic formalism,* the signature ideology of neoliberal capitalism. It is rendered operative through the law of social equivalence—rules that anticipate some correlative type of behavior. But this also implies a fundamental lack because the last thing rules are good for is telling us how to use them. That necessitates an *unruled* exterior of common knowhow.

What exactly is this background knowledge? How is it linked to the autonomy of the commons? Once again, Virno (2008) provides some insight. He builds on Wittgenstein's argument that any instruction must draw on a shared reflectivity about its successful enactment. And that reflectivity cannot itself be instructed by the same system of thought. A certain separation is required because "rules do not give instructions on how they should be applied in a particular case. Between norm and its concrete realization there exists a lasting hiatus, a real and true incommensurability" (Virno 2008: 33). The lasting hiatus alluded to here might be the closest definition of the social in a technocratic world. Improvisation and spontaneous creation prefigure the metrics of corporate calculability that seek to cash in on it.

It is now easier to see why self-organization is so important to biopolitical capitalism, especially under extreme neoliberalism, which by nature causes chaos. A number of researchers identify this requisite of worker self-management in the informal culture of the firm. Such invisible work falls beneath the management radar, remaining unpaid even when it is essential to make things happen in the office.[9] However, one of the best depictions of its importance can be found in a case where management openly sponsored its presence. Richard Edwards's (1979) study of Polaroid during the late 1970s recounts one of the first experiments in self-management typical of neoliberal corporate strategies to come. From the workers' perspective, of course, they simply did what they had always done, but were never formally recognized for. They pooled their knowhow, ignored many of the rules that impeded technical solutions, and managed themselves through flexible democratic forums. The big problem from management's standpoint soon became evident. The experiment *worked too well.* They realized that much of their official function was actually unnecessary, so the trial was swiftly terminated. A senior training manager explained why: "It was too successful. What were we going to do with the supervisors—the managers? We didn't need them anymore" (Edwards 1979: 156).

Other types of unseen self-organization act as moments of self-preservation, allowing workers to avoid the punitive repercussions that often befall them when formal systems fail. For example, in his ethnographic study of photocopy machine technicians, Orr (1996) noted the massive amount of surreptitious self-organization that helped bypass oppressive technocratic protocols (e.g., directive documentation). In reality, this kind of work involved skillful social awareness, uncodified experiential maps, and knowledge-sharing among workers. The official controls enforced by management frequently caused mayhem in the field. Unexpected variations and unforeseen events were endemic to the work. To accomplish the task, technicians secretly organized the labor process themselves. For example, they developed occupational practices like story-telling that surpassed the slow and cumbersome management system. Of course, the downside for the technicians was soon clear. It concerned the "adequacy of one's compensation . . . since it is unclear which activities require compensation as being part of one's work" (Orr 1996: 149).

## Free Self-Development

One of the most widespread criticisms of the modern corporation today concerns the way it steals ideas, creativity, and innovations from the public domain. Chapter 2 noted aspects of this trend. Many types of cultural goods, scientific breakthroughs, and social utilities frequently originate beyond (and sometimes against) the principles of private property. These are then tapped and appropriated for private gain, often with the help of predatory patenting laws. For example, there is now a substantial literature on how multinational firms engage in "biopiracy" or "bioprospecting" (see, for example, Shiva 2011; Hayden 2003). Plants, herbs, and other types of flora with inherent medicinal properties are systematically ring-fenced through various economic mechanisms. These goods are often considered free by the large conglomerates because they reside in the natural environment, or *terra nullius*. For more critical commentators, however, the true source of the so-called discoveries made by Monsanto and others are local indigenous peoples (Milun 2010).

This corporate enclosure of the natural commons is perhaps an enduring feature of capitalism, but has recently become its central business strategy when it pertains to the development of ideas, scientific inventions, and cultural innovations. Many inventions that have subsequently been patented by the multinational enterprise (related to health, technology, and media) required long-term incubation horizons, communal rather than secretive knowledge practices, and public access forums in order to mature. These conditions are generally anathema to those underlying the neoliberal firm. In his study of intellectual property law in the United States, Perelman (2002) argues that this underlies the increasing corporate privatization of public goods. His analysis of some key inventions in science and technology reveals the voracious nature of the modern enterprise as it enters its biopolitical phase. He reports that "73 percent of the main science papers cited by American industrial patents in two recent years were based on domestic and foreign research funded by government or nonprofit agencies. Even IBM—famous for its research prowess and numerous patents—was found to cite its own work 21 percent of the time" (Perelman 2002: 76).[10]

Apart from greed, much of the reason behind this parasitical business model, according to Perelman (2002), can be put down to its inability to engender the desired creativity within the confines of the private enterprise. Indeed, all of this should now be familiar to us given the conceptualization of economic rationality developed thus far. Perelman cites many cases in which neoliberalism on its own actually stunts creative development, from computer technology to transportation and public utilities—hence the strange perversity of intellectual property law. So much of it today serves aims that are diametrically opposed to the ones it professes—that is, not to protect the inventor (often an anonymous public) but to aid the corporate confiscation of otherwise freely available goods. Making matters even more interesting is that many social innovations (e.g., Youtube and intellectual domains) are often born *against* the basic premises of private property and commercial self-interest.

Corporations now have a litany of euphemistic terms to describe what is in truth the capture of labor conducted by the social commons free of charge—user innovation, co-production, prosumerism, crowdsourcing, distributed thinking, participatory design, and so forth.[11] Take the massive gaming industry, for example: the amateurism and artisanal cultures of on-line groups are used for unpaid R&D labor in many ways by private enterprise. Kücklich (2005) ironically calls this "playbour," since it utilizes the modifications of gamers outside the business circle to generate large private profits. As a result, "'mods' can not only increase the shelf-life of the games industry's products, but also inject a shot of much-needed innovation into an industry seemingly unable to afford taking commercial risks" (Kücklich 2005).

Almost all of this free self-development is immanently social. But I suggest that one kind occurs at the level of social innovation (e.g., technologies, fashions, bio-technical inventions, and counter-cultural forms of life) and the other kind is concerned with social personality (e.g., human capital, training, and communicative competence). The capture of the first is close to what Rifkin (2000) calls the "enclosure of the cultural commons" and Perelman (2002), the "corporate confiscation of creativity." And the capture of the second kind is now the foundation of neo–human capital theory (Hanlon 2013). Both forms of self-development are key targets for the corporation today, not only because they represent value difficult to foster in for-profit environments but also because they come free of charge.[12] While in-house investment in training and research/development is obviously still important, this emergent corporate trend indicates a more biocratic inclination. A wide range of empirical examples abound in the literature. But for the sake of brevity, let us discuss one striking case.

We are now just beginning to realize the extraordinary levels of post-industrial wealth that could not have emerged without the commercial cooptation of the *hacker ethos* that once thrived against private property. While the Bill Gateses and Steve Jobses of the industry cashed in on innovations that arguably would have emerged anyway, the working attitude underscoring these relentless innovative shifts required much more: an identity, a philosophy, and more importantly, an ethic of sharing that is fiercely communal, as evident in the decidedly anarchist "Hacker Manifesto." This hacker mentality animated the subcultures who wrote code for fun and who considered "the man" (the capitalist corporation) as a blockage to new ideas and interactive development.

The corporate appropriation of this IT counter-culture is painstakingly mapped by Liu (2004) in *The Laws of Cool.* Capitalism and large business enterprises discovered in these semi-visible undercurrents of resistance something useful, something it could not induce itself since this social underground was intrinsically open and collective. According to Liu and others including Perelman (2011), the message is simple. Corporations are by definition hopeless at creative cool so they must go looking for it (e.g., slackers). I also remind the reader of the sports apparel CEO quoted at the beginning of the book. Central here is the utilization of a network mindset so revered in IT subcultures. A network has no external point of reference, no outside. As a result, the disinterested slacker is put to work precisely through his or her quest to be authentic. Once enmeshed in the corporate logic (something the subculture was originally designed to avoid), it becomes difficult for the social entrepreneur to resist, as witnessed recently in relation to the D-I-Y credo among workers in the gaming industry (Abrahamson 2011).

## Conclusion

We can see now why free work is so closely connected to the way biopower is utilized to revive the flagging fortunes of the corporation today. In particular, unpaid work regimes reveal an important facet of neoliberal management practice, whereby it increasingly relies on living labor to make things happen. Most working people can relate to this, regardless of where they are placed on the social hierarchy. The demands of neoliberal (ir)rationality engender such a chaotic organizational climate that things would swiftly halt without the social common or R. E. Lucas's (1988) mysterious factor X. On the other side of the coin, however, are the negative externalities of this mode of accumulation: stress, uncertainty, tired minds, and a life of interminable work.

But we must not fall into the conceptual trap of *productivism*. Some critical investigations of the social factory and cognitive capitalism tend to display a desire to find work literally everywhere. But this is not how the current system functions. We must assign a special place in this analysis for non-work and the importance of surplus sociality pertaining to this mode of capitalism. One of the more disconcerting elements of neoliberal capitalism is the artificial promotion of free time rather than its demise, because, for reasons we have discussed, if the corporation were a perfect reflection of itself, it would swiftly cease.

That said, no critical analysis of these trends would be complete without investigating the contested and conflictual nature of any new corporate power relation. I suggest two avenues of resistance to free work capitalism can be noted among recent workers' initiatives. The first, unsurprisingly, demands valorization and remuneration. Similar to the feminist wages for housework rally-cry of the 1970s, trade unionism has been particularly vocal in insisting that the wealth generated by unpaid work ought to be justly rewarded. What was previously free time would now be rewarded with overtime pay or alternatively curtailed by more humane work/life balance solutions (Hochschild 1997). What was beforehand free self-organization would attract increased monetary rewards or a less hierarchical corporate structure to recognize, redistribute, and numerically measure unpaid labor previously hidden (Fletcher 2001). And free self-development is checked by more pluralistic corporate structures to recognize the worth of social entrepreneurship and appreciate the role of non-commercial ways of life (Svendsen 2008).

The second type of opposition is quite different. It seeks to *free* this free work from its corporatized environment and communally repossess it. According to Gorz (1989), a major proponent of this approach, the problem with the first mode of resistance is that it risks deepening the exploitative logic of work through accommodation. For sure, calls for better pay, better work conditions, and increased opportunities to learn on the job are laudable. This might moderate the more extreme effects of the neoliberal enterprise, but does not challenge its axiomatic principles. The overall fruits of work are still for someone else, for ends not self-determined or publicly debated.

Removing all of this free work from the instrumental logic of the corporation would allow us to reclaim the rich social autonomy so crucial to capitalism today. Truly free time, free self-organization, and free self-development might thus be the building blocks of an alternative understanding of work. If the modern enterprise has proliferated the ideology of work into all facets of life, then perhaps its overt reliance on free work might ironically sow the seeds for a new era that is truly *free from work*.

# 6

# How to Resist Work Today

So much worker militancy today is saddled with outdated notions about how we are to resist capitalism, especially as its idiom seeps into our dreams and desires. Oppositional strategies in the West still function as if the factory is the dominant template of corporate power. In doing so, it misses an important part of control in today's workplaces and beyond. An example might suffice to illustrate this, one unfolding as I write. In the United Kingdom, the university is becoming a hotbed of political unrest, with neo-managerialism in full swing and employee protest organizations readying for industrial action.

One of the leading teachers unions threatened to express their discontent by striking for one day. As planned, the strike went ahead. Did it cripple the university and bring it to a halt? Of course not. This institution is not like a car factory where the workforce clocks in and out around fixed times. Think about the young university lecturer I mentioned at the beginning of the book, meeting her goals even when it meant a rendezvous on Friday night. Similarly, on the day of the strike, most staff members were working from home as usual and not planning to be on campus anyway. And those scheduled to teach that day simply covered the missed material the following week—because of not managerial pressure, but student pressure. After all, their grades and their future careers were at stake. What might have brought a factory to a standstill didn't even cause a ripple in this biocorporate setting. What looked like an act of militancy fizzled out fairly quickly. None of this is to say that strikes (or the factory, for that matter) no longer matter. They undoubtedly do, perhaps more than ever. But biocracy is powerful precisely because it does not need to be situated in any confined space or time. This type of regulation resides in our ongoing social practices, ways of life, knowhow, and sensibilities. These qualities by nature transcend formal working hours. One might go so far as to suggest that it is biopower's very aim is to pull the rug out from under the feasibility of the conventional strike.

Of course, once one mentally departs the site of exploitation—be it to attend a strike or to exit in more permanent ways—things begin to look different. We start to see a livable life once again. But that sensible space of perspective is the first victim of biopower. Once we enter the terrain of biocracy, there appears to be no outside or end to work. It takes over everything, much as a small worry in the middle of the night makes us feel as if our whole world is at stake. Furthermore, the biopoliticized worker often displaces the real enemy (i.e., capitalism) onto a specific persona, tyrannical boss, backstabbing co-worker, or even him- or herself. If we ask what employees hate most about their jobs, what keeps them up at night, what gets under their skin, it is no longer "the man"—the old Fordist proxy for an exploitative company—but a real person. The neo-capitalist fetish is complete. When power truly goes virtual as biopower does, it paradoxically takes on an overly concrete or even personal quality that feels impossible to escape.

This is how work organizes us today. In its biopolitical setting, power pursues us from the side, as well as from above, and sometimes even from below. Accounts from contemporary employment show us that what ought to be basic class politics is displaced onto moments of stress, personal alienation, secret fears, and so forth. This overly personal tenor to the injuries of working today is due to the resource that biopower makes use of the most: our embodied intelligence, social networks, and self-management. And how does one resist a mode of regulation that puts life itself to work? This is a crucial problem because when employees try to resist work, it often feels like they are sabotaging themselves or their colleagues. Recall the lament of the "sleep worker," Rob Lucas (2010), in Chapter 1. He was well aware that if he engaged in factory-style resistance (foot-dragging, work-to-rule, sabotage, absenteeism), it would merely create havoc for him and his co-workers.

Making matters more complex are the discursive techniques that corporations now deploy to look like one of us, evoking themes sympathetic to emancipation and freedom. Harney and Oswick (2007) have argued that today it is ironically *management that is mostly against management,* making bizarre allusions to anarchy and anti-authoritarianism. Right-wing popular management gurus now gush over the benefits of modeling the firm after '68 slacker cool. Even the dark satire lampooning corporate life in the TV show *The Office* has made its way into human resource training programs (the icon of the bad-manager, David Brent, stars in the latest Microsoft induction video). Of course, amid all this, capitalism, exploitation, and private property remain very much intact, or even more so, which is perhaps the true objective of liberation management.

And the final challenge for those seeking to subvert biopower in the name of some post-capitalist future pertains to fear, a key emotional currency of neoliberal hegemony. In the halcyon days of Fordism, fear was a weapon of the workers' movement, imposing trepidation on the factory floor, often to the point where managers were too afraid to socialize with them over lunch. Things are different today. Workers are the ones deeply afraid. And there is no coincidence that this occurs precisely when capitalism becomes so reliant on living labor. Moreover, as the worker/manager/boss distinction is blurred via diffused hierarchical structures, that fear becomes a universal cultural metaphor. Its source feels objectless and thus inescapable, just like work itself.

This is more than just fear of possible unemployment or precarity. For that is an objectively rational response to the present situation. No, the widespread anxiety and hopelessness I am referring to is mostly needless, a political invention built into the very logic of work today. This makes its universalization seem inevitable and inescapable. In other words, when our jobs become *the* index for living as such, our fear becomes existential and seemingly without object. And the problem with fear is that it tends to individualize its victims, and we find it difficult to resist without turning on ourselves; it activates and promulgates the very power effects that we now need to refuse within the current biopolitical situation.

I am, however, in danger of making a bad mistake here. Have I not conferred far too much power on the corporate Leviathan and its ideology of work? Indeed, the title of this chapter is somewhat misleading given my argument so far. If we posit the commons—living social labor—as always in excess of the reductions that our jobs place on it, then perhaps we must turn the old political formula around once again. As workers continue to escape back into life, the corporate Leviathan only clocks moments of resistance. But as we now know, the resisting party here is the corporation itself. It rejects the full realization of the social openness most jobs parasitically rely on. This is why I have argued that biopower becomes a *qualitatively* dominant logic when capitalism can no longer organize itself sufficiently and turns to enlist us instead. Biopower always signals a major failure in this regard, which we need to keep in mind as the following argument develops.

So, if we are to appreciate how neoliberal control is counteracted and subverted by workers today, we must be sure to avoid surveying the scene from the viewpoint of capital. That perspective sees the corporation (capital) as first-mover and then awaits the resisting subject (labor). This popular formula cedes far too much constitutive energy to an otherwise ossified system, including neoliberalism more generally. It is living labor that generates worlds of wealth. Neocapitalism makes good use of this for sure. But the power of the commons represents an extra-capitalist political tendency, which the modern enterprise both requires and cannot completely capture.

The collective exit into life characterizes much labor struggle today. This chapter maps how the life-affirming qualities of this social surplus might escape its biopolitical prison and enjoy the freedoms already intrinsic to it. As stated above, time-tested acts of revolt like the strike are still very relevant. But counter-work opposition also needs to significantly rethink the meaning of refusal in light of these biopolitical trends.

## Refusing Work Today

In order to understand how and why biopower is refused at work today, three preliminary points must be made. First, and as I have also sought to emphasize throughout this book, we must appreciate the socially constructed nature of work. Our obsession with it in the West and its seemingly omnipotent influence over our lives is no longer linked to economic necessity. The bills and mortgage have to be paid, no doubt, but what we have called the ideology of work decouples our social energies from concrete shared needs, and may, in fact, be antithetical to the requirements of collective survival.

This is why work under biopolitical conditions (especially associated with neoliberal thought) generally feels imposed for its own sake. We need to realize that work today is a rather extreme ritual linked to a dying capitalist project. As a result, we cannot say to ourselves, "We have done enough," since like all rituals, it functions by way of a self-referential loop. The U.K. conservative government's controversial Back-to-Work scheme illustrates this perfectly. The unemployed are forced to sweat in fast-food restaurants without pay. The message is clear. This has nothing to do with material preservation; it is more about maintaining an ideological habit or addiction and the lack of perspective this engenders. This is also the case for the working poor who toil in multiple jobs and barely make a living (see Robinson-Tillett and Menon 2013). Wages are secondary to the ideological role of *looking like a worker*.[1] This realization is the first step toward refusing work. It must not be confused with refusing oneself or refusing economic necessity (i.e., survival). Indeed, the contrary.

This is not to say that there are not large groups of people whose work is directly linked to material subsistence, especially in the poor Global South and among the working poor in the North. And it is certainly true that any analysis of work in the West that omits the massive reliance on cheap and impoverished global labor would simply fetishize the category of work in rich countries. The ideology of work I am referring to, however, concerns the way in which almost every activity in Western societies appears to be linked to this sign of necessity—that is, work—which has now ballooned into an all-encompassing template for life itself. It must be remembered that before the arrival of capitalism, the average time spent working was about three days a week. Someone from another period would look at us and think we were crazy.[2]

Related to this, we should also be vigilant about the way the global ultra-poor are used by neoliberal apologists to justify the Western obsession with work. Someone might say to us, for example, "Hey, you think you've got it bad; just look at the Rat Catcher of Mumbai. . . . [Y]ou can't complain."[3] A nice double bind is thereby created. Accept your relatively well-off, overworked miserable life, because the only alternative is being knee-deep in effluent in a Third World sewer. Well, perhaps neither option is acceptable.

Of course, merely realizing that work is made up doesn't make being evicted any less real when you fail to pay the rent. This brings us to the second point. Successful acts of resisting biocracy begin by digging deeper into the causes of this strange over-ritualization of labor and identifying what it does to us individually and collectively. As I have argued throughout this book, it is the depressing feeling of endlessness that really defines the condition of working today, mainly because we are always carrying it with us, recognizing it in our gait and dreams, seeing a future that only reflects an impossible present.

Creating some kind of departure or rupture in this false infinitization of work becomes an important moment of refusal in the biopolitical workplace. As I mentioned in Chapter 1, we can see how this can be done in a self-destructive manner, especially when the body is mistaken for the boss function that works through it. An end to life is thought to be the only way out of a system that so fully harnesses life to the logic of production. Perhaps this is why so many attempts to induce a limit or afterwards to work life end up becoming individualistic acts of escape: passing out from too much alcohol, burnout, suicide, even yoga.

More optimistic strategies of detaching the social body from the parasite of work have a better image of what a post-work future means. In a growing plethora of communities, we can note the growing establishment of inoperative thresholds—that is, collective forms of life that are no more productive than they need to be.[4] The line is arbitrary, no doubt, and this makes it very powerful. We can bring the level of work to zero and live very well. Moreover, surplus or superfluous productiveness can be identified only through social endpoints that, for want of a better term, have been incredibly *de-worked*. We only need to consult the communism of uselessness in Charles Bukowski to see what this looks like.

The idea does not mean that nothing gets done. One of the key ideological traps that keep us wedded to work in its current form is the myth that society would stop without it. But, in fact, the opposite is the case. Social labor is freed from the impoverishing strictures of capitalist instrumentality so that purposeful activity can be pursued once again. This can be seen in jobs that we might already positively identify with and take pleasure in. It is the wonders of living labor we are enjoying rather than work, since its qualities are based on open self-determination rather than structured exploitation.

This can be explained in less esoteric terms. As we noted at the beginning of this book, the problem with capitalist work relations today is not about having too little time away from our jobs. Contemporary cognitive capitalism requires that we have plenty of that. Some take holidays (if they are lucky), weekends, and so forth. Neoliberalism does not function by totally colonizing these non-work spaces. It wouldn't survive if it did. All it needs to do is *index* them to the ideology of work. Recall the vignette discussed in the Introduction in which an overworked employee found it impossible to enjoy his vacation on a southern European beach. He viewed his free time as a horrible vacuum. Like a smoker who has decided to quit the habit, the temporal register of non-working is experienced as a vapid emptiness.

What appears to be a symptom of its power is, in fact, a weak link in the neoliberal fetish of employment. It is how we socially configure our free time that is critical. Once we get that right, then it's just a matter of escalating and expanding it into something new. Refusing biopower therefore means insisting that work has nothing to do with life. In other words, refusing work is a matter of exiting *into* life, reclaiming it back for ourselves so we can live again. But what exactly is a livable life? It depends, of course. But it might be defined as a way of living that does not pray for its own end, does not proceed on the basis that any kind of conclusion or terminus would be infinitely preferable.

And where might we find this livable life? Ironically, perhaps, everywhere. Is this not the open secret of neoliberal capitalism? If we had pure and unadulterated free markets, commercialization, private ownership, and individualism, society would implode under its own weight. Neoliberalism persists *despite* itself. Now we have arrived at the nub of the problem concerning the possibility of a post-work future. And this is our third point. Working today is not only mythological (rather than bound by economic necessity) but also extremely parasitical. The corporation and its obsession with work are being left behind by society. So it plunders the most progressive elements of the common to sustain itself, transforming those shared energies into an unbearable situation once again. Here is the imperative question. Can this collective threshold of non-productiveness be reclaimed toward more civilized ends? Or is it destined to remain what David Harvey (2012) labeled a "negative common," forever serving a parasitical capitalist system?

## Exit Capitalism

The multiple sites of what might be called "threshold soviets" currently emerging in society are symptomatic of the massive divestment in the social legitimacy of working today. Participation no longer feels like a sensible option in a system that is purely parasitical—hence the rise of non-participation politics, withdrawal, and self-valorization: put simply, *exit*.

It is interesting that this heightened desire to escape work (rather than fight for it in the name of inclusion or participation) is occurring at a time when unemployment is chronic and job security is so precarious. How do we explain this apparent contradiction? Why would we long to leave work behind when it is now so hard to come by? I think it is related to the way we have drastically changed our stance toward capitalism, neoliberal market society, and work more generally. These institutional realities now signify something unsalvageable and backward, with nothing left to offer us. As a militant workers' collective recently put it, "One does not tidy up in a home falling off a cliff" (Institute for Experimental Freedom 2009: 156).

### *The Gathering Exodus from Work*

While the evidence remains fragmented, the growing incidences of those wishing to exit employment are telling of the new biopolitical makeup of the workforce today. There has recently been an exponential growth in websites advising employees about the best way to quit. A Google search reveals that "How to Quit Your Job" is only second behind websites designed to help people kick smoking. It is rather sad how individualistic some of these websites are. The lessons they impart tend to be overwhelmingly psychological: When you are wedded to your immiserating job, unable to distinguish yourself from it, the boss, and the company, then the barrier stopping you is not the mortgage, the kids, or lack of alternatives—*it is you*.[5]

One might expect the over-exploited customer service worker or low-paid factory-hand to feel like escaping, but what about those in well-paid and relatively prestigious jobs? Here too the yearning to exit is evident. In an interview with the famed critic Terry Eagleton (Barker and Niven 2012), the scholar discusses impending retirement from his academic post. What he finds most notable about those in his profession today is the striking desire to exit their jobs that has gripped so many academics in the United Kingdom and elsewhere. As he puts it, "Most people I know in academia want to get out. Which is a pretty new situation. I've never encountered that before" (Barker and Niven 2012). According to a recent study, many people who hold Ph.D.s (especially women) do not even want to embark on an academic career after witnessing the nature of this work firsthand. For women, the intention to seek an academic position has "plummeted from 72% in the first year to 37% as they finish their studies" (Rice 2012).

We now turn to a very different occupation, the police force. In a recent employee morale survey of the U.K. police, the level of disillusionment was astounding. One police officer stated, "Morale is the lowest I have ever known. . . . I have worked for CID for over 15 years but due to the lack of front-line recruitment we are having to back-fill any uniform vacancies[;] I wish I could leave tomorrow" ("Four in Ten Female Officers" 2012). And in yet another example, the U.K. Border Agency (UKBA) has recently been severely compromised by its own redundancy program and needed to *recruit* new staff, since "more people than expected wanted to leave" ("Border Staff Being Cut Too Fast" 2012)

So much for the public sector. What about the private? Perhaps the most stunning example of this interest in exit can be found among members of ultra-pro-business circles, such as those who read the *Harvard Business Review*. In an article entitled *How to (Finally) Quit Your Job* (Gulati 2012), the writer offers advice for making the break, a decision that for many is perhaps as inconceivable as it is desirable. He contends:

> Since writing "Why You Won't Quit Your Job" earlier this year, I've been inundated with all kinds of public feedback, personal stories, and follow-up questions from people looking to overcome the psychological biases that trap them in unsatisfying roles and prevent them from doing work that matters. While these senior executives, 20-something bankers, and mid-career

marketers, analysts, and lawyers all knew that they wanted to leave their current roles, executing their plan proved to be a perennially insurmountable challenge. In fact, the most common question I got was "How can I overcome the hurdles to quitting and actually *quit?*" (Gulati 2012)

This is not an isolated case of exit work advice in the corporate sector; it is part of a broader trend including various types of self-help books, coaching advice and web-forum discussions.[6] A former manager told the author recently that he had never been so congratulated by his fellow workers as when announcing his resignation. Indeed, the idea that being jobless is some kind of social death might now be in the past. I would propose that *even the unemployed are quitting.* This is understandable given the laborious work that being unemployed in a neoliberal society entails. The U.K. government recently announced that the number of unemployed rose by 15,000 in the first part of 2013. However, unemployment benefit applicants *dropped* by 7,300, which might imply the unemployed are quitting their roles as defined by the punitive neoliberal state ("UK Unemployment Rises to 2.52 Million" 2013).

## Exit with Caution

This desire to depart the terrain of power might certainly be the result of an all-time low concerning the cultural worth of work today. As the budgets of large firms and the neoliberal state are reduced in times of austerity, work becomes intensified, stress rife, and the dream of getting out a soothing palliative—even when we would not seriously act on it. This might be the biopolitical version of Nietzsche's famous quip about suicidal thoughts being "a powerful comfort: by means of it one gets through many a bad night" (Nietzsche 1966: 281).

This would be too much of an apolitical reading of the trends noted above, however, since it abstracts the wish from the unique nature of corporate capitalism today. We need only to return to the 1970s to see how the vocabulary of the working class was animated not by exit, but by social democratic participation and inclusion. For many years under Fordism, working and survival were almost inextricably intertwined. Without a job, you perished. A good deal of pressure was placed on the workforce to make the best of their predicament and engage in political campaigns to be more fully recognized in the working project. More jobs, a deeper relationship with our work, and control over its objectives animated the guiding principle of the labor movement.

In the biopolitical era, as we have seen throughout this book, work is experienced in a much different way. Exacerbated by an over-ritualized economy, seemingly abstract and far away from economic necessity (in the West at least), our jobs feel sadly self-referential. The daily humiliations, micro-managed tasks, and permanent stress appear all the more unnecessary in the wake of this growing purposelessness. For many workers today, inclusion and recognition are no longer considered useful for counteracting domination, but actually tie us even tighter to our lifeless positions. This is why the mass hope to exit work represents a new development in the way we refuse capitalist subjugation. I believe this underlies Hardt and Negri's approach to what they call *exodus*. It is a process of

> *subtraction* from the relationship with capital by means of actualizing the potential autonomy of labor-power. Exodus is not a refusal of the productivity of bio-political labor power but rather a refusal of the increasingly restrictive fetters placed on its productive capacities by capital. . . . [E]xodus does not necessarily mean going elsewhere. We can pursue a line of flight while staying right here. . . . [E]xodus is possible only on the basis of the common. (2009: 152–153)

To reformulate this statement, exit is meaningful only if it involves a social evacuation from capitalist relations that consist of pure negativity. Exit is therefore not about escaping to somewhere else. On the contrary, if neoliberal capitalism relies on collective social riches that it cannot provide itself, then exodus simply means becoming more fully what we already are.

One of the problems that exit politics confronts is precisely this challenge from power to outline the terrain to which we are escaping: "What is your alternative?" I have no answer to this specific question.[7] It is the wrong question to ask, especially in the context of a neoliberal nightmare that would like us to believe its world is all there is. Indeed, the very nature of the question betrays a deeply conservative sentiment, because it contains its own answer: There is no alternative. This is why one of the most interesting qualities of exit politics, in my mind at least, is a resolute and confident *radical silence.*

## Common as Silence

Because the question "What's your alternative" is so laden in favor of shutting down the political imaginary of the working and unemployed 99 percenters who now want nothing more to do with capitalism, they are initially *silent.* And is this not symptomatic of the changing way in which neoliberalism and its plunder of life itself is being refused today?

Two recent events are illustrative here, both of which are linked to the legitimacy crisis of work that we are exploring. In the late summer of 2011, the streets of London were ablaze. After the police shot and killed Mark Duggin in the northern part of the city one warm afternoon, a large gathering of concerned citizens assembled outside the local police station. Feelings between them and the Tottenham constabulary had been tense for some time, and this appeared to be the final straw. The gathering was met with police hostility, and all-out violence ensued. The dispute spread throughout the city and other major U.K. centers, including Manchester and Birmingham. A good majority of those involved were younger people, in their teens, and proficient in the art of self-organization.

On the surface, such unrest is not that surprising. Like other large cities marked by excessive wealth and manufactured deprivation, London has long been prone to street fighting of this sort, as E. P. Thompson (1963) records in his history of the English working class. And as the media started to report on the events, the customary questions emerged almost immediately: *Why are they doing this? What is their rationale? What are they trying to achieve?* In the conservative press, typical scorn about ungrateful welfare recipients abounded. The looting was opportunistic, symptomatic of a Broken Britain whose light touch on unsocial behavior was now bearing fruit. On the other side of the coin, the liberal media gave more socio-economic explanations about alienated youth, bad jobs, and poverty.

Both sides of the media, of course, missed the point. One of the most striking aspects of these revolts was the outward *silence* of those involved, especially regarding their rationale and objectives. Official representation was solely the preserve of the middle-class media, policy pundits, and other moralists. And this silence confused the experts profoundly. When pressed to communicate the program motivating their behavior, no representative or leader emerged to speak, no charter was delivered. Only a taciturn withdrawal from the machinery of dialogue was evident.

Braving the second night of arson attacks, I wandered through my East London neighborhood eager to discover "their" side of the story. Many of the young people I approached were courteously disinterested in my inquiries as they regrouped around a large supermarket. I too was met with mute non-recognition. Of course, this did not mean that they were not talking among themselves, planning and deliberating on the nature of their refusal. A rich stratum of communication was clearly apparent. But when encouraged by power to represent their concerns, the mood decidedly changed. It was as if a secret compact had been made—best to remain opaque rather than gift to Prime Minister Cameron et al. what they so fervently sought: *our voice.*

## "*What's Your Alternative?*" *[Silence.]*

Detachment and exit from the unworkable neoliberal world is first signaled through the absence of representation. And did not this silence also frustrate many observers in 2011, when Wall Street was occupied, and then Zuccotti Park, and then so many other pseudo-public spaces, including St. Paul's in London? Commentators on both Left and Right were perplexed: What do they want? We ask them, but they seem to have no workable plan. They don't even seem to be interested in making a plan. And so on.

Of course, there were many experts at hand ready to speak on the occupiers' behalf. Even Bill Clinton and Slavoj Žižek got in on the act. Inside the movement, much debate and dialogue were pivotal for its political mobilization. Assemblies were held, political concepts debated, and new modes of democratic self-organization tested. But a curious structural silence prevailed. It was enough simply to state, "We are the 99 percent"; we are you. This reticence was no more evident than when called on by the extreme neoliberal apparatus to testify and deliver a policy, a point-by-point charter of demands. Spray-painted on a wall in East London (Norton Folgate Street), the anonymous reply to this invitation was borrowed from the streets of 1968 Paris: *We ask nothing; we will demand nothing; we will take; we will occupy.*

Understanding the logic of this silence tells us much about the groundswell gathering against biopolitics today, especially when the means of representation appear to have been so irrevocably compromised by power. The first point we must observe is that the refusal to represent is not itself bereft of words or expression. In fact, the opposite is true. The Occupy Movement, for example, was a swarming din of plans, alternatives, and molecular moments of collective exchange. It simply chose not to talk to power, especially in the manner that power wanted them to. Occupiers refused to enter into the discursive mirror game that is now governing so much neoliberal discourse. The erstwhile radical clarion call to be recognized (e.g., Habermas 1987; Honneth 1996) is displaced by what we have termed *post-recognition politics.* Many are now suspicious about speaking up and being counted. Recognition by the powerful is just another way of being sucked back into a one-sided arrangement with its pointless commitments. The refusal to be recognized might therefore convey a kind of resilience. As Kolowratnik and Miessen (2012) conclude, awakening from the nightmare of participation means reclaiming the means of social self-defense.

Perhaps, then, neoliberal capitalism is maintained today not by too few words, but by too many to the wrong people. When we speak to the manager, the teacher, the police officer, the bureaucrat, even transgressively, we are identified once more, fixed within a constellation that will never accept us. What Moten and Harney (2012) call managed self-management functions via a plethora of accounts (to be accountable), responses (to be responsible), and reports (to be reportable). Hence there is a confusing paradox: "Today nobody can hear you over the noise of talk" (Moten and Harney 2012).

And yet, there is so much silence. Why would we want to theorize about it, conserve it, strategize it, share it, enrich it, or occupy it in relation to the politics of work today? I experiment here with the idea that silence might be suggestive of an emergent kind of under-commons, no doubt transitory, but demonstrably collective in its opposition to the ideology of employment. Its commonality is founded on the shared misgiving that the neoliberal project now gains sustenance from any kind of communicative participation between it and the 99 percent. In its dying stage of development, corporate hegemony even welcomes *dissenting* discourse into its language game, as long as it abides by the prefixed rules.

Accordingly, I propose that the silent commons is anything but reserved quietude or fearful seclusion. At the present juncture at least, in which a myopic economic formalism has colonized so many modes of social representation, mute opacity in the face of participation politics might tilt toward something transversal, truly communal, and classless.

## The Poverty of Silence?

Complications do arise, however, at this stage in the argument. Refusing work and activating the threshold soviet, as theorized above, through silence entail characteristics long considered regressive in social theory. When it comes to the functioning of power and domination, is silence not a synonym for elite secrecy and agenda setting—and on the other side of the coin, consent, capitulation, and fear? A long tradition of thought has convincingly cautioned that those rendered speechless before the law pose a double travesty. Silence according to this viewpoint indicates not only (1) the sheer enormity of an individual's or group's oppression (for Anne Frank in her secret attic or Winston Smith in Orwell's *1984,* speaking would surely equal death) but also (2) a dangerous opportunity for oppressors themselves to speak on the behalf of the silenced. The circle of power is thus closed.

The case against silence has antecedents in recognition politics championed in the United States. The influential community power debates during the 1960s are illustrative here. C. Wright Mills among others revealed how elites partially manage populations by erasing certain issues from public discourse, especially those that might reveal hypocrisy (Lukes 2005). The cold war context undoubtedly inspired some of these observations. A key tool of totalitarian societies is to constrain the very words used (and not used) in everyday parlance. During the dark years of Stalinism in the Soviet Union, party officials hoped that manufactured non-signification would disappear the very thought denoted by the word.[8]

But is this deficit the only component of public silence? Or might it have hidden strengths of its own? This is the problem Jean Baudrillard grapples with in his book *In the Shadow of the Silent Majorities* (2007).

He argues that the social—or its living modes of representation apropos classes, peoples, cultures, and nations—has been dissolved into a sheer single nothingness, only capable of being symbolized through abstract surveys and opinion polls. Silence despite obvious injustices is now one of the most characteristic elements of this inscrutable mass. Behind the abstraction is a voiceless universe that merely absorbs, observes, and sinks back into anonymous oblivion. The political orientation of this silence is uncertain. On the one hand, it is symptomatic of a new constellation of dissent, one that emerges from a long and fruitless battle with modernity. This could well become "an absolute weapon" (Baudrillard 2007: 49) if its ironic signature disrupts the din of capitalist talk and lays the ground for a more transformative engagement with power.

On the other hand, however, without any new and positive referents the silent majority will never assemble enough explosive capacity to overcome its own negative content. In other words, Baudrillard insists that we characterize the silent crowd as yet another instance of the oppressed failing to speak out. This makes it both refreshingly inaccessible to classical schemas—including emancipatory ones—and also inert and pliant: "The mass is dumb like beasts, and its silence is equal to the silence of beasts. . . . [I]t says neither whether the truth is to the left or to the right, nor whether it prefers revolution or repression. . . . [I]t is without conscience and without unconscious" (Baudrillard 2007: 54). Because the silent majority is unreadable, it can never enter the lexicon of democratic exchange. It therefore becomes the nothingness of its own non-existence, something encouraged by the neoliberal rebuttal of all imaginative alternatives.

## *The Radicalized Silent Worker*

How then might we analytically connect the silent biocratic worker with a moment of collective escape and departure—that is, the refusal of work? We might begin by revisiting Marx and some of the most striking pages of *Capital* ([1867] 1972) where he gives graphic details of what factory work does to people, especially in the dark and dirty English workhouses of the early nineteenth century. The passages in "The Working Day" (about overwork), "The Division of Labor and Manufacture" (about exploitation), and "Machinery and Large-Scale Industry" (about forced submission) are still remarkable in how they depict the human misery underlying capitalist wealth production. But as Jameson (2011) argues in his rereading of *Capital,* something very strange is occurring here, which is essential to Marx's critique. As opposed to other reports on the horrors of life in the factory (or the coal mine, the nascent bureaucratic offices emerging at the time, and so on), Marx consistently refuses to describe hired labor power as living, breathing people. Even in the most disturbing sections, a worker's singular anguish must remain secondary to the whir of a nonfigurative process.

Dickens breathes life into his workers so that we might identify with their predicament. The Utopian Socialists cradle them in effusive sentiment to shed light on the dreadfulness of work. Marx remains stubbornly stone cold. Jameson (2011) highlights this strange paradox, since the Bible of Labor ultimately leaves its humanity mysteriously unrepresented—but why? According to Jameson, this is crucially necessary if Marx is to remain faithful to his understanding of capitalist exploitation. To imbue work with human qualities would fudge the reality of the labor process, inadvertently (and ideologically) transporting us "outside of the realm of capital, which is not in the lived qualities of work as such, but only its quantity and the surplus values to be extracted" (Jameson 2011: 112). Abstract labor cannot speak, for it is strictly lifeless, formalized dead time. It is only when the *impossibility* of the capital accumulation process appears—overworked bodies collapsing, overproduction of commodities, unsustainable immiseration—that individual personages with singular histories are allowed to emerge in *Capital.* This sort of vanishing point of impossibility is necessarily extraneous to the accumulation process but, more importantly, it is indicative of something preceding the dominance of dead time. This is the social surplus of living labor.

This thematic of impossibility is so central to Marx's analysis that hired labor power must remain mute if it is not to be crowned with the false virtues of bourgeois reconciliation. A silent workforce remains truthful to what it is in the eyes of capital, a conscious bearer of an unfeasible world. To speak to the boss or manager would participate in the fantasy that some kind of life under capitalism might be viable after all, blinding us to its untenable nature. This point was well understood by activists during the May 1968 events in Paris, especially the Situationist Internationale. Public dialogue had to be approached with extreme caution. Otherwise it might sanctify an outmoded (and strictly unreproducible) way of life. Meaningful anti-work protest can only be instigated in the idiom of a voiced impossibility. More recently, we saw this during the French *banlieues* riots in November 2005. As some astute commentators put it, "The rioters didn't demand anything[;] they attacked their own condition[;] they made everything that produces and defines them a target" (Théorie Communiste 2012: 49). In other words, it was their very own impossibility that spoke with bricks and fire.

It is here that Vaneigem (2001) points to the combative elements of silence: "Our freedom is that of an abstract temporality in which we are named in the language of power, with choice left to us to find officially recognized synonyms for ourselves. In contrast, the space of our authentic realization (the space of everyday life) is under the dominion of silence. There is no name to name the space of lived experience" (2001: 56). Any naming would betray the unworkable social existence that currently passes for living under capitalist conditions. Moreover, like a governmental consultation meeting that invites multiple views to legitimate an authoritarian decision that has already been made, the form kills the content. Why so? First, even critically addressing power perpetuates the mistaken notion that this power has not reduced us to nothing (i.e., abstract, dead labor). This grants capitalism certain synergies with life, something it doesn't deserve. Second, the post-capitalist kernel contained in abstract labor's own impossibility is forsaken, since the struggle becomes overcoded through its very relation to the enemy—hence the event's capture, delivered back to us as an inescapable *post-limit* that is purely self-referential, without end or coda. In rather crass terms, think here of the stockbroker wearing a Capitalism Sucks T-shirt with an image of Lenin giving the finger.

## Silence as an Exit Weapon

The analysis forwarded in this book has attempted to demonstrate that a society based purely on neoliberalism—or any type of capitalism—would not last a day. Due to its anti-social precepts, it cannot reproduce itself on its own terms and thus requires shared sociality to continue. This is how we might define the social today, a communist underbelly that both absorbs the shocks of extreme capitalism and provides the living sustenance it needs. Henceforth, living labor can be conceptualized as something autonomous or in excess to the datum of capital accumulation, since the latter could never exist in a world that perfectly reflected its own principles.

Life itself must be recruited for the capitalist enterprise to persist despite itself. In order for this to happen, it needs to cultivate ways of gaining our recognition, attention, and interest. Speaking to power in this parasitical setting, even critically, thus risks granting it something, implying worth to the addressee. Perhaps this is why emergent political movements are so reluctant to enter into dialogue with the corporation, the state, the military, and so forth. From the enigmatic provocations of the Invisible Committee to the anti-work cooperatives in the largest cities of Europe and the Americas, exit or opting out (Jones 2012) appears to be galvanizing democratic praxis. But what does "exit" mean here and how is it related to radical silence?

Hardly anyone today fears being abandoned by power. That would be a blessing. No—what really frightens us is the idea of being included, forced to participate in an unwinnable mirror game with the Master. To make matters worse, the Master is now diffuse and increasingly difficult to identify. Kolowratnik and Miessen (2012) encapsulate this in their analysis of the nightmare of participation around distributed work systems. From corporate community liaison meetings to the consultative listening exercises of multinational firms to team-building meetings in the postmodern workplace, the new injunction is to enter a no-win domain—and speak. Its objective, of course, is to render one's voice truly silent, truly impotent.

Some critical elements of this *radical silence* can be traced back to Foucault's ([1982] 1997, 2011) far-reaching insights regarding how biopower grips us in neoliberal societies. In an interview conducted in 1982 he suggested that silence might be weapon for the weak only when voice loses its disruptive content, overcoded by a reductive form (religious settings, bourgeois mannerisms, fake parliamentary exchange, and so on). Whatever we say in these settings, no matter how seditious, merely reinforces its totalizing setting. No proper rupture is possible. The speaking subject is also the subject of the statement, as Foucault (1978) famously cautioned. An obvious example is the catholic confessional, but so too is the frenetic compulsion to speak under liberalism and now, neoliberalism (also see Foucault 2011). There is undoubtedly an aspect of flippancy in the philosopher's remarks: "Silence might be a much more interesting way of having a relation with people" (Foucault [1982] 1997: 122). The tone, however, belies the seriousness of his investigations at the time. This becomes evident in his last set of annual lectures entitled *The Courage of Truth* (Foucault 2011).[9]

Toward the end of his life, Foucault returned to ancient Greek thought in order to conceptually reassemble something like a pre-disciplinary subject. There is no romanticism or nostalgia here, but a strategic reinvention of techniques that might allow us to fight an enemy that has been inserted into our everyday subjectivity. As Hardt (2010b) points out, this is especially important in the biopolitical society where economic optimization is seemingly indistinguishable from living itself. This is why, according to Foucault, biopower operates unlike anything we have seen before. Its currency is permanent visibility, binding us to a strange talking-person-machine, or what the right-wing economist Gary Becker preferred to call human capital. And perhaps this is also why personal authenticity is so salient in recent management ideology: "What is unique about *you,* what makes *you* standout, and how can it be enhanced, used, and traded?" But what happens when human capital replies? Not unlike Marx's factory worker of yesteryear, it camouflages its own impossibility, having us believe that abstract labor might somehow have a life.

Any kind of visibility in a biopolitical clearing, no matter how radical and subversive, reconnects us to the subordinating flows we are all keen to escape. Perhaps what Foucault (2011: 17) calls "structural silence" is wise because it points to social goods lying beyond the operative grid of neoliberal sociality. And if silence provides a space for inscrutable communication, then might it not also engender inflections of solidarity with those who have already awoken from the nightmare of work?

If so, then the silent common is more than just a reclamation of dignity despite everything (see Foucault 2011). Nor is it a stylization of politics, since that too is exactly what the unstated majoritarian now seeks to break away from. It is more a *turning away from power.* Again, in order to conceptualize this, we have to purge our analysis of any Hobbesian presuppositions. Rather than picturing the laboring majority as tragically dependent on (yet systematically excluded from) an unfair institutional edifice that produces our world, we ought to reverse the scenario. Capitalism is a pure subtraction that feeds on modes of life that struggle to supersede the stupidity of private property, timetables, and an obsession with pointless employment.

Now we can appreciate why the multitude is refusing to recognize or be recognized by power as they attempt to exit the ideology of work. Silence here does not aim to send a signal to capitalism (i.e., a moment of aplomb amid adversity). Nor does it attempt to bamboozle its laws of domination by remaining mute amid violent demands for our acknowledgment. It is more like a background after-image that flares up as we turn our backs on a world of useless work and disappear. Non-signification is all that remains once the bioproletariat escapes back into life.

## Conclusion

We can now make some brief concluding points regarding the nature of refusal at work today. How do we resist biopower once it enters the workplace? First, the free social time that we actually do have is amplified and expanded, pushing its threshold to all corners of the social body. This means abandoning the apparatus of fear that would have us believe that life would cease without work. We have found that the opposite is the case because the virus of biopolitical employment has very little to do with economic necessity. We can live better without it. Second, we reclaim a good life from the parasite of the corporate enterprise by way of exit. Escaping work is not about forgoing the social, but repossessing its collective means of life for deeper democratic ends. And third, refusal means turning our back on the recognition machine of neoliberal capitalism, transforming silence into a weapon against the tyranny slowly working us to death.

An Australian palliative care nurse, Bonnie Ware, recently published a moving account of her conversations with people very close to death. Across a broad range of patients, she noted a striking similarity concerning the things they regretted most about their lives. At the top of the list was not having pursued the life they had really desired—their lost opportunities for authentic happiness. And a close second was regret for having worked too much; it seemed such a waste of a life. For them it was too late, but what about for us? If only we could collectively embody that final realization throughout our entire lives, workplaces, neighborhoods, homes, and desires.

# Conclusion

*Working after Neoliberalism*

Clearly we are living in extreme times. When the conservative commentator Peter Hitchens was recently asked if there were alternatives to capitalism, he replied: "I have no idea. I guess there could be alternatives. Dead silence, starvation and the end of the world … it's like asking if there is an alternative to the weather" ("Masters of Money" 2012).

Statements that a few years ago would have been dismissed as dim-witted, like those of Hitchens, are now considered wise. There is no alternative to capitalism. Questioning its value is like questioning the forces of nature and even life itself. The same has happened to the idea of work. The radical historical bubble we find ourselves trapped in today—let us half-jokingly call it a workers society—is treated like the weather. Sometimes inclement, other times fine, but always there no matter what.

Although this book has introduced some rather epochal terms to describe this new world of employment, including biopower and biocracy, the transition itself was subtle and relatively rapid, building on basic principles of capitalist society that have not changed a great deal. Structures of direct exploitation were multiplied through techniques of *self-exploitation*.[1] To demonstrate the nature of this transition, two accounts of working life in the United States from the 1970s and

1980s are useful. They are only ten years apart, but reveal two distinct political universes.

In his wonderful and almost forgotten essay *Counter-planning on the Shop Floor*, published in 1971, Bill Watson revealed the emergence of a new type of radicalism in the factory. Employee self-organization bypassed both managerial prescriptions, mostly because they were useless in practice, and union norms, which were considered too closely aligned with capitalist objectives. The counter-planning sub-culture created a secret code of self-governance and autonomy. Friends were smuggled across the shop floor to be closer together, lunch breaks were swapped, and production decisions shared, all of which made the factory environment much easier to deal with. For example, when senior management announced that a scheduled inventory ought to take up to six weeks to complete, the counter-planning ability of workers was activated. They knew it could be done in just four days. And the remaining five weeks would allow for a more civilized pace in the factory.

So they trained each other, pooled their expertise, and evoked support networks to finish the task. Watson reports that things were on track until something strange happened. Management discovered the counter-planning and banned it immediately, even though the inventory was being conducted in a far superior manner than they could envisage.[2] It was evident that "any attempt to assert an alternative plan of action on the part of workers was deemed a constant threat to management" (Watson 1971: 8). At the end of the essay, Watson reflected on the emancipatory potential of this self-management among the workforce. Maybe "within these new independent forms of workers organization lies a foundation of social relations at the point of production which can potentially come forward to seize power in a crisis situation and give new direction to society" (Watson 1971: 9).

Now, fast-forward ten years to the early 1980s. Neoliberalism has arrived and is radically reshaping society, individual values, and the way we work together. This period in U.S. labor history is vividly captured in Jefferson Cowie's *Stayin' Alive* (2010), and particularly the demise of working-class solidarity following Reagan's election. He opens his book with a description of the suave twenty-six-year-old autoworker, Dewey Burton. He has rugged sideburns and blue jeans and represents a new type of anti-capitalist. In the early 1970s he would not have been out of place in Watson's study above: "As

Dewey explained, workers were harnessed to union pay but longed to run free of the deadening nature of work itself—and sometimes free of the union-leaders who spoke on their behalf" (Cowie 2010: 7). Dewey was especially adamant that worker control over the factories or counter-planning would be one of the most heated labor relation issues in the coming years. Workers on the shop floor knew that they could run the plant far better than management, and frequently did just that, albeit informally. It helped make life on the line more bearable. As Cowie reports, for a short time in the mid-1970s Dewey even became semi-famous as the new face of labor radicalism. This innovative militancy rallied against everything about exploitation, against the staid unions that thrived on capitalism, and it exuded a romantic independence.[3]

And then comes the surprising hook of the story. By 1980, like so many other working-class whites, Dewey had strangely become a staunch Ronald Reagan supporter. What on earth had happened? How did counter-planning, deemed so radical by the establishment in 1971, turn out to be the central motif of a new brand of extreme capitalist ideology ten years later?

A number of studies have endeavored to understand this rupture in U.S. working-class politics, especially in relation to the rise of the religious Right (see Frank 2005; Bageant 2007).[4] Building on the discussion in previous chapters, we might present an explanation that traces two colliding trends in the persona of Dewey Burton, the effects of which define how we work today. First, the 1970s was marked by a new kind of radicalism, which balked against the very notion of work itself. These workers wanted to *live,* not be ordered around all day by timetables and useless supervisors. Union leaders found this type of recalcitrance particularly difficult to understand. For them, wages were good, life was stable, and the labor question was practically solved. Biopolitical methods of management were a strategic response to this threatening, militant energy, recalibrating the nature of work to incorporate its potency and demands toward exploitative ends. Bios was put to work.

A second trend points to the rise of neoliberal society as the governing classes attempted to retract many social concessions they made to labor following the post-war compromise. The crisis of Fordism in the 1970s provided the perfect alibi to usher in this new world. Unbridled profiteering, extreme inequalities in income distribution, and an almost Hitler-like assault on trade unions were the result. For the elites of industry, however, there was a catch. Neoliberalism is such a confused method of economic (dis)organization, even by its own standards, that every living fiber of labor needed commandeering to get things done. Counter-planning around the tenets of economic reason soon becomes good for the corporation, and bad for the rest of us.

## The "Bio-shock" of Working Today

This book has investigated what the world of work means in the shadow of these historical transformations. Most changes in the way jobs are conducted in Western societies today have been overwhelmingly regressive, even when draped in the language of empowerment, flexibility, and lifestyle. What Watson called counter-planning is now an expected norm. An entire paradigm of management has been invented to make the most of it. This means that work has taken on some eccentric characteristics that we must explain. For example, even the most unskilled jobs—say, the music store retail assistant or home care associate—have become overly embodied, enrolling our social skills and non-work energies into the production process. I use the word "overly" because we see the organism physically exhausted from the weight of work, by its social pressures and psychic demands. The body and its affectations becomes a new kind of living battleground. This is why so many workers are tempted to fight when hemmed in by biocracy, with some disturbing consequences, as we have noted.

So while the term "immaterial labor" correctly signifies the way many occupations have detached from factory-like tasks, such as mindlessly screwing on a bolt, it still must be used with caution for a number of reasons. The most obvious one is that more people are working in factories and fields now than ever, but mostly in the poor Global South. And they supply the North with more than it is willing to acknowledge. Closer to our argument, however, concerns the exceedingly tangible nature of immaterial labor. It has very little to do with service work or the nature of certain jobs in post-industrial society. Biopower represents a particular configuration of power especially manifest in the dissolution of work versus non-work divisions. It employs the body by activating contact points with the modulations we make outside direct exploitation. Constantly agitated, always concerned with what needs to be done, the organism lives this shock as a way of life.

The body blow of work is also highly *socialized* in Western economies. And, as such, it becomes a horizontal force, accumulating over time, which makes it difficult to distinguish from the difficulties of life more generally. The rich but emotionally destroyed banker can undoubtedly read the byproduct of biopower on his body, but this is also the primary medium through which exploitation flows as it seeks the social materials it needs. Our damaged torsos, high blood pressure, and stiff joints are a fetishistic reminder of a world we have not chosen, to the point where even our illnesses feel foreign to us. Is this not the underlying message of the film *Fight Club* (Fincher 1999)? If we are going to be systematically damaged by our jobs, why not short-circuit the process with bruises and black eyes that can be truly *owned*—a proper return to the body as ours.[5]

Those who have been labeled the working poor, of course, experience the violence of employment in a more brutal manner. Moreover, the externalized costs of their exploitation are wider felt, since a vast amount of social support is required to function as a shock absorber to maintain their precarity (see G. Thompson 2010). Many in this group have been relegated to low-paid occupations from better jobs following the economic downturn.[6] It is telling how quickly savings and friendship networks are exhausted in order for these workers to make do. Those barely making a living with multiple jobs, are, ironically enough, enormously expensive to maintain from the biopolitical perspective. Again, this cost is highly socialized, carried by the commons: friends, family, charities, churches, loved ones, and credit cards, all of which are effectively subsidizing exploitative fast-food restaurants, catering firms, universities, and so forth.

This brings us to another central claim of the book. These trends have been precipitated by the neoliberal mission to reduce almost every facet of our lives to the index of work. Individuals become permanent pieces of human capital or human resources, a commodity whose market value is *qualitative* (e.g., personality, emotional intelligence, and education) rather than just quantitative (e.g., how many hours we can put in at the office). When this occurs, the social experience of our work takes on a hue of endlessness. We now *are* our jobs.[7]

Why is neoliberalism so obsessed with the idea that we should be indistinguishable from the work we do? On the basis of the preceding investigation, two explanations might be advanced. First, I do not think it is coincidence that this intense ideological reduction of life to work has occurred precisely when its scarcity and precarity has reached new levels, not just in the West but also around the world (see Foster and McChesney 2012). This tells us a few important things. With the availability of huge amounts of non-work time, which is a structural implication of neoliberal economic policy, how that time is socially used becomes a major concern for the authorities. The generalization of work aims to keep this free time in check. If you don't have a job, then do not enjoy your free time, index everything to the principles of employment more than ever. And if you do have a job, be extremely grateful and willing to sacrifice all for it. We become indebted to work, owe our very social existence to it. This myth is integral to the way class domination functions today.

The second reason why life feels so saturated with work pertains to the *inoperative* nature of the neoliberal paradigm itself. This is especially evident in the contemporary workplace, which would grind to an abrupt halt if the principles of individualism, competition, and private property alone prevailed.[8] Let us approach the problem from another angle. Mark Fisher (2009) recently wrote a fascinating account about how neoliberalism psychologically shuts down alternatives. This he called "capitalist realism," since it inserts a pervasive business ontology into the center of social existence. Clearly better and more just worlds begin to look unrealistic in comparison. Even in the face of impending environmental disaster, a rogue financial system, and nigh-impossible levels of unemployment, asking about alternatives is like, well, questioning the weather.

This ideological conceit certainly succeeded for a while. But we have now passed an important tipping point. Is not the current mood characterized by an all-pervading capitalist *unrealism,* in which the unworkable truth of the corporate enterprise, labor market, and neoliberal state is obvious to everyone? The crisis-struck economies of the West are painful examples of institutionalized incompetence, intentionally disorganized and in a state of disarray. To paraphrase Jean Baudrillard (2010), late capitalism appears to have embezzled reality, functioning through a paradoxical anti-ontology that no one understands. Things are no different inside the corporation or any workplace feeling the heat. Management hierarchies and workflow systems exist almost solely to impede job performance. What Spicer and Alvesson (2012) call *management stupidity* is so endemic that it is a wonder anything gets achieved.[9] It could be the case that corporate managers and the proponents of neoliberalism are unintelligent. I would not argue otherwise. However, it might be prudent to explore another explanation. To paraphrase Marx, capitalism is difficult to perceive because it formats perception itself. And not every society does that. How do we overcome this analytical impasse? First, forget the inevitable shortcomings of real people for a moment and tackle the problem in its abstraction. The *totality* is stupid, but why? Because it clearly cannot reproduce itself. And that is a serious problem for the ruling class. Biopower steps into the breach to solve that problem. And that defines our predicament today. From the bottom of the pyramid to the very top, the abstract impossibility of late capitalism is suddenly linked to our own intimate problems. Even our ambitions and most agreeable successes are implicated. Counter-planning within the confines of the capitalist social factory might have once been a path to life, but not anymore.

Once biopower is introduced in this manner, we might assume that control from above would cease as a decisive factor in the exploitation process. However, this is not the case. The corporate utilization of life itself in the workplace does not lead to less bureaucracy or direct surveillance as might be expected. The proponents of liberation management and Results Only Work Environments forget to tell us this. Traditional hierarchical controls exponentially increase for a number of reasons. As we already know, management has always been about enforcement rather than coordination since it aims to keep a lid on the conflict of interests at the heart of the employment situation. This must be observed, even if it appears to periodically undermine productivity. Even managers find this dysfunctionally coercive aspect of their role difficult to comprehend (Scase and Goffee 1989).[10]

Biopower amplifies the inherent class contradiction between labor and capital, spreading it throughout the social body. On the side of capital, putting life itself to work in order to generate profits requires stringent management systems to keep it in order. This is why those subjected to the just-be-yourself corporate philosophy frequently complain that the exhortation is valid only up to a point. They cannot *really* be themselves—like sleeping for 5 hours on the job or setting the building on fire when frustrated with a rude customer.

Old-fashioned discipline accompanies biopower into the workplace for another reason. There is still something dangerously indeterminate about life once unleashed in the office. It can so easily turn on the firm. The corporation depends on its vibrant social energy more now than ever, but also sees something that is antithetical to its existence, a quality that exceeds capitalism itself. This is why control does not disappear with the introduction of biopower, but leads to *more* management.

## This Is Not Neoliberalism—It Is Worse

Yet it appears that neoliberalism is persisting unabated, organizing our lives on a scale that Von Hayek and Thatcher would have considered wonderful. That said, the present juncture is interesting. Just as neoliberal thought is crashing and burning around us, its discursive influence is becoming ever more pervasive. The austerity measures in Western Europe—a direct result of applied neoclassical economics and the restriction on monetary supply—are now so self-destructive that even the International Monetary Fund admits they are hurting the economy ("Professor Ngaire Woods" 2013). This pattern defines the nature of work as well. At the very moment its cultural kudos seems irretrievably damaged and unemployment has reached levels not seen since the Great Depression, it begins to govern our lives on an unprecedented scale.

I guess this is why so many commentaries use the notion of the living dead to explain the present period of Western capitalism. According to Quiggin (2010), most policy makers are haunted by zombie economics, deploying assumptions that have long been discredited in observable practice. Other books, such as *Zombie Capitalism* (Harman 2009) and my own *Dead Man Working* (2012), reveal the living death of many jobs today. The inexplicable persistence of neoliberal thought is described by Crouch (2011) as a "strange non-death" because the only people who still believe in it are the 1 percent no longer dependent on the shameful travesty that is now the privatized British railway system, for example. As one English journalist put it, "Staring dumbfounded at the lessons unlearned in Britain, Europe and the United States, it strikes me that the entire structure of neoliberal thought is a fraud. The demands of the ultra-rich have been dressed up as sophisticated economic theory and applied regardless of the outcome. The complete failure of this world-scale experiment is no impediment to its repetition. This has nothing to do with economics. It has everything to do with power" (Monbiot 2013b).

The real question is, then, why does the system continue if only the 1 percent (or more accurately, the 0.01 percent, according to Runciman [2013]) still have faith in its virtues? Naked economic power is one obvious answer. In addition, years of brutal individualization have taken their toll. Most of us are now so dependent on institutions that we know are corrupt, but we are too tired and isolated to do anything about it. But I would venture something else is happening here as well. It is clear that the 99 percent do not believe in neoliberalism. We know that its rituals make life harder when applied to even the most basic facets of life, including work. Treating the workplace as a competitive marketplace, for example, merely creates chaos. And here is the crucial point: neoliberalism propaganda does not try to convince *us* to believe in it. The wool is pulled over our eyes when it persuades us that those at the top still believe in it. But perhaps they don't.

This, of course, makes our predicament much worse. What exactly is it that Rupert Murdoch, David Cameron, and other elites of the corporate power structure would like us to believe *they believe*? Let us take a few examples. The privileging of free markets leads to wider prosperity and more effective/responsive services. The 99 percent know this to be deeply untrue. Corporatism in fact, destroys markets and manipulates prices via privatization, which ultimately denies large numbers of people access to basic necessities.[11] Indeed, the dominance of the anti-market corporation over our lives has become so pronounced that some left-wing thinkers have proposed the bizarre notion of free market communism as a possible antidote to capitalist control (see Holland 2011).[12]

So much for free markets. What about a non-interventionist state, a key emblem of neoliberal thought? No; in the United Kingdom, for example, taxation of the middle classes has reached crippling levels, especially in the context of conspicuous tax relief for corporations, most of which are based in tax havens anyway (Shaxson 2012). Indeed, state intervention has been exceedingly intrusive and brutal for most working people amid the current financial crisis. Moreover, the banking bailouts following the 2008 financial crisis in the United States and the United Kingdom thoroughly debunked the myth that government and big business were ever semi-autonomous.[13] And as oil-poor superpowers in the Global North forcibly secure their supplies, the inordinate subsidization of the military complex reveals the crucial role of the capitalist state apparatus today.[14]

Next we could mention the much-celebrated sovereignty of the consumer, the savior of the free world according to Milton Friedman; he equated it with democratic voting rights. As the innumerable accounts of large multinational food companies have now revealed, monopolization and substandard products have left most consumers choiceless over the last ten years (see Quinn 2005; Simms 2007). In addition, the concentration of capital coupled with the reduction of real wages from the 1980s onward has seen not a reduction, but an overall hike in consumer prices, something so-called neoliberal governments condone.[15] Price gouging is the new norm.

As for the intrinsic worth of work, this book has presented an extended critique of what our jobs have done to us. The neoliberal vision of the workers' society depicts a fantasyland: morally contented citizens, empowered by the skills they acquire, justly rewarded with rising living standards, gratefully benefiting from open meritocratic career paths and personal security, and so forth. Almost everybody knows that this version of society is very inaccurate. It has absolutely no bearing on the reality of working life for most of us today. Our workers society is nearer to a nightmare we are hoping to soon wake up from.

The vast majority knows this well, but perhaps also the elite. For example, in the United Kingdom, the Conservative Work and Pensions Minister of Parliament claimed in 2013 that he could survive on £53 (US$81.31) a week. A petition signed by over four hundred thousand British people challenged him to try. The public didn't believe anyone could live on £53 a week. But that was not the point of the claim; the ministerial claim was purely ideological. As long as the otherwise disbelieving 99 percent continue to believe that the 1 percent still believe in free market capitalism, the distortion is successful.

This ideological mechanism of secondary belief—that those at the top are Friedmanian fanatics who stubbornly hold onto the ideals of the work ethic and consumer sovereignty—aims to conceal a perverse truth. This is not neoliberalism—it is worse, if that is at all possible. The neoliberal state is indeed dead. Even though leaders of industry and the corporatized governing class audaciously profess its morals, the reality for most even Milton Friedman would find fairly alien.

Our society is more of a hybrid *capitalist feudalism,* a backward system governed by oligarchical privilege and the aggressive protection of inherited wealth—and for the rest of us not born into this corporatized clique, authoritarianism, financial disorder, and above all, manufactured *fear.*[16]

Duménil and Lévy state in their analysis of global capitalism, "The contemporary crisis revealed the strategy's unsustainable character. . . . [N]eoliberal trends ultimately unsettled the foundations of the economy of the 'secure base' of the upper classes" (2011: 1). This might also explain the self-destructive tendency in capitalist governance structures today. We have certainly noted the social effects of this among the overworked multitude, especially when they become the "fix-it" crew for an economic paradigm that never really worked.[17] But now the agents of capitalist power too are displaying such tendencies. For example, on her first day at the helm, the CEO of a well-known U.S. internet firm made a startling announcement to all employees working from home (for is the boundary-less firm not the quintessential symptom of biopower today?): There will be no more telecommuting. Everyone is now required to be present at the office, with no excuses—a peculiar decision, given the accepted view that remote working in this industry can substantially increase effectiveness and productivity. Perhaps we are witnessing the advent of a modern kind of despotic leadership, one that actually resents employees who have a life, even if that means potentially undermining key performance indicators of the firm.

This represents an interesting shift in the cultural antinomies of capitalist employment arrangements today. Not only has self-harm become the working norm for so many tired employees, but the benefactors of profit are also turning on themselves. One might suspect that, similar to the brooding feudal oligarchy of pre-capitalist society, there is something disturbingly *suicidal* about this final phase of neoliberalism, from the austerity policies rocking the European Union, to the draconian immigration initiatives that drive away global talent from languishing sectors in New York and London, to Ponzi schemes and stock-trading activities that entail eye-watering levels of risk, to policies on the natural environment that beggar belief. In other words, these economic practices appear to be not only blindly self-destructive but also deliberately bent on self-ruin.

If this is indeed a time of transition from neoliberalism to some

other future state, then we might call it "*nihi*liberalism."[18] What do
Rupert Murdoch and Company really believe in if they do not sin-
cerely care whether neoliberalism works? Who knows—but maybe
*nothing.* The nihilism of the ruling classes today is almost palpable.
The immense hoarding of resources in the post-2008 period and the
open hedonism amid crushing poverty is certainly symptomatic of
this. It might also explain the increasingly vindictive stance that big
business takes toward the public sphere, a sector that is slowly reviving
after so many years of corporate capture.[19] For example, when individuals from the anti-corporate group "No Dash for Gas" recently spoke
out against a large energy firm, the response was disproportionately
malicious, designed to devastate the activists' lives forever (Monbiot
2013a). The action was widely reported as "corporate and PR suicide," but perhaps that was the point. What can only be described as
a scorched-earth policy is indicative of a once robust class offensive
in retreat. As members of the neoliberal oligarchy reconsolidate in
their securitized mansions and Learjets, we might be witnessing a sea
change in capitalist politics, perhaps pointing to a future free from
work.

## The End of the Age of Work?

We have revealed some disturbing truths about capitalist society
in its declining phase. Work is but a pointless ritual designed to
maintain an extreme class configuration. Even members of the corporatized elite do not believe in their own rhetoric. But what does
the truth matter? Once we realize that no one really believes in the
neoliberal project, not even the infinitesimal minority who benefit
from it, then it might seem that unmasking this open secret could
be a radical gesture. Unfortunately, this misses another important
facet of the ideology currently enrolling our participation in an extreme situation, even when we categorically do not believe in it. As
Deleuze brilliantly puts it concerning the psychosis of late capitalism,
"Nothing is secret, at least in principle and according to the 'code.'
And yet nothing is admissible. . . . [B]y contrast to other societies,
it is a regime that is both public *and* inadmissible. A very special de-
lirium" (Deleuze 2004: 263). Our public revelations about the ills of
capitalism can sometimes feed into the ideological *false truth telling*
of domination itself, whereby the blatant harms of corporate coloni-

zation are hidden in plain sight.[20] Some critical truths are ironically good for big business.

A few examples illustrate how this functions. A former employee of a large European weapons manufacturer told me about this strange exercise on his first day on the job. A company official places a bullet-ridden military helmet on the table, confessing, "This is what you sell." Only then does the company go on to argue that the firm does everything it can to abide by international law, human rights, and so forth. British Petroleum (or BP) no longer bothers with its green Beyond Petroleum campaign, since even a child would incredulously deride such cynicism. Set against images of lush rainforests and smiling villagers from an impoverished country, BP's webpage revised what Beyond Petroleum really means: "It is shorthand for what we do: exploring, developing and producing more fossil fuels to meet growing demand." In other words, the unsustainable exploitation of a finite resource! And more recently, the multinational mining corporation Vale—voted the world's worst company in 2012 by the Public Eye Award—chooses not to conceal its controversial labor relations record. Instead, it sponsors a London retrospective of photographer Sebastião Salgado, whose images have previously raised awareness about the dire conditions of miners in South America and Africa.

Practical criticism must therefore take this deceptive element into consideration. For we can unmask the discursive tactics of corporate hegemony as much as we like; the danger is that our very ability to speak is used to erroneously vindicate the system's commitment to freedom. This is why, I would argue, *post-recognition* politics is central to an emergent radical labor movement. This has been prompted partly by outrage fatigue (Mieville 2012), whereby protest seems both frustratingly ineffectual yet somehow useful to those at the top. But it also arises from a different understanding of how power functions today. Successfully refusing capitalism is not about finding better ways to be included in its extractive work structures or gaining concessions and recognition from a ruling anti-democratic minority who does not actually care whether we like them or not (but would like us to believe they do), for they already know that the age of work is over. They realize that its overwhelming presence is a manufactured tool designed to enhance class control. But so long as the dialogue continues—no matter how critical—the mythology of the neoliberal mindset is assured: without work and the multinational firm, we are nothing.

This book has endeavored to demonstrate that work and the corporation do not enrich our worlds or gift us with life. We are not the products of its coordinated efforts, and indeed, on the contrary, especially today as capitalism moves into a noticeably parasitical phase. This analytical conclusion is the only realistic way to envision an age beyond work. Three points are decisive.

First, what is presented to us as normal is actually an extreme historical situation. We sometimes do not see this because we lose perspective. But we sense it, feel it, and see it in the eyes of others. Our frenetic attachment to work (while despising everything about it) is a self-referential ritual with little functionality or necessity other than maintaining a certain class relation.

Second, there is nothing progressive or modern about this stage of corporatized capitalism. In fact, as I have noted throughout this book, there is something very pre-modern, undemocratic, and backward about it. Rather than being the great provider of transport, medicine, communication, and leisure, the modern firm stunts free social development, heralding a strange feudal-like impasse. That neoliberalism presents itself as the highest order of civilization merely indicates that it too has foreseen its own redundancy.

And third, the practical twin of post-recognition politics is collective *self-valorization*. When workers begin to appreciate how overly reliant capitalism is on its living labor today, refusal is no longer enacted in the name of some far away utopia. A vast non-capitalist social wealth is already present *before the refusal itself*, for that is what the 1 percent relies on to sustain its unsustainable paradigm. Self-valorization is simply the collective repossession of what was ours all along, for ends that are truly shared.

It is often said that working-class solidarity was the first casualty of the neoliberal revolution. This certainly appears to be the case. However, might not the thorough universalization of work under biopolitical circumstances also yield new trends in cross-factional commonness? As I have argued in the preceding chapters, the blight of life at work is a widespread experience, which is not unusual given the way our society has singularly reduced everything to it. Biopower installs the template of production into everyone, even the unemployed. As such, managers and bankers complain of overwork as much as those at the bottom, despite their radically different life chances.

It is possible, then, that the very nature of biopower and its prodigious indifference to boundaries, categories, and divisions might inadvertently engender a new collective experience against corporatized work. While the capital/labor, employer/employee, and manager/managed dichotomies are still very relevant, biopower is hegemonic precisely because it partially cuts across these divides. For the modern worker, the real struggle is not simply between capital and labor as it was under Fordism, but between *capital and life*. And because this life or human resource is such a generalized quality, we all begin to count ourselves as workers. A number of leading labor activist groups in Western Europe have noted this. One stated, "Historical conflict no longer opposes two massive molar heaps, two classes—the exploited and the exploiters, the dominant and the dominated, managers and workers—among which one could differentiate. The front line no longer cuts through the middle of society; it now runs through the middle of each of us" (Tiqqun 2011: 12).

The excerpt is certainly bleak. But could we not invert it for emancipatory purposes? If exploitative work has become a universal principle that cuts through all of us in the social factory, then so must the non-capitalist other that it requires to subsist. In other words, the pervasive socialization of the means of production following the biopolitical turn has unwittingly placed the post-work imaginary at the heart of society. And as such, might we be witnessing the emergence of a new universal class like the proletariat of yesteryear?[21] Perhaps it is still too far off to be clearly seen, but I wager that it is the future to come.

# Notes

## INTRODUCTION

1. We must remain cautious about deploying new times terminology without circumspection, as Bradley et al. (2000) and, more recently, Doogan (2009) argue. Arguments such as Sennett's (2006) concerning the new culture of capitalism and Boltanski and Chiapello (2005) about the new spirit of capitalism risk missing some key continuities between present and past logics of capitalist rationality (e.g., private property, commoditization, and exploitation). This book instead notes recent shifts *within* the broader constellation of capitalism, some of which might spell its coming demise.

2. This transition between institutional spheres is not that great. Indeed, this book does not make a major distinction between public institutions and for-profit businesses, since the demarcation has long lost its importance following the neoliberal revolution. As Collini (2012) notes in relation to the U.K. university sector, the business analogy is now central to its institutional logic, especially in terms of labor relations.

3. See the report "2012 Trends in Global Employee Engagement," conducted by the company Aon Hewitt (2012).

4. For useful studies of labor intensification in the mainstream U.S. employment sector, see Green's (2007) *Demanding Work* and Schor's *The Overworked American* (1993). Both tend to emphasize increasing hours spent at work rather than the qualitative changes explored here.

5. Following Davis and Monk (2007), we might call London an evil paradise, especially for many of its workers. As a central hub for the European

workforce, it is both an attractive location to seek employment and extremely unworkable for those who find it, even for the so-called middle classes (see Boyle 2013). According to Mieville (2012), this curious contradiction represents a deep-seated sado-monetarism within the city.

6. Here, it is important to avoid imputing any functionality or equilibrium between the social common and capitalist exploitation. It always involves an uncontainable struggle. As Hardt and Negri express it, "The communism of capital can absorb all values within its movement, and can represent to the fullest the general social goal of development, but it can never expropriate that particularity of the working class that is its hatred of exploitation, its uncontainability at any given level of equilibrium" (1994: 51).

7. For an inside perspective on the huge amount of work conducted by unemployed people, see Ehrenreich's (2006) *Bait and Switch* and Southwood's (2011) *Non-stop Inertia*.

8. Howker and Malik's (2013) excellent analysis of the "jilted generation" in the United Kingdom strikingly makes this point when they quote a recent newspaper report: "For the first time, a grandmother in her eighties can expect to enjoy higher living standards than someone in their twenties who is working" ("Jinxed Generation's Plight Worsening" 2012). Add race and gender inequalities to this, and the picture becomes especially bleak. And no, it is not the grandmother's fault!

9. This attitude of pointlessness toward work could easily be mistaken for cynicism, particularly the *cynical ideology* that Žižek (1989) noted in the 1980s. The cynical individual exclaims, "We don't believe in capitalism, we can see through its propaganda, but we nevertheless act *as if* we believe." Under cynical ideology, we still believed in our disbelief, and that kept the capitalist totality in place. But what we might call the current *post-cynical condition* is quite different, because we don't even believe in our cynicism anymore, in our disbelief. This is personified by today's unhappy worker, who knows that they cannot go on like this . . . but do anyway.

10. As Nancy (1991: 31) puts it rather cryptically, "This is why community cannot arise in the domain of *work* . . . community necessarily takes place in what Blanchot has called 'unworking', referring to that which, before and beyond the work, withdraws from the work, and which, no longer having anything to do with either production or with completion, encounters interruption, fragmentation, suspension." In other words, community can never be an instrumental process or finalized outcome of action, but is something that has paradoxically never arrived and can thus only be enjoyed on those terms.

11. It might be objected that I don't give enough importance to cooperatives like Mondragon in Spain. Such non-capitalist experiments are unarguably laudable for the way they make worker democracy a central organizing

principle. But Mondragon, for example, still competes in a divided and conflictual global economy, inevitably leading to compromise once it looks beyond the collective's boundaries. As Marszalek (2012) recently put it:

> Mondragon Corporation abides by outstanding principles regarding the dignity of work and the betterment of their community, but when the corporation enters the arena of international trade, these ethical premises are challenged by the bottom-line mentality. This conundrum cannot be ignored. Every worker cooperative must deal with the marketplace and its diktats and limit, to the best of its ability, their corrosive effects on daily operations. Mondragon, since it contends with these issues on such an immense scale, attempts to balance the real world's ethical compromises with their internal values with increasing difficulty. Its overseas investments, for instance, are motivated solely by financial concerns; they do not invest to create cooperatives with the 15,000 workers they employee in other countries.

12. See Milkman, Bloom, and Narro's (2010) *Working for Justice* concerning these emergent workers movements and their claims. And for a fascinating analysis of "alternative unionism," see Eidelson's (2013) investigation of "alt labor" in the United States. In relation to Europe, see the report "27% of Spaniards Are Out of Work: Yet in One Town Everyone Has a Job" (2013).

## CHAPTER 1

1. This idea is different from the "responsible autonomy" (A. Friedman 1977) noted in earlier studies of Fordist employment because it seeks to capture what is already present rather than trust employees to follow the rules in the supervisor's absence. Even counter-management activities are harnessed by ROWE, which would have once been labeled shirking within the responsible autonomy paradigm.

2. To the best of my knowledge, the term "biocracy" was first used by Lifton (1986) in his analysis of Nazi eugenics, as noted by Esposito (2008: xxv).

3. I have explored and elaborated on this *aporia* underlying corporate social responsibility in a previous work, *The End of Corporate Social Responsibility* (Fleming and Jones 2013).

4. As Negri argues, "The subsumption of society by capital, rather than closing the contradictions of exploitation, actually extends them indefinitely over the entire social terrain" (2008: 15).

5. Without this conceptual precaution we are also open to the criticism that the analysis overly romanticizes social relations outside of work, that they are somehow untainted by capitalism—clearly a problematic proposition.

This is where Gorz gets it wrong. He argues that immaterial workers "come into the production process with all the cultural baggage they have acquired through games, team sports, campaigns, arguments, musical and theatrical activities" (Gorz 2010: 10). Unfortunately, the culture industry has made these activities outside of work fairly capitalist as well. This is why we must approach non-labor from a qualitative perspective. Just as work is not quantitatively everywhere but feels like it is when it poisons the totality of our lives (like a troubled sleeper worrying about his or her job at 3:00 A.M.), the register of non-work similarly haunts the neoliberal system like an inscrutable ghost in the machine—hence its radical potential today.

6. As Michael Hardt convincingly argues, Marx "does not make this claim, of course, in quantitative terms. Industrial production at the time made up a small fraction of the economy even in England, the most industrialized country. Marx's claim is instead qualitative: all forms of production will be forced to adopt the qualities of industrial production" (2010a: 134).

7. It is very instructive to compare this understandable sentiment with classic observations of *successful* output restriction in the Fordist factory, such as those reported by Roy (1952). There, the signs of biopower are nowhere to be seen.

8. This is especially so with the recent surge in job-related suicides, including overpaid bankers, Chinese factory workers, and middle-management bureaucrats (e.g., France Telecom). Indeed, it is telling of how biopower functions to universalize work when some employees might consider death over the comparatively minor gesture of simply quitting their job or going on strike.

9. In their book *Escape Routes,* Papadopoulos, Stephenson, and Tsianos explain the rationale of exit politics when they argue, "Of course, sovereignty digests resistance: active forms of resistance are continually co-opted. But this twin movement of flight and capture only appears catastrophic if we insist that there must be an ultimate solution to social conflicts. We do not. . . . [E]scape is not opposed to or against the regimes of control in which it emerges; escape betrays the regime of control by carefully evacuating its terrain" (2008: 74–75).

10. There is, of course, a rich history of work refusal in the labor movement (often rubbing up against organized unionism, which has tended to fetishize work), as noted by Seidman (1991) and Black (1985). This book will be concerned specifically with refusal in the context of neoliberal capitalism.

## CHAPTER 2

1. Friedman's suggestion is not new. The argument builds on a long history of Enlightenment thought—including Adam Smith and Montesquieu—that commerce has a pacifying effect on populations. Self-interest and impersonal

market relations were thought to temper the passions, since certainty, peace, and rule of law are prerequisites for business (Hirschman 1997). But as Graeber (2011) notes in his excellent historical analysis of debt, the opposite is actually the case. Violence is the founding principle of a money-based economy, since impersonal measurement generally arises around warfare, punishment, and retribution. When war-besieged soldiers arrive in your town, money becomes important since you cannot trust them to return a favor in any practical way.

2. We have to look no further than Baudelaire's prose poem "Crowds" to see that joyous individuality (which is very different from serial individualism) is but another name for the productive nature of what we have called the sociality of gain: "The multitude, solitude. Identical terms. . . . [T]he man who is unable to people his solitude is equally unable to be alone in a crowd. The solitary and thoughtful stroller finds a singular intoxication in this universal communion" (Baudelaire, [1869] 1970). Only together, open, and communal in human exchange, as Marx would have it, can we really be ourselves.

3. See Joseph's (2002) excellent critique of the uses and abuses of the notion of community in the U.S. tradition of political thought.

4. See Kordela (2007) for the philosophical import of surplus in the Spinozist tradition. Also see Papadopoulos, Stephenson, and Tsianos's (2008) discussion of surplus in relation to the social potentials that may provide an escape route from work.

5. In the life sciences, for example, Cooper defines life itself as surplus since it is "intrinsically expansive . . . thus accumulating a relentlessly surplus of free energy above and beyond the chemical deposits already available on earth" (Cooper 2008: 35).

6. Panzieri provides an excellent analysis of technology from this perspective in his essay "The Capitalist Uses of Machinery" ([1961] 2009). The reliance on independent thought among the workforce provides the momentum for challenging the capitalist system as a whole. He writes, "Since self-management demands are not posed merely as demands for 'cognitive' participation, but affect the concrete relationship of rationalization/hierarchy/power, they do not remain closed within the ambit of the firm. Instead, they are precisely directed against the 'despotism' which capital projects and exercises over society as a whole, at all levels, and they are expressed as the need for a total overthrow of the system, by means of a global prise de conscience and a general struggle of the working class as such."

7. Žižek protests, "In the same way the brain sciences teach us how there is no central Self, so the new society of the multitude which rules itself will be like today's cognitive notion of the ego as a pandemonium of interacting agents with no central authority running the show. . . . No wonder Negri's notion of communism comes uncannily close to that of 'post modern' digital capitalism" (2009: 56).

## CHAPTER 3

1. Corporate-dominated markets are key here. As Patel puts it, "There's more than enough food on earth to feed the world one and half times over. The reason people go hungry is the way we distribute food through the market, as private property, and the people who starve are simply too poor to afford it" (2011: 94).

2. According to Chomsky (1991), the state has always been a capitalist one, via subsidies, preferential treatment, and tax credits. "There's nothing remotely like capitalism in existence. To the extent there ever was, it had disappeared by the 1920s or 1930s. Every industrial society is one form or another of *state* capitalism. But we'll use the term 'capitalism,' since that is more or less its present meaning."

3. In his analysis of the corporate takeover of individual life, a similar sentiment is reported by Court (2003) whereby three-fourths of Americans believed the corporation had "too much power over their lives" (Court 2003: 11).

4. I am thankful to Gerry Hanlon for alerting me to this document.

5. Lustig (1979) makes one of the most convincing arguments about how the early proponents of corporatization were well aware of its tendency to curb both democratic participation and the efficient management of collective goods. Also see Djelic's (2013) fascinating business history of similar debates in England around the enfranchisement of capital.

6. This idea of subduing labor by transforming them into minor capitalists via the stock market returned during the 1980s, especially in relation to the dwindling middle classes. Some commentators even heralded a coming post-capitalist era since everybody had an ownership stake in capital (see Drucker 1993). The way in which the winners and losers were divided following the 1987 crash swiftly revealed how class relations remained distinctly capitalist in character.

7. Also see Stout's (2012) analysis of this trend in *The Shareholder Value Myth*.

8. In his classic essay, "What Do Bosses Do?" Marglin draws out the crucial implications of this observation: "If it turns out that the origin and function of capitalist hierarchy has little to do with efficiency, then it becomes an open question whether or not hierarchical production is necessary for a high material standard of living" (1974: 20).

9. As Shenhav also demonstrates in his extensive archival study of Tayloristic methods of management, "It is particularly significant that flash points of labor strikes during the early Progressive era were located in the very industries that were being rationalized and systematized" (2002: 122).

10. One might also see the introduction of the Wagner Act in 1933— which legalized unionism in order to placate angry workers—as symptomatic of the deep hostility that the human relations movement inspired among the working class (see Panitch and Gindin, 2012: 59).

11. Perelman argues that this is why "deep down, most political and business leaders are keenly aware that market forces, without any outside guidance, will and often do produce catastrophic results. . . . [P]ure capitalism suffers from such severe internal contradictions that it could never survive on its own" (2006: 15).

12. It is important to note that the corporatization of the state not only invested in life through biopolitical means but also degraded and destroyed it as it sought to gain total control over society. The shock was felt most severely in post-communist countries, for obvious reasons. According to the study "Death Surge Linked with Mass Privatization," by Oxford University (2009), "As many as one million working-age men died due to the economic shock of mass privatization policies followed by post-communist countries in the 1990s." Also see Stuckler and Basu (2013) in relation to the way economic austerity kills.

13. For an interesting analysis of this trend in the post-crisis United Kingdom, see Ha-Joon Chang's (2013) thought piece entitled "Britain: A Nation in Decay," regarding infrastructural decline. The blog "Ripped Off Britons" (2013) is also incisive on this point.

14. The antecedents of other inventions like the Human Genome Project are so historically variegated that it is difficult to discern all the preceding strands of influence and luck. But this is a point that ought to be used *against* intellectual property law rather than for it. Hyde's (2011) *Common as Air* eloquently makes this argument with respect to artistic commercialism, in which private property must almost be deemed an oxymoron given the social nature of artistic creation.

15. Krippner's (2011) *Capitalizing on Crisis* and Mirowski's (2013) *Never Let a Serious Crisis Go to Waste* are interesting in this respect regarding global capitalism. In relation to European economies, see the paper by Transnational Institute in Amsterdam (2013) entitled "Privatizing Europe: Using the Crisis to Entrench Neoliberalism."

## CHAPTER 4

1. Cynicism was perhaps one of the key responses to culture management among the workforce. Kunda noted Tech staff calling its managed culture "California bathtub crap." And in the U.K. firm he studied, Collinson (1992) reported employees deriding it as "Yankee hypnosis" and the newsletter as "Goebbel's gazette."

2. Regarding sexuality, we have seen a major shift in the way it has been approached in workplace settings. As Burrell (1984) demonstrates in his study, sexuality was shunned from the workplace because of its counter-productive connotations. Compare this to the firms that Ross (2004) and Fleming (2009) studied, whereby sexual display was almost *expected* from employees by management.

In an extensive international study on workplace intimacy by Kakabadse and Kakabadse, the authors found, "The blurring of the work and private life has clearly emerged from this survey. . . . [I]n the eyes of many, intimacy at work is no longer a problem, is on the increase and many report improvements in work performance resulting from the exhilaration of intimacy experiences" (Kakabadse and Kakabadse 2004: 5). In other words, biopower has entered the building.

3. No wonder these closed and tightly circumscribed institutions began to look like cults, especially when they became preoccupied with screening out any dangerous external contaminants such as family and private lives. See O'Reilly and Chatman's (1996) excellent comparison of culture management and brainwashing cults.

4. It is important to note that culture management was reserved for not only office work but also manual labor jobs where unionization was still relatively high, including automobile factories (Hamper 1992) and, bizarrely, even a slaughterhouse (Ackroyd and Crowdy 1990).

5. This observation confirms the findings of previous studies about the way emotion and rationality can be perversely wedded under authoritarian regimes (e.g., Marcuse 1964), as well as prefiguring future studies noting the calculative subordination of love, shame, and commitment within highly administrative settings (e.g., Illouz 2007).

6. The celebration of diversity also has a moral dimension, since it absorbs liberalist motifs apropos of minorities such as gays and ethnic groups who are often disenfranchised in Western corporate settings (see Florida 2004a, 2004b). The message is that difference along these dimensions should be encouraged and used by the firm for productive ends (for example, see Janssens and Zanoni 2005; Raeburn 2004).

7. This is true, but only up to a point. For example, employees are not free to be themselves by joining a union. Moreover, one employee I observed in a call center was among those who decided to just be themselves, but his method was to give hash-cookies to his teammates. He was fired (Fleming 2009).

8. This gives us a different take on Harvey's (2001) observation that sickness under capitalism is defined as the inability to work. Sickness is now an integral part of work-life culture—one must almost *physically* reflect the debilitating nature of work itself to participate in its bodily regime. Visible suffering is now an emblem of being a good employee under neoliberal capitalism.

9. This is why radical groups like the Invisible Committee place so much emphasis on worker anonymity, which, again, would seem out of place under conditions defined by the Fordist social compact in which voice was central. They write:

> Turn anonymity into a defensive position. In a demonstration, a union member tears the mask off an anonymous person who has just broken a window. "Take responsibility for what you're doing instead of hiding

yourself." But to be visible is to be exposed, that is to say above all, vulnerable. When Leftists everywhere continually make their cause more "visible"—whether that of the homeless, of women or of undocumented immigrants—in hopes that it will get dealt with, they're doing exactly the contrary of what must be done. Not making ourselves visible, but instead turning the anonymity to which we've been relegated to our advantage, and through conspiracy, nocturnal or faceless actions, creating an invulnerable position of attack. (Invisible Committee 2009: 112–113)

## CHAPTER 5

1. This observation is, of course, important for the feminist critique of capitalism, as a huge amount of unpaid labor time was required to reproduce the conditions of capitalist production. In the home this was (and still is) highly gendered in nature (see Weeks 2011 for an excellent overview and evaluation of this kind of feminist analysis).

2. For example, a U.K. budget airline has recently announced that pilots will be rehired as self-employed agents: "The pilots are then paid for the work they do but have to pay for all their own expenses, including uniforms, identity cards, transport, and hotel accommodation. The contracted pilots have no pension scheme or medical insurance unless they set it up themselves" ("You Thought Ryanair's Stewards Had It Bad?" 2013).

3. For Land and Böhm, "Facebook labor" represents a dominant practice in the capital accumulation process today: "If labor is understood as 'value producing activity,' then updating your status, liking a website, or 'friending' someone, creates Facebook's basic commodity. It produces marketing data about you, which they can leverage for market research purposes and to better target advertising you might be interested in. It also produces an audience, as your 'friends' receive updates, follow your links, or log on to Facebook to join a conversation" (2012).

4. If hiring interns was once a civic duty, it is now highly exploitative and fundamental to corporate productivity. We often think of interning as a temporary "foot in the door" path to full paid employment. But not anymore, given the current era of the permanent intern ("The Age of the Permanent Intern" 2013).

5. This integration process was not easily accomplished, given ingrained customary rights and societal structures that were still not conducive to a waged way of life. Workers had to be frightened into compliance, which is where public hangings were particularly effective (Linebaugh 2006).

6. Academic publishing is another good example of this corporate logic. In the U.K. university system, for example, public funds pay academics to

write articles and submit them to academic journals. However, these journals are now mostly owned by private companies, which then sell the articles back to the public university, charging massive subscription fees. One guesses the gross profit margins must be staggering (see Monbiot 2011).

7. It is no coincidence that Florida's (2004b) conservative (yet perplexingly popular) theory of the "creative class" is heavily indebted to this work.

8. Bizarrely enough, it might even be the case that the firm would dissuade workers from such "sleep work" given that employees might arrive to work the next morning impaired, fatigued, and disengaged.

9. For an interesting sociological account of this invisible work, see Wadel's (1979) discussion of the hidden work underlying everyday life, which resonates with more recent workplace investigations too, such as Fletcher's (2001) concern with unseen labor.

10. Mazzucato (2013: 93) presents some fascinating examples of this appropriation of public innovations in her analysis of the entrepreneurial state. She reveals that the Apple iPhone, for example, almost completely consists of state-led (i.e., publically funded) inventions: "Apple concentrates its ingenuity not on *developing* new technologies and components, but on *integrating* them … its great in-house product designs are, like that of many 'smart phone' producers, mostly invented somewhere else, often backed by tax dollars" (emphasis in original). She also presents evidence regarding the way workers in the public sector are often the true source of many of these so-called privately owned ideas.

11. See Von Hippel (2006: 133) for an extended analysis of these trends of capitalist capture and how the corporation can "profit by systematically searching for innovations developed by lead users" free of charge.

12. In this respect, it is interesting to note the rise of the "creativity management" genre of popular business books, such as Pink's *Drive* (2011). They, too, realize that the logic of innovation and the profit-maximization imperative tend to be at odds with each other. So they devise new methods of management that would look communist to most CEOs. Thus, once more the fantasy of capitalism without capitalism underscores much neoliberal discourse.

## CHAPTER 6

1. An even better way of observing this curious ideology of work is from the side of those who don't need to work but still do in order to appear like a worker—those at the top of the hierarchy. How else can we explain the obsession with work among rich capitalists—isn't it bizarre that they don't stop and relax with their millions?

2. For example, see Clastres's excellent *Society against the State*, where he describes the relationship between technology, work, and leisure in primitive societies: "The advantage of a metal axe over a stone axe is too obvious to re-

quire much discussion: one can do perhaps ten times as much work with the first in the same amount of time as with the second; or else, complete the same amount of work in one-tenth the time. And when the Indians discovered the productive superiority of the white men's axes, they wanted them not in order to produce more in the same amount of time, but to produce as much in a period of time ten times shorter." (1989: 194).

3. The Rat Catcher of Mumbai was recently reported to be the worst job in the world, as depicted in Miriam Chandy Menacherry 2012's excellent documentary, *The Rat Race*.

4. Patel (2011) makes a related point with respect to the natural commons when he suggests that "commoning involves other people putting limits on what resources you can exploit, how much you can accumulate, how things will be shared. The free market has none of those constraints" (Patel 2011: 112). For our purposes, this tells us that an inoperative threshold would delimit our hyper-worked lives in a manner that is both social and imminently democratic.

5. One of the most amusing comments in the vast number of advice columns on this topic is by James Altucher (2013), writing in the *Huffington Post*. He suggests no fewer than ten reasons why we should quit our jobs this year: "Your hands are not made to type out memos. Or put paper through fax machines. Or hold a phone up while you talk to people you dislike. 100 years from now your hands will rot like dust in your grave. You have to make wonderful use of those hands now. Kiss your hands so they can make magic."

6. For a fascinating example targeted directly at rich corporate workers, see a book by the anonymous author Escape the City (2012) entitled *The Escape Manifesto: Quit Your Corporate Job, Do Something Different*.

7. That is, I have no answer other than the collective ownership of the means of production (or democracy) (see Wolff 2012 and Albert 2003).

8. Comrade Beria knew of the magical power of discourse in carving up the social world as well as any contemporary post-modernist. Who could ever forget those wonderful propaganda posters picturing a stern peasant woman, forefinger pressed to her lips: "Keep your mouth shut! Yabbering goes hand in hand with treason!"

9. Although he does not say, I suggest that Foucault gains inspiration for his approach to silence from Nietzsche: "I do not want to wage war against what is ugly. I do not want to accuse; I do not even want to accuse those who accuse. *Looking away* shall be my only negation. And all in all and on the whole: someday I wish to be only a Yes-sayer" (Nietzsche 1974: 223).

## CONCLUSION

1. The term "self-exploitation" must be used with caution, since—and following Deleuze and Guattari's (2004) *Anti-Oedipus*—it misses the moment

of desire that frequently accompanies someone's over-identification with his or her own domination. Desire introduces the importance of the other into the subjective matrix, whereas the term "self-exploitation" does not capture the subjective dissymmetry occurring here. In other words, there is no way that biopower can be at one with the individual in question.

2. It must be noted that a number of studies have revealed the way management frequently turned a blind eye to such counter-planning as well. This was for the very reason that it led to more efficient and voluminous output (see Mars 1982; Bensman and Gerver 1962). But it also provides managers with ample justification for punitive measures that might be enacted in the future, especially around unionization (see Gouldner 1954).

3. Aronowitz and DiFazio nicely capture the deep discontent with unions among militant workers like Dewey during this period: "Organized labor has hitched its fate to capital. . . . [U]nion leaders believe that capitalism is in their, as well as their members', best interests, and to go into systemic opposition is to commit political and economic suicide" (2010: xxiii).

4. According to Bageant's (2007) exceptionally depressing *Deer Hunting with Jesus: Dispatches from America's Class War,* the combination of job loss through outsourcing, religious zealotry, personal debt, and a stringent rightwing campaign of fear resulted in the old social democratic Left becoming Republican by default rather than by desire.

5. If *Fight Club* represents a reclamation of the body from the damages of work *and consumption,* then biopower and its ideological tyranny of employability is more about the surrender of the body, especially with regard to obesity and painfully invasive body-sculpting as described by Blum (2003) in her *Flesh Wounds: The Culture of Cosmetic Surgery.*

6. For example, regarding the struggles of multi-part-time work in the United Kingdom, see "Work Doesn't Pay for Multi-Part-Time Employees" (2013).

7. Of course, we are neither our jobs nor human capital—but the neoliberal fantasy of work would like us to see ourselves in this manner. And to paraphrase Gilles Deleuze, once you're trapped in the fantasy of the other (or human capital) you're fucked. Something deeply inhuman is intrinsic to human capital.

8. This point is often missed in even the most strident criticisms of neoliberalism, like those leveled by Mirowski (2013: 124) when he avers, "This is how neoliberalism works." In fact, it does not work at all and was never designed to.

9. Also see Curtis's (2012) *Idiotism: Capitalism and the Privatization of Life,* where he argues that the anti-cooperative nature of neoliberalism leads to idiotic decisions and statements.

10. In this sense, along the biocratic dimension of capitalist hegemony, managers too are subject to the forces of exploitation and neoliberal disar-

ray, while of course much better paid. The proposition that managers are not workers like the rest of us, therefore, ought to be treated with caution.

11. The corporation has historically been antithetical to free markets, as Braudel's (1982) and Arrighi's (1994) discussions of *contre-marché* reveal. Neoliberal preaching about the corporation's central role in promoting free markets seems even more ludicrous in light of the historical evidence.

12. In this regard, I completely agree with Graeber's (2011) argument that a critique of capitalism must not rule out the idea of the market per se, since it was useful for serving collective needs long before the appearance of capitalism (also see K. Polanyi [1944] 2002). But the very concept of a market—its political and social function—must now be radically rethought, inclusive of different values and registers of social experience. I am not sure the idea of market communism quite does this.

13. This idea is slowly emerging in conservative analysis as well, as Bremmer's (2013) *The End of the Free Market* indicates. How it will gel with the putative abhorrence neoliberalism has for the state will be fascinating to observe.

14. For an extended analysis, see Muttitt's (2011) excellent *Fuel on the Fire: Oil and Politics in Occupied Iraq*.

15. See William Davies's excellent essay on "After Markets" (2012). He refers to the way in which the U.K. government stepped in to regulate the price of alcohol. This is not a trivial thing because

> by this definition, a society in which it is illegal to sell a bottle of wine for £4.50, no matter how profitable it is to do so, nor how much demand there is for it, is no longer a neoliberal society. A different set of assumptions is built into such a policy. Unlike so-called "sin taxes" that governments have long levied on tobacco and alcohol as a morally righteous way to increase their own revenue, a state-enforced price has no fiscal rationale, other than the longer-term reduction of health spending. Evidently, it is no longer assumed that individuals are necessarily the best judges of their own welfare. And although a price still exists, it is no longer set only by the magical forces of supply and demand. Expert decree now has a place. To put this another way, policymakers are recognizing that there is a limit to how much consumer freedom we can cope with.

16. As Morin (2013: 61) also points out in *A World without Wall Street?* "We are therefore in the presence of a privileged caste which appropriates a major part of the resources of 6.7 billion people. This caste constitutes the 'new aristocracy.'"

17. One way this self-destructive neoliberal paradigm compels us to work even harder is to ideologically invert the temptation to rest or relax. Now *non-activity* is seen to be self-destructive, as one overworked temp-employee in-

terviewed by Brooks stated: "There's a very self-destructive tendency to just relax, not look for that other job until you have had a couple of days to relax" (2012: 127–128).

18. This phrase was wonderfully coined by Mark Fisher after he heard me present on the connections between nihilism and neoliberal class politics.

19. In relation to the media and the multinational firm, see Dan Hind's (2010) analysis in his thoughtful *The Return of the Public.*

20. Abbas (2012: 11) perfectly captures the dynamics of this lie as truth when he recounts an old Freudian joke about a conversation between two men: "Where are you going?" asked one. "To Cracow," was the answer. "What a liar you are!" broke out the other. "If you say you're going to Cracow, you want me to believe you're going to Lemberg. But I know that in fact you're going to Cracow. So why are you lying to me?"

21. Here, of course, I am thinking of Lukács ([1923] 1971). Perhaps another book remains to be written on updating his concept of totality in light of the bioproletariat's position within the late capitalist situation.

# References

Abbas, A. 2012. "Adorno and the Weather: Critical Theory in the Era of Climate Change." *Radical Philosophy* 174:7–14.

Abrahamson, E. 1997. "The Emergence and Prevalence of Employee Management Rhetorics: The Effects of Long Waves, Labor Unions, and Turnover, 1875 to 1992." *Academy of Management Journal* 40:491–533.

———. 2011. "The Iron Cage: Ugly, Uncool and Unfashionable." *Organization Studies* 32 (5): 615–629.

Absensour, M. 2011. *Democracy against the State.* Cambridge, UK: Polity.

Ackroyd, S., and P. A. Crowdy. 1990. "Can Culture Be Managed? Working with 'Raw' Material: The Case of the English Slaughtermen." *Personnel Review* 19 (5): 3–13.

Ackroyd, S., and P. Thompson. 1999. *Organizational Misbehaviour.* London: Sage.

Adler, P. S., and B. Borys. 1996. "Two Types of Bureaucracy: Enabling and Coercive." *Administrative Science Quarterly* 41 (1): 61–89.

Agamben, G. 1998. *Homo Sacer: Sovereign Power and Bare Life.* Stanford, CA: Stanford University Press.

———. 2000. *Means without Ends: Notes on Politics.* Minneapolis: University of Minnesota Press.

"Age of the Permanent Intern, The." 2013. *The Washingtonian,* 6 February. Available at http://www.washingtonian.com/articles/people/the-age-of-the-permanent-in.

Albert, M. 2003. *Parecon: Life after Capitalism.* London: Verso.

Altucher, J. 2013. "Ten Reasons Why You Have to Quit Your Job This Year." *Huffington Post*, 5 April. Available at http://www.huffingtonpost.com/james-altucher/10-reasons-to-quit-your-job_b_3020829.html.

Alvesson, M., and H. Willmott. 1992. "On the Idea of Emancipation in Management and Organization Studies." *Academy of Management Review* 17 (3): 432–464.

Aon Hewitt. 2012. "2012 Trends in Global Employee Engagement." Available at http://www.aon.com/attachments/human-capital consulting/2012_TrendsInGlobalEngagement_Final_v11.pdf.

Aronowitz, S., and W. DiFazio. 2010. *The Jobless Future.* 2nd ed. Minneapolis: University of Minnesota Press.

Arrighi, G. 1994. *The Long Twentieth Century: Money, Power, and the Origins of Our Times.* London: Verso Books.

Augustine. 1961. *Confessions.* London: Penguin.

Bageant, J. 2007. *Deer Hunting with Jesus: Dispatches from America's Class War.* Melbourne, Australia: Scribe.

Bains, Gurnek, et al. 2007. *Meaning Inc.: The Blueprint for Business Success in the 21st Century.* London: Profile Books.

Bakan, J. 2005. *The Corporation: The Pathological Pursuit of Profit and Power.* New York: Free Press.

Barker, A., and A. Niven. 2012. "An Interview with Terry Eagleton." *Oxonian Review* 19 (4). Available at http://www.oxonianreview.org/wp/an-interview-with-terry-eagleton/.

Barker, J. R. 1993. "Tightening the Iron Cage: Concertive Control in Self-Managing Teams." *Administrative Science Quarterly* 38 (4): 408–437.

Barley, S. R., and G. Kunda. 1992. "Design and Devotion: Surges of Rational and Normative Ideologies of Control in Managerial Discourse." *Administrative Science Quarterly* 37:363–399.

Barnes, P. 2006. *Capitalism 3.0: A Guide for Reclaiming the Commons.* San Francisco: Berrett-Koehl.

Baudelaire, C. (1869) 1970. *Paris Spleen.* New York: New Direction Books.

Baudrillard, J. 2007. *In the Shadow of the Silent Majorities.* Los Angeles: Semiotext(e).

———. 2010. *The Agony of Power.* Los Angeles: Semiotex(e).

Becker, G. 1976. *The Economic Approach to Human Behavior.* Chicago: University of Chicago Press.

Beder, S. 2009. *This Little Kiddy Went to Market.* London: Pluto Press.

Bendix, R. 1956. *Work and Authority in Industry: Managerial Ideologies in the Course of Industrialization.* Hoboken, NJ: John Wiley and Sons.

Bensman, J., and I. Gerver. 1962. "Crime and Punishment in the Factory: The Function of Deviancy in Maintaining the Social System." *American Sociological Review* 28 (4): 588–598.

Berle, A., and G. Means. 1932. *The Modern Corporation and Private Property.* New York: Harcourt, Brace and World.

Beynon, H. 1973. *Working for Ford.* London: Allen Lane.

Black, B. 1985. *The Abolition of Work and Other Essays.* Port Townsend, WA: Loompanics Unlimited.

Blau, P. 1955. *The Dynamics of Bureaucracy.* Chicago: University of Chicago Press.

Blum, V. 2003. *Flesh Wounds: The Culture of Cosmetic Surgery.* Los Angeles: University of California Press.

Boltanski, L., and E. Chiapello. 2005. *The New Spirit of Capitalism.* London: Verso.

"Border Staff Being Cut Too Fast." 2012. BBC, 12 July. Available at http://www.bbc.co.uk/news/uk-politics-18861902.

Bowman, S. 1996. *The Modern Corporation in American Political Thought: Law, Power and Ideology.* University Park: Pennsylvania State University Press.

Boyle, D. 2013. *Broke: Who Killed the Middle Class?* London: Forth Estate.

Bradley, H., M. Erickson, C. Stephenson, and S. Williams. 2000. *Myths at Work.* Cambridge, UK: Polity.

Bramel, D., and R. Friend. 1981. "Hawthorne: The Myth of the Docile Workers and Class Bias in Psychology." *American Psychologist* 36 (8): 867–878.

Braudel, F. 1982. *The Wheels of Commerce.* New York: Harper and Row.

Braverman, H. 1974. *Labor and Monopoly Capitalism: The Degradation of Work in the Twentieth Century.* New York: Monthly Review Press.

Bremmer, I. 2013. *The End of the Free Market: Who Wins the War between States and Corporations?* New York: Penguin.

Brooks, D. 2011. *The Social Animal.* New York: Random House.

Brooks, R. A. 2012. *Cheaper by the Hour: Temporary Lawyers and the Deprofessionalization of the Law.* Philadelphia: Temple University Press.

"Burnout Is Bigger Heart Attack Risk Than Smoking." 2013. *Metro,* 14 March.

Burrell, G. 1984. "Sex and Organization Analysis." *Organization Studies* 5 (2): 197–218.

Callaghan, G., and P. Thompson. 2002. "'We Recruit Attitude': The Selection and Shaping of Call Centre Labour." *Journal of Management Studies* 39 (2): 233–254.

Casarino, C. 2008. "Surplus Common." In *In Praise of the Common,* by C. Casarino and A. Negri. Minneapolis: University of Minnesota Press.

Cederström, C., and P. Fleming. 2012. *Dead Man Working.* London: Zero Books.

Chandler, A. 1977. *The Visible Hand: The Managerial Revolution in American Business.* New York: Belknap Press.

Chang, H.-J. 2013. "Britain: A Nation in Decay." *The Guardian,* 8 March.

Available at http://www.guardian.co.uk/commentisfree/2013/mar/08/britain-economy-long-term-fix.

Chesworth, N. 2012. "I Really Am a One-Man Band." *Evening Standard*, 26 June.

Chomsky, N. 1991. "On Capitalism—Interviewed by David Finkel." Available at http://www.chomsky.info/interviews/1991----02.htm.

Clastres, P. 1989. *Society against the State.* Trans. Robert Hurley. New York: Zone Books.

Collini, S. 2012. *What Are Universities For?* London: Penguin.

Collins, H. M. 2001. "Tacit Knowledge, Trust and the Q of Sapphire." *Social Studies of Science* 31 (1): 71–85.

Collinson, D. 1992. *Managing the Shop Floor: Subjectivity, Masculinity and Workplace Culture.* Berlin: De Gruyter.

Cooper, M. 2008. *Life as Surplus: Biotechnology and Capitalism in the Neoliberal Era.* Seattle: University of Washington Press.

Coser, L. 1974. *Greedy Institutions: Patterns in Undivided Commitment.* New York: Free Press.

Costas, J., and P. Fleming. 2009. "Beyond Dis-identification: Towards a Discursive Approach to Self-Alienation in Contemporary Organizations." *Human Relations* 62 (3): 353–378.

Courpasson, D. 2006. *Soft Constraint, Liberal Organizations and Domination.* Copenhagen: Liber and Copenhagen Business School Press.

Court, J. 2003. *Corporateering: How Corporate Power Steals Your Personal Freedom.* New York: Penguin.

Cowie, J. 2010. *Stayin' Alive: The 1970s and the Last Days of the Working Class.* New York: New Press.

Crouch, C. 2011. *The Strange Non-death of Neo-liberalism.* Cambridge, UK: Polity.

Crozier, M. 1964. *The Bureaucratic Phenomenon.* Chicago: University of Chicago Press.

Curtis, N. 2012. *Idiotism: Capitalism and the Privatization of Life.* London: Pluto Press.

Davies, W. 2012. "After Markets." *Aeon Magazine.* Available at http://www.aeonmagazine.com/living-together/after-neoliberalism/.

Davis, M., and D. B. Monk. 2007. *Evil Paradises: Dreamworlds of Neoliberalism.* New York: New Press.

Deal, T., and A. Kennedy. 1982. *Corporate Cultures: The Rites and Rituals of Corporate Life.* New York: Perseus Books.

"Death Surge Linked with Mass Privatization." 2009. Oxford University Press release. Available at http://www.ox.ac.uk/media/news_stories/2009/090115.html.

Deleuze, G. 2004. "On Capitalism and Desire." In *Desert Islands and Other Texts: 1953–1974.* Los Angeles: Semiotext(e).

———. 2006. *Foucault*. New York: Continuum.

Deleuze, G., and F. Guattari. 1987. *A Thousand Plateaus: Capitalism and Schizophrenia*. Trans. B. Massumi. Minneapolis: University of Minnesota Press.

———. 2004. *Anti-Oedipus*. London: Continuum.

Djelic, M. L. 2013. "When Limited Liability Was (Still) an Issue: Mobilization and Politics of Signification in 19th Century England." *Organization Studies* 3 (5): 595–621.

Doogan, K. 2009. *New Capitalism? The Transformation of Work*. Cambridge, UK: Polity.

Drucker, P. 1946. *The Concept of the Corporation*. New York: John Day.

———. 1993. *Post-capitalist Society*. New York: HarperBusiness.

Duménil, G., and D. Lévy. 2004. *Capital Resurgent: Roots of the Neoliberal Revolution*. Trans. Derek Jeffers. Cambridge, MA: Harvard University Press.

———. 2011. *The Crisis of Neoliberalism*. Cambridge, MA: Harvard University Press.

Edwards, R. 1979. *Contested Terrain: The Transformation of the Workplace in the Twentieth Century*. New York: Basic Books.

Ehrenberg, A. 2010. *The Weariness of the Self*. Montreal: McGill-Queens University Press.

Ehrenreich, B. 2006. *Bait and Switch: The Futile Pursuit of the Corporate Dream*. London: Granta Books.

Eidelson, J. 2013. "Will 'Alt-Labor' Replace Unions?" *Salon*, 29 January. Available at http://www.salon.com/2013/01/29/will_alt_labor_replace_unions_labor/.

Escape the City. 2012. *The Escape Manifesto: Quit Your Corporate Job, Do Something Different*. London: Capstone.

Esposito, R. 2008. *Bios: Biopolitics and Philosophy*. Minneapolis: Minnesota University Press.

Felstead, A., N. Jewson, and S. Walters. 2005. *Changing Places of Work*. London: Palgrave.

Fincher, D. (director). 1999. *Fight Club*. Film. Regency Enterprises.

Fisher, M. 2009. *Capitalist Realism: Is There No Alternative?* London: Zero Books.

Fleming, P. 2009. *Authenticity and the Cultural Politics of Work*. Oxford: Oxford University Press.

Fleming, P., and M. Jones. 2013. *The End of Corporate Social Responsibility*. London: Sage.

Fleming, P., and A. Sturdy. 2011. "Being Yourself in the Electronic Sweatshop: New Forms of Normative Control." *Human Relations* 64 (2): 177–200.

Fletcher, J. 2001. *Disappearing Acts: Generation, Power and Relational Practice at Work*. Boston: MIT Press.

Fligstein, N. 1990. *The Transformation of Corporate Control.* Cambridge, MA: Harvard University Press.

Florida, R. 2004a. *Cities and the Creative Class.* New York: Routledge.

———. 2004b. *The Rise of the Creative Class.* New York: Basic Books.

Foster, J. B., and R. W. McChesney. 2012. *The Endless Crisis: How Monopoly-Finance Capital Produces Stagnation and Upheaval from the USA to China.* New York: Monthly Review Press.

Foster, R., and S. Kaplan. 2001. *Creative Destruction: Why Companies That Are Built to Last Underperform the Market—and How to Successfully Transform Them.* New York: Crown Business.

Foucault, M. 1977. *Discipline and Punish: The Birth of the Prison.* London: Penguin.

———. 1978. *History of Sexuality. Volume 1, An Introduction.* London: Allen Lane.

———. (1982) 1997. "Michel Foucault: An Interview with Stephen Riggins." In *Ethics: Subjectivity and Truth (Essential Works of Michel Foucault, 1954–1984),* by Michel Foucault. Ed. P. Rabinow. New York: Penguin.

———. 2001. *Fearless Speech.* Los Angeles: Semiotext(e).

———. 2008. *The Birth of Biopolitics: Lectures at the Collège de France, 1978–1979.* London: Palgrave.

———. 2011. *The Courage of Truth: Lectures at the Collège de France, 1983–1984.* London: Palgrave.

"Four in Ten Female Officers Have Considered Quitting the Force." 2012. *The Guardian,* 14 July.

Frank, T. 2005. *What's the Matter with Kansas? How the Conservatives Won the Heart of America.* New York: Holt McDougal.

Freeland, G. 2012. *Plutocrats: The Rise of the Global Super Rich.* New York: Allen Lane.

Friedman, A. 1977. *Labor and Industry: Class Struggle at Work and Monopoly Capitalism.* London: Mcmillan.

Friedman, T. 1999. *The Lexus and the Olive Tree.* New York: Picador.

Gillespie, R. 1991. *Manufacturing Knowledge: A History of the Hawthorne Experiments.* Cambridge, UK: Cambridge University Press.

Gillick, L. 2009. "The Good of Work." In *Are You Working Too Much?* ed. J. Aranda, B. Wood, and A. Vidokle. London: Sternberg Press.

Goffman, E. 1961. *Asylums: Essays on the Social Situation of Mental Patients and Other Inmates.* New York: Anchor.

Gordon, D. 1996. *Fat and Mean: The Corporate Squeeze of Working Americana and the Myth of Managerial "Down Sizing."* New York: Martin Kessler Books.

Gorz, A. 1989. *Critique of Economic Rationality.* London: Verso.

———. 2005. *Reclaiming Work.* Cambridge, UK: Polity.

————. 2010. *Immaterial*. London: Seagull Books.

Gouldner, A. 1954. *Patterns of Industrial Bureaucracy: A Case Study of Modern Factory Administration*. New York: Free Press.

Graeber, D. 2011. *Debt: The First Five Thousand Years*. London: Melville.

Grassman, P. R. 2012. "The Economy of Dissociation: Organizing Identity through Loss, Jouissance and the Virtual." Ph.D. diss., University of the West of England.

Greece Solidarity Campaign. 2013. "Factory in Greece Starts Production under Workers' Control." Available at http://eagainst.com/articles/factory-in-greece-starts-production-under-workers-control.

Green, F. 2007. *Demanding Work: The Paradox of Job Quality in an Affluent Economy*. Princeton, NJ: Princeton University Press.

Gregg, M. 2011. *Work's Intimacy*. Cambridge, UK: Polity.

Grenier, G. 1987. *Inhuman Relations: Quality Circles and Anti-unionism in American Industry*. Philadelphia: Temple University Press.

Grey, C. 1999. "We Are All Managers Now; We Always Were: On the Emergence and Demise of Management." *Journal of Management Studies* 36:561–586.

Gross, E. 1956. "Review of Work and Authority in Industry." *American Sociological Review* 21 (4): 789–791.

Gulati, D. 2012. "How to (Finally) Quit Your Job." *Harvard Business Review*, 12 July. Blog. Available at http://blogs.hbr.org/cs/2012/07/how_to_finally_quit_your_job.html.

Habermas, J. 1987. *The Theory of Communicative Action*. Vol. 2. *Lifeworld and System*. Cambridge, UK: Polity.

Haiven, M. 2013. "Finance Depends on Resistance, Finance Is Resistance, and Anyway, Resistance Is Futile." *Mediations* 26, nos. 1–2. Available at http://www.mediationsjournal.org/articles/finance-depends-on-resistance.

Hamper, B. 1992. *Rivethead: Tales from the Assembly Line*. New York: Warner Books.

Hanlon, G. 2013. "From Profit to Rent: The Google Model of Production." Working paper, Queen Mary College, University of London.

Hardt, M. 2010a. "The Common in Communism." In *The Idea of Communism*, ed. Costas Douzinas and Slavoj Žižek. London: Verso.

————. 2010b. "Militant Life." *New Left Review* 64:151–160.

Hardt, M., and A. Negri. 1994. *The Labor of Dionysus: A Critique of the State Form*. Minneapolis: University of Minnesota Press.

————. 1999. *Empire*. Cambridge, MA: Harvard University Press.

————. 2009. *Commonwealth*. Cambridge, MA: Harvard University Press.

Harman, C. 2009. *Zombie Capitalism: Global Crisis and the Relevance of Marx*. London: Bookmarks.

Harney, S., and C. Oswick. 2007. "Regulation and Freedom in Global Business Education." *International Journal of Sociology and Social Policy* 26 (3/4): 97–109.

Harvey, D. 2001. *Spaces of Hope: Towards a Critical Geography.* Edinburgh: University of Edinburgh Press.

———. 2012. *Rebel Cities: From the Right to the City to the Urban Revolution.* London: Verso.

Hayden, C. 2003. *When Nature Goes Public.* Princeton, NJ: Princeton University Press.

Himanen, P. 2001. *The Hacker Ethic and the Spirit of the Information Age.* New York: Random House.

Hind, D. 2010. *The Return of the Public.* London: Verso.

Hirschman, A. O. 1997. *The Passions and the Interests: Political Arguments for Capitalism before Its Triumph.* Princeton, NJ: Princeton University Press.

Hobbes, T. (1651) 2010. *Leviathan.* London: Penguin.

Hochschild, A. 1997. *Time Bind: When Work Becomes Home and Home Becomes Work.* New York: Owl Books.

Holland, E. 2011. *Nomad Citizenship: Free-Market Communism and the Slow Motion General Strike.* Minneapolis: University of Minnesota Press.

Honneth, A. 1996. *The Struggle for Recognition.* Cambridge, MA: MIT Press.

Howker, E., and S. Malik. 2013. *Jilted Generation: How Britain Has Bankrupted Its Youth.* London: Icon Books.

Hyde, L. 2011. *Common as Air.* New York: Farrar, Straus and Giroux.

Illouz, E. 2007. *Cold Intimacies: The Making of Emotional Capitalism.* Cambridge, UK: Polity.

Institute for Experimental Freedom. 2009. *Politics Is Not a Banana.* Available at http://www.infoshop.org/pdfs/politics-banana3.pdf.

Invisible Committee. 2009. *The Coming Insurrection.* Los Angeles: Semiotext(e).

"It's Companies Like G4S That Embody the 'Something for Nothing' Culture." 2012. *New Statesman,* 16 July.

Jacoby, S. M. 1985. *Employing Bureaucracy: Managers, Unions and the Transformation of Work in American Industry.* New York: Columbia University Press.

Jacques, R. 1996. *Manufacturing the Employee: Managing Knowledge from the 19th to the 21st Centuries.* London: Sage.

Jameson, F. 2011. *Representing Capital: A Reading of Volume One.* London: Verso.

"Jinxed Generation's Plight Worsening." 2012. *Financial Times,* 12 December. Available at Timeshttp://www.ft.com/cms/s/0/a2f9471e-1f6e-11e2-b273-00144feabdc0.html#axzz2kzN5qqZK.

Jones, B. E. 2012. *Women Who Opt Out.* New York: New York University Press.

Joseph, M. 2002. *Against the Romance of Community.* Minneapolis: University of Minnesota Press.

Kakabadse, A., and N. Kakabadse. 2004. *Intimacy: An International Survey of the Sex Lives of People at Work.* London: Palgrave.

Kelly, M. 2001. *The Divine Right of Capital: Dethroning the Corporate Aristocracy.* San Francisco: Berrett-Koehler.

Kolowratnik, N. V., and M. Miessen. 2012. *Waking Up from the Nightmare of Participation.* Utrecht, Neth.: Expodium.

Kordela, A. K. 2007. *$urplus: Spinoza, Lacan.* New York: State University of New York Press.

Korten, D. 1995. *When Corporations Rule the World.* New York: Berrett-Koehler.

Krippner, G. 2011. *Capitalizing on Crisis: The Political Origins of the Rise of Finance.* Cambridge, MA: Harvard University Press.

Kücklich, J. 2005. "FCJ-025 Precarious Playbour: Modders and the Digital Games Industry." *Fibre Culture Journal.* Available at http://five.fibreculturejournal.org/fcj-025-precarious-playbour-modders-and-the-digital-games-industry/.

Kuhn, T. 2006. "A 'Demented Work Ethic' and a 'Lifestyle Firm': Discourse, Identity, and Workplace Time Commitments." *Organization Studies* 27 (9): 1339–1358.

Kunda, G. 1992. *Engineering Culture: Control and Commitment in a High-Tech Corporation.* Philadelphia: Temple University Press.

Land, C., and S. Böhm. 2012. "'From Whom Does Facebook Extract Exchange Value?" Organizations, Occupations and Work: A Section of the American Sociological Association (blog). Available at http://oowsection.org/2012/03/03/from-whom-does-facebook-extract-exchange-value/.

Land, C., and S. Taylor. 2010. "Surf's Up: Life, Balance and Brand in a New Age Capitalist Organization." *Sociology* 44 (3): 395–413.

Lash, S., and C. Lury. 2007. *The Global Culture Industry.* Cambridge, UK: Polity.

Lave, J., and E. Wenger. 1991. *Situated Learning: Legitimate Peripheral Participation.* Cambridge, UK: Cambridge University Press.

Lazzarato, M. 1996. "Immaterial Labor." In *Radical Thought in Italy: A Potential Politics,* ed. Paulo Virno and Michael Hardt. Minneapolis: University of Minnesota Press.

"Learning How to Vacation." 2012. *New York Times,* 15 July.

"Lessons in Leadership." 2008. University of Southern California, 9 October. Available at http://www.youtube.com/watch?v=OBMZIBuFbSI.

Lifton, R. 1986. *The Nazi Doctors: Medical Killing and the Psychology of Genocide.* New York: Basic Books.

Linebaugh, P. 2006. *The London Hanged: Crime and Civil Society in the Eighteenth Century.* London: Verso.

Liu, A. 2004. *The Laws of Cool: Knowledge Work and the Culture of Information.* Chicago: University of Chicago Press.

Lucas, R. E. 1972. "Expectations and the Neutrality of Money." *Journal of Economic Theory* 4 (2): 103–124.

———. 1988. "On the Mechanics of Economic Development." *Journal of Monetary Economics* 22 (1): 3–42.

Lucas, Rob. 2010. "Dreaming in Code." *New Left Review* 62:125–132.

Lukács, G. (1923) 1971. *History and Class Consciousness: Studies in Marxist Dialectics.* London: Merlin Press.

Lukes, S. 2005. *Power: A Radical View.* 2nd ed. London: Macmillan.

Lustig, J. 1979. *Corporate Liberalism: The Origins of American Political Theory, 1890–1920.* New York: Praeger.

Marcuse, H. 1964. *One-Dimensional Man: Studies in the Ideology of Advanced Industrial Society.* New York: Beacon Press.

Marglin, S. 1974. "What Do Bosses Do? The Origins and Functions of Hierarchy in Capitalist Production." *Review of Radical Political Economics* 6:60–112.

Mars, G. 1982. *Cheats at Work: An Anthropology of Workplace Crime.* London: George Allen and Unwin.

Marszalek, B. 2012. "The Meaning of Mondragon." Available at http://www.counterpunch.org/2012/07/13/the-meaning-of-mondragon.

Martin, R. 2002. *The Financialization of Daily Life.* Philadelphia: Temple University Press.

Marx, K. (1844) 2013. "Comments on James Mill, *Éléments D'économie Politique*," ed. anonymous. Available at http://www.marxists.org/archive/marx/works/1844/james-mill/index.htm.

———. (1847) 2008. *Wage Labor and Capital.* Rockville, MD: Wildside Press.

———. (1858) 1973. *Grundrisse.* London: Penguin.

———. (1867) 1972. *Capital.* Vol. 1. London: Penguin.

———. (1894) 1981. *Capital.* Vol. 3. Trans. David Fernbach. London: Penguin.

"Masters of Money: Karl Marx." 2012. *BBC Television Two.* Available at http://www.youtube.com/watch?v=Obh2LZpkQOE.

Mayer, C. 2013. *Firm Commitment: Why the Corporation Is Failing Us and How to Restore Trust in It.* Oxford, UK: Oxford University Press.

Mazzucato, M. 2013. *The Entrepreneurial State: Debunking the Public vs. Private Sectors Myth.* London: Anthem Press.

McDermott, R., and D. Archibald. 2010. "Harnessing Your Staff's Informal Networks." *Harvard Business Review* 88:18–21.

Menacherry, M. (director). 2012. *The Rat Race.* Film. Filament Pictures.

Meyerson, D. 2011. *Tempered Radicals: How People Use Difference to Inspire Change at Work.* Cambridge, MA: Harvard Business School Press.

Michel, A. 2012. "Transcending Socialization: A Nine-Year Ethnography of the Body's Role in Organizational Control and Knowledge Workers Transformation." *Administrative Science Quarterly* 56 (3): 325–368.

Mieville, C. 2012. *London's Overthrow.* London: Westbourne Press.

Milkman, R., J. Bloom, and N. Narro. 2010. *Working for Justice.* Ithaca, NY: ILR Press.

Mirowski, P. 2013. *Never Let a Serious Crisis Go to Waste: How Neoliberalism Survived the Financial Meltdown.* London: Verso.

Monbiot, G. 2011. "Academic Publishers Make Murdoch Look like a Socialist." *The Guardian,* 29 August.

———. 2013a. "EDF's Vengeful £5m 'No Dash for Gas' Lawsuit Corporate and PR Suicide." *The Guardian,* 28 February.

———. 2013b. "If You Think We're Done with Neoliberalism, Think Again." *The Guardian,* 14 January.

Montgomery, D. 1988. *The Fall of the House of Labor: The Workplace, the State, and American Labor Activism, 1865–1925.* Cambridge, UK: Cambridge University Press.

Moore, M. (director). 2009. *Capitalism: A Love Story.* Film. The Weinstein Company, Dog Eat Dog Films.

Morin, F. 2013. *A World without Wall Street?* London: Seagull Books.

Moten, F., and S. Harney. 2012. "Blackness and Governance." In *Beyond Biopolitics: Essays on the Governance of Life and Death,* ed. P. T. Clough and C. Willse. Durham, NC: Duke University Press.

Muttitt, G. 2011. *Fuel on the Fire: Oil and Politics in Occupied Iraq.* London: Bodley Head.

Nancy, J. L. 1991. *The Inoperative Community.* Trans. Michael Hardt. Minneapolis: University of Minnesota Press.

———. 2000. *Being Singular Plural.* Stanford, CA: Stanford University Press.

Negri, A. 1991. *The Savage Anomaly: The Power of Spinoza's Metaphysics and Politics.* Trans. M. Hardt. Minneapolis: University of Minnesota Press.

———. 2008. "Vicissitudes of Constituent Thought." In *In Praise of the Common,* by C. Casarino and A. Negri. Minneapolis: University of Minnesota Press.

———. 2009. *The Labor of Job.* Trans. M. Mandarini. Durham, NC: Duke University Press.

Nelson, M., H. Paek, and M. Rademacher. 2007. "Downshifting Consumer, Upshifting Citizen? An Examination of a Local Freecycle Community." *ANNALS of the American Academy of Political and Social Science* 611: 141–156.

Nietzsche, F. 1966. *Beyond Good and Evil.* Trans. Walter Kaufman. New York: Vintage.

———. 1974. *Gay Science.* Trans. R. J. Hollingdale. New York: Vintage.

Nonaka, I., and G. von Krogh. 2009. "Tacit Knowledge and Knowledge Conversion: Controversy and Advancement in Organizational Knowledge Creation Theory." *Organization Science* 20 (3): 635–652.

O'Reilly, C., and J. Chatman. 1996. "Culture as Social Control: Corporations, Cults, and Commitment." In *Research in Organizational Behavior,* ed. B. Staw and L. Cummings. Greenwich, CT: JAI Press.

Orr, J. 1996. *Talking about Machines: An Ethnography of a Modern Job.* New York: Cornell University Press.

Panitch, L., and Gindin, S. 2012. *The Making of Global Capitalism: The Political Economy of American Empire.* London: Verso.

Panzieri, R. (1961) 2009. "The Capitalist Uses of Machinery: Marx versus the Objectivists." Available at http://operaismoinenglish.files.wordpress.com/2010/09/capitalist-use-machinery.pdf.

Papadopoulos, D., N. Stephenson, and V. Tsianos. 2008. *Escape Routes: Control and Subversion in the 21st Century.* London: Pluto Press.

Parker, M. 2000. *Organizational Culture and Identity.* London: Sage.

Patel, R. 2011. *The Value of Nothing: How to Reshape Market Society and Redefine Democracy.* London: Portobello Books.

Perelman, M. 2002. *Steal This Idea: Intellectual Property Rights and the Corporate Confiscation of Creativity.* New York: Palgrave.

———. 2006. *Railroading Economics: The Creation of Free Market Mythology.* New York: Monthly Review Press.

———. 2011. *The Invisible Handcuffs of Capitalism: How Market Tyranny Stifles the Economy by Stunting Workers.* New York: Monthly Review Press.

Perlin, R. 2011. *Intern Nation: How to Earn Nothing and Learn Little in the Brave New Economy.* London: Verso.

Perrow, C. 2002. *Organizing America: Wealth, Power, and the Origins of Corporate Capitalism.* Princeton, NJ: Princeton University Press.

Peters, T. 1994. *The Tom Peters Seminar: Crazy Times Call for Crazy Organizations.* London: Macmillan.

———. 2003. *Re-imagine! Business Excellence in a Disruptive Age.* London: Dorling Kindersley.

Peters, T., and R. H. Waterman. 1982. *In Search of Excellence.* New York: Harper and Row.

"Petitions and Remonstrances Relating to Amherst Carriage Company. Remonstrance of George W. Cushing & others, journeymen carriage makers, against a petition of Robert C. Kid and others to be incorporated as the Amherst Carriage Company." 1838. Massachusetts Legislator. Archival document available at Harvard University, Houghton Library.

Pink, D. 2011. *Drive: The Surprising Truth about What Motivates Us.* London: Cannon Gate.

Polanyi, K. (1944) 2002. *The Great Transformation: The Political and Economic Origins of Our Time.* New York: Beacon Press.

Polanyi, M. 1966. *The Tacit Dimension.* Garden City, NY: Doubleday.

Porter, M., and M. Kramer. 2011. "Creating Shared Value." *Harvard Business Review,* Spring, 3–17.

"Professor Ngaire Woods—IMF Have Learnt Lessons from Austerity." 2013.

BBC, 7 January. Available at http://news.bbc.co.uk/today/hi/today/news id_9782000/9782405.stm.

Quiggin, J. 2010. *Zombie Economics: How Dead Ideas Still Walk among Us.* Princeton, NJ: Princeton University Press.

Quinn, B. 2005. *How Wal-Mart Is Destroying America (and the World).* New York: Ten Speed Press.

"Radical Tilt at Governance Failures, A." 2013. *Financial Times,* 25 March.

Ramaswamy, V., and F. Gouillart. 2010. "Building the Co-creative Enterprise." *Harvard Business Review,* 11–21 October.

Ramsay, H. 1977. "Cycles of Control: Worker Participation in Sociological and Historical Perspective." *Sociology* 11 (3): 481–506.

Reich, R. 1992. *The Work of Nations: Preparing Ourselves for 21st Century Capitalism.* New York: Vintage.

Ressler, C., and J. Thompson. 2011. *Why Work Sucks and How to Fix It: The Results Only Revolution.* New York: Portfolio.

Rice, C. "Why Women Leave Academia and Why Universities Should Be Worried." 2012. *The Guardian,* 24 May.

Rifkin, J. 1995. *The End of Work.* New York: Putnam Publishing Group.

———. 2000. *The Age of Access: How the Change from Ownership to Access Is Changing Everything.* London: Penguin.

"Ripped Off Britons." 2013. Blog. Available at http://www.blog.rippedoffbritons.com/2013/03/outsourcing-public-services-case-of.html.

Robin, M.-M. (director). 2008. *The World according to Monsanto.* Film. National Film Board of Canada.

Robins, N. 2006. *The Corporation That Changed the World: How the East India Company Shaped the Modern Multinational.* London: Pluto.

Robinson-Tillett, S., and C. Menon. 2013. "Work Doesn't Pay for Multi-Part-Time Employees." *The Guardian,* 13 April.

Ross, A. 2004. *No-Collar: The Humane Workplace and Its Hidden Costs.* Philadelphia: Temple University Press.

Roy, D. 1952. "Quota Restriction and Goldbricking in a Machine Shop." *American Journal of Sociology* 57 (5): 427–442.

Runciman, D. 2013. "Stiffed." *London Review of Books* 34 (20): 7–9.

Sam, A. 2009. *Checkout.* London: Gallic Books.

Scase, R., and R. Goffee. 1989. *Reluctant Managers.* London: Routledge.

Schein, E. 1985. *Organizational Culture and Leadership.* New York: Jossey-Bass.

Schor, J. 1993. *The Overworked American: The Unexpected Decline of Leisure.* New York: Basic Books.

Schrader, D. 1993. *The Corporation as Anomaly.* Cambridge, UK: Cambridge University Press.

Seidman, M. 1991. *Workers against Work: Labor in Paris and Barcelona during the Popular Fronts.* Berkeley: University of California Press.

Sellers, C. 1991. *The Market Revolution.* New York: Oxford University Press.

Semler, R. 2007. *The Seven-Day Weekend.* New York: Penguin.

Senge, P. 1990. *The Fifth Discipline.* New York: Doubleday.

Sennett, R. 2006. *The New Culture of Capitalism.* London: Penguin.

———. 2009. *The Craftsman.* London: Penguin.

———. 2012. *Together: The Rituals, Pleasures and Politics of Co-operation.* New York: Allen and Lane.

Shaxson, N. 2012. *Treasure Islands: Tax Havens and the Men Who Stole the World.* London: Vintage.

Shenhav, Y. 2002. *Manufacturing Rationality: The Engineering Foundations of the Managerial Revolution.* Oxford, UK: Oxford University Press.

Shershow, S. C. 2004. *The Work and the Gift.* Chicago: University of Chicago Press.

Shiva, V. 2011. *Biopiracy: The Plunder of Nature and Knowledge.* New Delhi: Natraj Publishers.

Silver, B. 2003. *Forces of Labor: Workers' Movements and Globalization since 1870.* Cambridge: Cambridge University Press.

Simms, A. 2007. *Tescopoly: How One Shop Came Out on Top and Why It Matters.* London: Constable.

Socialist Patients Collective. 1972. *Turn Illness into a Weapon.* Heidelberg, Germ.: Krrim.

Southwood, I. 2011. *Non-stop Inertia.* London: Zero.

Spicer, A., and M. Alvesson. 2012. "A Stupidity-Based Theory of Organizations." *Journal of Management Studies* 49 (7): 1194–1220.

Spinoza, B. (1677) 1996. *Ethics.* Trans. Edwin Curley. London: Penguin.

Stout, L. 2012. *The Shareholder Value Myth: How Putting Shareholders First Harms Investors, Corporations, and the Public.* San Francisco: Berrett-Koehler.

Stuckler, D., and D. Basu. 2013. *The Body Economic: Why Austerity Kills.* London: Allen Lane.

Svendsen, L. 2008. *Work.* Durham, UK: Acumen.

Tapscott, D., and A. Williams. 2008. *Wikinomics: How Mass Collaboration Changes Everything.* London: Atlantic Books.

Terranova, T. 2003. "Free Labor: Producing Culture for the Digital Economy." *Technocapitalism.* Available at http://www.electronicbookreview .com/thread/technocapitalism/voluntary.

Théorie Communiste. 2012. "Communization in the Present Tense." In *Communization and Its Discontents,* ed. B. Noys. London: Autonomedia.

Thompson, E. P. 1963. *The Making of the English Working Class.* London: Penguin.

Thompson, G. 2010. *Working in the Shadows: A Year of Doing the Jobs Most Americans Won't Do.* New York: Nation Books.

Tiqqun. 2011. *This Is Not a Program*. Trans. D. Jordan. Los Angeles: Semiotext(e).

Transnational Institute in Amsterdam. 2013. "Privatizing Europe: Using the Crisis to Entrench Neoliberalism." Available at http://www.tni.org/sites/ www.tni.org/files/download/privatising_europe.pdf.

Tronti, M. 1966. *Operai i capitale*. Turin, Italy: Einaudi.

———. 1980. "The Strategy of Refusal." In *Autonomia: Post-political Politics*, ed. S. Lotringer and C. Marazzi. New York: Semiotext(e).

"27% of Spaniards Are Out of Work: Yet in One Town Everyone Has a Job." 2013. *The Independent*, 12 May.

"UK Unemployment Rises to 2.52 Million." 2013. BBC, 15 May. Available at http://www.bbc.co.uk/news/business-22536437.

Vaneigem, R. 2001. "Totality for Kids." In *Beneath the Paving Stones: Situationalists and the Beach, May 1968,* ed. Dark Star. New York: AK Press.

Virno, P. 2004. *A Grammar of the Multitude: For an Analysis of Contemporary Forms of Life*. Los Angeles: Semiotext(e).

———. 2008. *Multitude: Between Innovation and Negation*. Los Angeles: Semiotex(e).

Von Hippel, E. 2006. *Democratizing Innovation*. Cambridge, MA: MIT Press.

Wadel, C. 1979. "The Hidden Work of Everyday Life." In *Social Anthropology of Work,* ed. S. Wallman. London: Academic Press.

Watson, B. 1971. *Counter-planning on the Shop Floor*. Boston: New England Free Press.

Weber, M. 1946. *From Max Weber: Essays in Sociology*. New York: Oxford University Press.

Weeks, K. 2011. *The Problem of Work: Feminism, Marxism, Anti-work Politics and Postwork Imaginaries*. Durham, NC: Duke University Press.

Whyte, W. F. 1955. *Money and Motivation*. New York: Harper and Row.

———. 1956. *The Organizational Man*. New York: Simon and Schuster.

Willmott, H. 1993. "Strength Is Ignorance; Slavery Is Freedom: Managing Cultures in Modern Organizations." *Journal of Management Studies* 30 (4): 515–552.

Wolff, R. 2012. *Democracy at Work: A Cure for Capitalism*. Chicago: Haymarket Books.

Wright, S. 2002. *Storming Heaven: Class Composition and Struggle in Italian Autonomist Marxism*. London: Pluto.

"You Thought Ryanair Stewards Had It Bad? Wait 'til You Hear about Their Pilots." 2013. *The Independent*, 18 May.

Žižek, S. 1989. *The Sublime Object of Ideology*. London: Verso.

———. 2009. *First as Tragedy, Then as Farce*. London: Verso.

# Index

Abbas, A., 174n20
Abrahamson, E., 76
absenteeism from work, 35, 41, 126
academic institutions, 1, 2, 161n2; free
    labor in, 104; public and private
    interests in, 80, 169–170n6; publish-
    ing in, 169–170n6; retirement from,
    132; strikes in, 124–125
accumulation of capital. *See* capital
    accumulation
Agamben, G., 44, 58
age discrimination, 96
age of work, end of, 156–159
allegiance to firm, 97
Altucher, James, 171n5
Alvesson, M., 151
Amherst Carriage Company, 68–69
*Animal Farm* (Orwell), 90
anonymity of workers, 168–169n9
*Anti-Oedipus* (Deleuze and Guattari),
    171–172n1
Apple iPhones, 170n10
Argentina, recovered factories in,
    20–21, 42
Aronowitz, S., 172n3

Arrighi, G., 173n11
artisans, skilled, early incorporation
    affecting, 69
AT&T, 73
attitudes toward work, 4, 16, 162n9; in
    expression of non-work interests at
    work, 24; as life, 33, 34; as necessity
    (*see* necessity of work); as pointless,
    16, 162n9; regrets about time spent
    at, 144
Augustine, 49–50
authenticity, 96; demand for, 78; in
    management ideology, 143; in non-
    work at work, 24, 33, 93
authority, and identity of community,
    50–51
autonomy, 42, 57, 59–60, 81; of the
    commons, 20, 60, 117; in corporate
    culture, 91; definition of, 59; in
    free time, 10; of living labor, 56,
    141; responsible, 163n1; and self-
    organization in free work capitalism,
    116–118; of skilled artisans, early
    incorporation affecting, 69; Spinoza
    on, 47

class relations, 67–68; antagonism in, 114; in autonomy of the commons, 60; in biopower, 38, 151; in capitalist employment, 17; and control strategies, 72–75; in corporations, 12, 30, 72–75; historical aspects of, 69–70; management function in, 117; in neoliberalism, 6, 19, 29; non-dialectical analysis of, 67; post-industrial, 58; in worker refusal strategies, 56
Clastres, P., 170–171n2
Clinton, Bill, 136
cognitive capitalism, 38, 114, 122, 130
collaboration, profitable business ideas from, 112
Collini, S., 161n2
Collinson, D., 167n1
colonization, corporate, 10
commercialization, 77–81; of public sector, 78–81; of society, 77–78
*Common as Air* (Hyde), 167n14
the commons, 2, 43–61; autonomy of, 20, 60, 117; and biopolitical capitalism, 94; and biopower, 86; and community at work, 17–19; enclosure and capture of, 32, 119, 120; exploitation of, 55, 56, 113–114, 162n6; gender politics affecting, 7; general intellect of, 54–56; intellectual and creative property of, 112–113; materialization of, 56; and neoliberal capitalism, 10, 19, 28; reliance of corporations on, 51; silence of, 138, 143; social excess of, 127
communication: and silence in resistance, 135–144; in workplace dialogue, 100
communism, 112; of capital, 54, 55–56; free market, 153, 173n12; of uselessness, 129
communitarian movement, 50
community, 50–51, 165n3; and *Gemeinschaft*, 50–51; Hobbes on, 46, 47; at work, 17–19, 162n10
*Confessions* (Augustine), 49–50
conformity in corporate culture, 84, 94–95

control and regulation: in biocracy, 104; biopolitical, 35, 87, 95; in biopower, 5, 26–30, 59, 151; in blending of work and non-work, 99; bureaucratic, 74; in capitalism, 5, 6, 30; class character of, 72–75; corporate culture in, 87–88, 89, 90, 92–93; in domination and hegemony, 39–40; evolution of, 67; in Fordism, 29, 92, 98; labor history of, 71–78; by management, 12; management ideology on, 75–78; in materialization of the commons, 56; in neoliberalism, 55, 127; overabundance of, 38; at point of production, 107; resistance to, 125, 127; supervisor monitoring in, 73; surplus regulation in, 36–38; technical, 73–74; tolerance of unsanctioned activities in, 109
Cooper, M., 165n5
cooperation, 17–18, 30; general intellect in, 55; in liberation management, 61; Marx on, 53
co-production, free labor in, 113, 120
*Corporate Cultures: The Rites and Rituals of Corporate Life* (Deal and Kennedy), 88
*The Corporation: The Pathological Pursuit of Profit and Power* (Bakan), 62–63
corporations and firms: birth of, 66–71; blending of work and non-work in (*see* blending of work and non-work); capturing life at workplace, 24–25, 110–113; class relations in, 12, 30, 72–75; and the commons, 43–61; compared to public institutions, 161n2; culture in, 84–102 (*see also* culture, corporate); definition of, 62; early form of, 68–71; enclosure movement in, 23–42, 64; engagement of employees in, 4; free work capitalism of, 103–123; as guarantor, 96; historical aspects of, 62–83; human capital required for profitability of, 30; impersonality of, 62; importance of external social relations to,

Fordism, 5, 8, 147; control in, 29, 92, 98; fear in, 126; non-work in, 13, 24; official and unofficial work time in, 104–105; responsible autonomy in, 163n1; successful output restriction in, 164n7; and Welfare State, 79; work and survival in, 133
Ford Motor Company, 108
Foster, R., 95
Foucault, Michel, 26–27, 28, 34, 39, 61, 66, 142–143
"Fragment on Machines" (Marx), 53–54
France: events of 1968 in, 137, 140; riots of 2005 in, 141
Frank, Anne, 138
freedom, 60; demand among workforce for, 78; and diversity in corporate culture, 95–96, 168n7; to do it yourself, 96; to express life at work, 87; illusion of, in non-work at work, 98
free enterprise, 63
Freeland, G., 78
free markets, 153, 173nn11–13
free time: anxiety and boredom in, 10; as concern for authorities, 150; extension of work into, 8–10; in free work capitalism, 115–116, 122, 123; and non-activity as self-destructive, 173–174n17; in resistance to bio-power, 144; in vacations, 8–10, 130
free work capitalism, 103–123; capturing life in workplace, 110–113; feminist analysis of, 169n1; free time in, 115–116, 122, 123; hacker ethos in, 120–121; harvesting external ideas, 112; intern workers in, 105, 113–114, 169n4; normalization of, 106; productivity in, 9, 104; resistance to, 122–123; scattered points of production in, 106–113; self-development in, 118–121, 122, 123; self-organization and autonomy in, 116–118, 122, 123; unemployment requirements in, 10, 128; unpaid labor in (*see* unpaid labor)
Friedman, A., 163n1
Friedman, Milton, 82, 154

Friedman, Thomas, 44
*Fuel on the Fire: Oil and Politics in Occupied Iraq* (Muttitt), 173n13
fun activities at work, 23, 24, 110
functional creep, 36
functional sociology, 12
"funsultants," 24

gaming industry, 120, 121
Gates, Bill, 120
*Gemeinschaft,* 50–51
gender politics, 7
general intellect, 53, 54–56, 60, 98
generational differences, 16, 162n8
Gillespie, R., 77
global capitalism, 44
global economic crisis (2008), 4
Google, 131; model of production in, 98
Gordon, D., 117
Gorz, A., 16, 37, 59, 94, 101, 105, 122, 164n5
Gouldner, A., 105, 109
governmentality, neoliberal, 32
Graeber, D., 107, 165n1, 173n12
Grassman, P. R., 98
Great Depression, 77, 79, 152
Greece, recovered factories in, 42
Green, F., 161n4
Gregg, M., 9, 35–36, 37–38, 40, 115–116
Gross, E., 76
*Grundrisse* (Marx), 53
Guattari, F., 171–172n1

Habermas, J., 100
*The Hacker Ethic and the Spirit of the Information Age* (Himanen), 6
hacker ethos, 120
Haiven, M., 81
Hanlon, G., 79–80
Hardt, M., 9, 14, 28, 29, 57–58, 59, 60, 134, 143, 162n6, 164n6
"Harnessing Your Staff's Informal Networks" (McDermott and Archibald), 111
Harney, S., 126, 137

management: biopolitical methods of, 147; controls used by, 12, 71–78; distrust of, 38, 172–173n10; encouraging non-work at work, 13–14, 23–25; exploitation of, 172–173n10; function of, 116–117, 118, 151; humanized practices, 60; human relations approach, 75, 76, 77, 89, 166n10; in Japan, 88; liberation, 23, 24, 37, 55, 61, 93, 96, 111, 126, 151; lifestyle approach to, 24–25, 33, 98; response to counter-planning, 146, 172n2; scientific, 55; stupidity of, 151; in Taylorism, 76

managerialism, 11, 66, 68, 77, 89, 93, 106; biopower as crisis in, 41; corporate, 25, 55

Marcuse, H., 37

Marglin, S., 117, 166n8

markets, free, 153, 173nn11–13

Marszalek, B., 163n11

Martin, R., 81

Marx, Karl, 59; on autonomous free association, 50; on barriers to capitalist production, 30; on capital, 57, 139–140; *Capital*, 53, 139; on capitalism as dead labor, 52; on capitalists as leaders of industry, 65; on factory system, 39; on false society and false social experience, 19; "Fragment on Machines," 53–54; *Grundrisse*, 53; on industrial production, 164n6; on living labor, 7, 51, 52–53; on real and formal subsumption, 51; on social character of workers, 13; on technological determinism, 35; on unproductive labor, 108; on wage exploitation, 103; "Wage Labor and Capital," 67

materialism, radical, of Spinoza, 47

Mayer, C., 82

Mazzucato, M., 170n10

Means, G., 71

measurement systems, 11, 12, 37–38; in Results Only Work Environments, 25

medicine, public and private investments in, 80

Menacherry, M., 171n3

Michel, A., 32, 33, 93, 99

micromanagement, 37

micro-powers, 39

Microsoft, 126

middle class, debt of, 81

Miessen, M., 137, 142

Mieville, C., 162n5

militancy, worker, 42, 57, 69, 70, 76, 77, 101, 124, 147, 172n3

Milkman, R., 163n12

Mills, C. Wright, 138

mind-control tactics, 97

Mirowski, P., 167n15, 172n8

mobile technology, 35–36, 115–116

Mondragon Corporation, 162–163n11

monetarism, 78

Monk, D. B., 161–162n5

Monsanto, 119

Montesquieu, 164n1

Moore, M., 63

"more to life," 64, 67

Morin, F., 173n16

Moten, F., 137

motivation of employees, 95, 96

the multitude, 46, 48, 59–60

Mumbai, rat catcher job in, 128, 171n3

Murdoch, Rupert, 153, 156

Muttitt, G., 173n13

Nancy, J. L., 162n10

Narro, N., 163n12

natural selection, 75

necessity of work, 115; blending of work and non-work in, 99; myth of, 5–7, 42, 99, 128, 133–134, 144; for personal sense of individuality and social value, 5; for survival, 6, 42, 114, 128, 133

Negri, A., 9, 14, 28, 29, 47, 52, 57–58, 59, 60, 134, 162n6, 163n4

neo-human capital theory, 120

neo-human relations movement, 89

neoliberal capitalism, 9–10; biopower in, 13, 27, 28; exit from, 60; health impact of, 168n8; illusion of permanence in, 115; perceptions on future

trust, 49; and distrust of management, 38, 172–173n10
Tsianos, V., 164n9, 165n4

unemployment, 6, 131, 133; fear of, 126; work requirement in, 10, 128, 162n7
unions, 164n10; alternative, 163n12; and corporate culture, 89; management ideology in response to, 76; for manual labor jobs, 168n4; in response to technical control, 74; rise of neoliberalism affecting, 148
United Kingdom: attitude toward bankers in, 15; biocracy in, 98; corporate culture in, 98; cost of living in, 154; cycles of control and commitment in, 89; exit from work in, 132; free work capitalism in, 103, 105, 106, 107; gender differences in wages in, 7; historical worker militancy in, 69; income and living costs in, 7, 161–162n5; infrastructure decline in, 167n13; jilted generation in, 162n8; limited liability protection in, 70; multiple part-time jobs in, 172n6; non-work at work in, 13–14; sale of railways in, 78; self-employment in, 104, 169n2; street fighting and unrest in, 135–136; taxation in, 153; unemployment in, 10, 128, 133; working class in, 72
universalization of work, 33, 158
universities. *See* academic institutions
unpaid labor, 105, 106, 107, 115, 120; in biopower, 115; feminist analysis of, 169n1; of interns, 105, 113–114, 169n4; in invisible work, 117; in overtime, 106; in research and development, 113, 120; wealth generated by, 122
user innovations, 120, 170n11
U.S. Steel Corporation, 71, 73

vacation time, 8–10, 130
Vale mining corporation, 157

value: blurring of life and labor in creation of, 33; labor theory of, 52, 57; surplus, 52, 53, 107
Vaneigem, R., 141
violence and war: and pacifying effect of commerce, 44, 164–165n1; potential of the multitude for, 48
Virno, Paolo, 3, 12–13, 28, 31, 46, 48, 54, 55, 115, 117
*The Visible Hand: The Managerial Revolution in American Business* (Chandler), 44

Wadel, C., 170n9
*Wage Labor and Capital* (Marx), 67
wages: compared to living costs, 7, 161–162n5; gender politics affecting, 7; and productivity, 103, 106; reduction in, 154
Wagner Act (1933), 166n10
Wall Street occupation, 136
war and violence: and pacifying effect of commerce, 44, 164–165n1; potential of the multitude for, 48
Ware, Bonnie, 144
Waterman, R. H., 88, 89, 91, 92
Watson, Bill, 146, 148
wealth creation: in capitalism, 18, 57, 64, 82, 140; inequality in, 16; investment function of corporations in, 71; living labor in, 127; social surplus in, 14, 45; unpaid labor in, 120, 122
Weber, M., 23, 91, 92, 108
Weeks, K., 9, 52
welfare capitalism, 70
Welfare State, 78, 79; decline of, 81; privatization of, 79
"What Do Bosses Do? The Origins and Functions of Hierarchy in Capitalist Production" (Marglin), 166n8
*When Corporations Rule the World* (Korten), 63
*Why Work Sucks and How to Fix It: The Results Only Revolution* (Ressler and Thompson), 25, 85

**Peter Fleming** is a Professor of Business and Society at Cass Business School, City University London. He is the co-author of several books, including *Contesting the Corporation: Struggle, Power and Resistance in Organizations* (with André Spicer), *Dead Man Working* (with Carl Cederström), and *The End of Corporate Social Responsibility: Crisis and Critique* (with Marc T. Jones).